T. S. Eliot

MODERN LITERATURE SERIES

GENERAL EDITOR: Philip Winsor

In the same series:

S .Y. AGNON   *Harold Fisch*
SHERWOOD ANDERSON   *Welford Dunaway Taylor*
LEONID ANDREYEV   *Josephine M. Newcombe*
ISAAC BABEL   *R. W. Hallett*
JAMES BALDWIN   *Carolyn Wedin Sylvander*
SIMONE DE BEAUVOIR   *Robert Cottrell*
SAUL BELLOW   *Brigitte Scheer-Schäzler*
JORGE LUIS BORGES   *George R. McMurray*
BERTOLD BRECHT   *Willy Haas*
ANTHONY BURGESS   *Samuel Coale*
ALBERT CAMUS   *Carol Petersen*
TRUMAN CAPOTE   *Helen S. Garson*
WILLA CATHER   *Dorothy Tuck McFarland*
JOHN CHEEVER   *Samuel Coale*
COLETTE   *Robert Cottrell*
JOSEPH CONRAD   *Martin Tucker*
JULIO CORTÁZAR   *Evelyn Picon Garfield*
JOAN DIDION   *Katherine Usher Henderson*
JOHN DOS PASSOS   *George J. Becker*
THEODORE DREISER   *James Lundquist*
FRIEDRICH DÜRRENMATT   *Armin Arnold*
T. S. ELIOT   *Burton Raffel*
WILLIAM FAULKNER   *Joachim Seyppel*
F. SCOTT FITZGERALD   *Rose Adrienne Gallo*
FORD MADOX FORD   *Sondra J. Stang*
JOHN FOWLES   *Barry N. Olshen*
MAX FRISCH   *Carol Petersen*
ROBERT FROST   *Elaine Barry*
GABRIEL GARCÍA MÁRQUEZ   *George R. McMurray*
ELLEN GLASGOW   *Marcelle Thiébaux*
MAKSIM GORKI   *Gerhard Habermann*
GÜNTER GRASS   *Kurt Lothar Tank*
ROBERT GRAVES   *Katherine Snipes*
PETER HANDKE   *Nicholas Hern*
LILLIAN HELLMAN   *Doris V. Falk*
ERNEST HEMINGWAY   *Samuel Shaw*
HERMANN HESSE   *Franz Baumer*
CHESTER HIMES   *James Lundquist*
HUGO VON HOFMANNSTHAL   *Lowell W. Bangerter*
JOHN IRVING   *Gabriel Miller*
CHRISTOPHER ISHERWOOD   *Claude J. Summers*
SARAH ORNE JEWETT   *Josephine Donovan*
UWE JOHNSON   *Mark Boulby*
JAMES JOYCE   *Armin Arnold*

(*continued on last page of book*)

T. S. ELIOT

Burton Raffel

Frederick Ungar Publishing Co.
New York

Library of Congress Cataloging in Publication Data

Raffel, Burton.
  T.S. Eliot.

  (Modern literature series)
  Bibliography: p.
  Includes index.
  1. Eliot, T.S. (Thomas Stearns), 1888-1965—
Criticism and interpretation.   I.   Title.
II.   Series.
PS3509.L43Z816   821′.912   81-70119
ISBN 0-8044-2708-9   AACR2

Contents

vi

Chronology

1888:   Thomas Stearns Eliot is born in St. Louis, Missouri, on September 26

189?–1904: He attends Smith Academy, St. Louis

1904–1906: He attends Milton Academy, Massachusetts

1906–1909: He attends Harvard, completes his B.A. degree

1909–1910: He attends Harvard as a graduate student in English literature, completes M.A. degree

1910–1911: He spends academic year at Sorbonne, Paris

1911–1914: He attends Harvard as a graduate student in philosophy, completes course work for the Ph.D. degree, begins doctoral dissertation on F. H. Bradley

1914:   He attends Marburg University, Germany, July–early August 1914

1914–1915: He resides in Oxford

1915:   He marries Vivienne Haigh-Wood, moves to London, takes post as a teacher, first at High Wycombe School, briefly, and then for a longer period at Highgate Junior School; first poems published in *Blast, Poetry*

1916:   He finishes his dissertation, which is submitted to Harvard and approved

1917:   He takes a post in the Colonial and Foreign Branch of Lloyds Bank; *The Love Song of J. Alfred Prufrock and Other Observations* is published; serves as assistant editor of *The Egoist*, 1917–1919; begins to be known in English literary circles

1919:   *Poems 1919* is published by Leonard and Virginia Woolf at the Hogarth Press; "Gerontion" is published

1920:   *Poems, 1920* (*Ara Vos Prec*, in England) is published in U.S. by Knopf; *The Sacred Wood* is published

1922:   *The Waste Land* is published; he becomes editor of the *Criterion*

1924:   *Four Elizabethan Dramatists* is published

1925:   He, and the *Criterion*, join the publishing firm of Faber and Gwyer, later Faber and Faber; "The Hollow Men" is published; *Poems 1909–1925* is published

1926:   *Fragment of a Prologue* is published (one portion of *Sweeney Agonistes*)

1927:   Eliot becomes an Anglo-Catholic, and a British citizen; *Fragment of an Agon* (second part of *Sweeney Agonistes*) is published; "Journey of the Magi" is published

1928:   *For Lancelot Andrewes* is published, Eliot's preface announcing that his "general point of view may be described as classicist in literature, royalist in politics, and anglo-catholic in religion"

1929:   *Dante* is published

1930:   *Ash-Wednesday* is published

1932:   The first edition of *Selected Essays* is published

1932–1933: He lectures in the United States; separates from his first wife

1933:   *The Use of Poetry & the Use of Criticism* is published

1934:   *After Strange Gods* is published; *The Rock* is written, performed, and published

1935:   *Murder in the Cathedral* is written, performed, and published; *Burnt Norton* is published
1939:   *The Family Reunion* is performed and published; *Old Possum's Book of Practical Cats* and *The Idea of a Christian Society* are published
1940:   *East Coker* is published
1941:   *The Dry Salvages* is published
1942:   *Little Gidding* is published
1947:   Vivienne Eliot dies
1948:   He is awarded the Nobel Prize
1949:   *Notes towards a Definition of Culture* is published
1950:   *The Cocktail Party* is performed and published
1955:   *The Confidential Clerk* is performed and published
1957:   He marries Valerie Fletcher
1959:   *The Elder Statesman* is performed and published
1965:   He dies on January 4

to the memory of Louie May Miner,
who taught me Eliot, and Yeats,
and discipline, and a degree of
moderation, and who gave me the
crucial support and encouragement
that only a great teacher and
a deeply caring human being is
capable of giving

Preface

Sometimes politicians, painters, or poets seem to catch and hold our attention. They may not be the best politicians, painters, or poets, but they have the quality that all sports fans know, the charisma, the special drama, that compels our notice. For some performers, the rise to what we now call "superstar" status happens, almost as if by magic, at the very start of their career. Lord Byron was an instant celebrity at age twenty-four when he published the first cantos of *Childe Harold.* Thomas Hardy, on the other hand, who lived fifty-two years more than Byron, was truly famous only at the end of his very long life. And Hardy's longevity probably had a good deal to do with his rise in critical reputation. In our own time, the novelist Philip Roth is a prime example of the almost instantaneous "superstar." Roth was twenty-six when he won a National Book Award and unbroken national attention for his *Goodbye, Columbus.* There may well have been better books of fiction published in 1959—but the Reggie Jacksons of the literary world do not have to hit home runs in order to claim, and to keep, the limelight. It is indeed in some ways a mysterious process.

1

T. S. Eliot, a shy, introspective man who had been an even shyer and more solitary boy, achieved immense, worldwide fame in his early thirties, after a literary career only half a dozen years long. Publication of *The Waste Land* in 1922 established him as a benchmark figure against whom other writers would thereafter be measured. He had been reasonably well-known in the English-speaking world even before 1922; in England, in particular, he had become very much a member of the literary establishment, known both as a poet and as a critic and journalist. But after *The Waste Land,* everything he did was important. What he wrote was imitated, attacked, and defended. What he believed became as important as what he wrote: his conversion to Anglo-Catholicism in 1927 reverberated for decades in the minds and hearts of young writers, bringing into the ecclesiastical fold many sheep who would, without Eliot's vast and potent influence, probably have remained outside. If he did not single-handedly start the movement toward poetic drama, he was certainly one of its sparkplugs. The New Criticism, which dominated both academic and nonacademic literary circles for much of the 1930s and 1940s, owed at least as much to Eliot's influence as to any other critic. Indeed, Eliot sparked off any number of literary revivals, notably of the work of Dante and John Donne. And his animadversions on Shelley, and to some extent against John Milton (though he later modified his dislike of Milton), shaped critical battle lines for years afterward. For more than four decades chance remarks of his were taken far more seriously than he wanted them to be taken. His very phrasing in his poems and criticism passed into something like Scriptural status and was quoted and requoted, explained and re-explained by friends and foes alike. Young poets especially had to deal with Eliot's example before they could hope to find their own styles and their own subject matters.

What is it that gives a man, most particularly a poet, such resounding importance? It is too easy to talk vaguely and abstractly of "genius," or to cover up incomprehension with fine-sounding phrases like "identification with the *Zeitgeist,*" or "distillation of the spirit of the Age." Sigmund Freud, for example, is specifically one of the prime movers of our century, because he more than any other man opened the road inward. Freud's fame rests squarely on his driving curiosity about and passionate inquiry into the workings of the human psyche. Karl Marx, contrariwise, is famous both because he perceived fundamental tensions in industrialized society and because, since his death, other men have used his name (if not always his ideas) just as the followers of Islam use the name of Mohammed and Christians use the name of Jesus Christ.

Eliot won the Nobel Prize for Literature in 1948, but his was not a narrowly literary achievement. He was one of the great poets of the twentieth century: that alone would have been enough to make him a major figure, a "superstar." But he was also one of the great literary critics of the twentieth century, every bit as seminal, powerful, and influential as he was in poetry. The audience for criticism is, to be sure, not so large, nor (in my view) is criticism of the same importance. But books are written, and deserve to be written, about the intricacies of Eliot's critical thought. Additionally, Eliot was an important theatrical figure—not so large and weighty a playwright as he was a poet and critic, but important nevertheless. He was also a religious and social polemicist and taken seriously in those roles. He was a leading figure in one of the English-speaking world's important publishing houses, Faber and Faber in London.

It is my feeling, and I shall try to document that feeling in this book, that Eliot is a multifaceted but unitary figure, no matter what role we consider him in. His energies, like the energies of virtually all multifaceted human beings, were restless, turning sometimes this way, sometimes that. Not everything he did even as poet and as critic was successful, or even important. He started projects he could not finish. He announced books he would never write, he planned and sometimes worked hard to prepare for careers he then discarded—for instance, he completed the work for a Ph.D. but never bothered to claim it, and prepared to become a school teacher but very quickly abandoned teaching. But in all his work and in all his roles, Eliot was first and foremost a man of high passion in a world which no longer welcomes the depth and intimacy of true passion. Though I do not want to exaggerate or distort the intentions of a man for whom I have profound respect, it seems to me Eliot was probing basic and deeply sensitive veins of twentieth-century existence just as surely as, albeit in different ways from, Freud and Marx. This is peculiarly true of Eliot as a poet. William Butler Yeats and Wallace Stevens, other major twentieth century poets, do not have the same sort of social focus. Yeats's passions tend to be personal; even when they are political, or in some sense social, it is Yeats himself who stands at the center of his poetry and his poetic concern. Stevens, though he is surely a passionate man, tends toward the passion of the mind.[1]

Accordingly, though I have no intention of embarking upon a "re-evaluation" of Eliot, it is necessary that I begin my consideration of his work by placing somewhat unusual stress on an early poem sequence, "Preludes," which has not seemed to other writers to be of comparable importance.[2] The first chapter of this book will be devoted to an intensive and fairly detailed examination of the four poems in this sequence, written when Eliot was in his early twenties. When I have taught Eliot's work in university seminars, I have similarly begun with "Preludes," spending hours of class time in an analysis of both the individual poems and of the sequence. It seems to me that it is impossible to understand the nature and depth of Eliot's passion without understanding this early work. And as I have said, it seems to me impossible to understand the entirety of Eliot's career without a careful and sympathetic attempt to recognize the passional keys to that career— and most especially to his poetry. I will deal with Eliot as poet, as critic, as playwright, and as social thinker. But it is to his poetry that I will devote the largest portion of this book.

Accordingly, though this book is intended for students and the general reader rather than for academic specialists, its perspectives are distinctly different from the majority of writers on Eliot, though I freely admit my debt to those earlier critics. I have been trying to unravel what Professor Elisabeth W. Schneider calls "the pattern in the carpet" for more than thirty years.[3] My first long paper on Eliot was written when I was an undergraduate in 1947, and was followed by an even longer Master's thesis in 1949. I do not deceive myself that my understanding of Eliot is, *tout court,* immeasurably greater than that of the many fine critics who have devoted so much effort and intelligence to the same truthseeking with which I have been concerned. We agree, those critics and I, in a great many important matters. But I *would* be deceiving myself —and my readers—if I pretended that my overall sense of Eliot's literary career, its chronological arc, and also its wellsprings, was substantially identical to theirs. Again, much of whatever value this study may have will, I think, rest quite specifically on the different perspective of Eliot offered in these pages. No perspective is or ever will be definitive; but if no perspective, mine included, can ever be definitive, every perspective ought to be illuminating: if I

have achieved that goal in the pages which follow, I will
be more than satisfied.

1

The early poem, "Preludes," subjected to detailed analysis and presented as a keystone to all of Eliot's work

W hether "Preludes" was written in 1915 or in 1910–1911,[1] and whether the four sections are the parts of a tightly unified poem, as I understand them to be, or simply four poems grouped together, as Professor Elisabeth Schneider suspects them of being,[2] all seem to me matters of less importance here than what the poem itself says, and how it says it, and what "Preludes" can tell us about the young T. S. Eliot's preoccupations. The message, if not the tone, of "Preludes" is I think very different from that which is usually attributed to Eliot—it is far more passionately concerned with ordinary urban existence and its problems, far more compassionate toward the ordinary human beings involved in that urban existence, and as I shall demonstrate far more intimately and importantly connected with Eliot's other poetry, early and late, than has ever been understood. I want to demonstrate, too, that there is to my mind a very tight and powerful structure to "Preludes." I find it impossible, myself, to see the sequence as anything but a unified structure, a single poem.

The first section begins:

> The winter evening settles down
> With smell of steaks in passageways.
> Six o'clock.
> The burnt-out ends of smoky days.

Grover Smith, whose job it is to uncover sources, and who has performed that job extremely well, notes that "Eliot owed much of the atmosphere found . . . in 'Preludes' . . ." to two novels by the self-educated French author of studies of common folk, Charles-Louis Philippe (1874–1909).[3] But it would be a serious mistake to attribute lines like these to anything but direct personal experience. No source more esoteric than daily living is required to understand, sympathetically, the heaviness embodied so beautifully in "settles down." Seen romantically, a "winter

8

evening" can be perceived as a light, even feathery, cover-
ing cloak of darkness, and so on. What Eliot is implicitly
but firmly informing us, however, is that in this poem we
are not to be given a romantic, but a realistic perception
of urban life.

And not just any urban life, for in the second line we
are informed, perhaps even more emphatically, that the
poem's concern is with lower levels of society, with working people, and those, in fact, who live their lives out "in
passageways," and with the "smell of steaks." And we are
also informed, though rather more subtly, that for the
moment at least the particular perspective from which the
poem proposes to operate is a neutral one. That is, we do
not see through the eyes of any human being—and though
"your feet" in line 7 plainly suggests the physical presence
of a human observer, there is no human activity at all in
this entire first section. There is no direct sentient activity
of any kind, until we are shown, in the last three lines, the
"lonely cab-horse" which, "at the corner of the street
. . . steams and stamps." And only after that warm-blood-
ed sign of life, "lonely" and animal, but still sentient, does
darkness and desolation give way to the section's final
image, "the lighting of the lamps."

The whole poem is very strictly controlled. What the
poet allows us to see, to experience, is governed by the key
tones established very early on: the "winter evening," the
"smell of steaks," and perhaps most of all by "the burnt-
out ends of smoky days." This is a personification, but
utterly unlike the sorts of personifications used by more
romantic poets. The "days" of this poem, understood as
a measure of the life being described as well as a chronological indicator, are smoky with fog and assorted urban
particulates, but they are also personified as discarded
cigarettes, consumed, and now useless. So too, accordingly, are we shown "the grimy scraps / Of withered leaves,"

and the "newspapers from vacant lots," which a "gusty shower wraps . . . about your feet." That is, the essentially working-class imagery framed in lines 1–4 is here carried forward, and intensified, with additional visualizations from the same levels of urban existence. The "blinds and chimneypots" of this scene are inevitably "broken." "Your feet" are passive, unmoving, unsentient.

No reader new to "Preludes" will, of course, be fully aware of the progressions I have been discussing. Nor will that reader sense, as I have also suggested, that in lines 1–10 literally nothing moves of its volition. Everything is repetitive, neutrally inspired, even, perhaps, spiritlessly inspired—everything, let me emphasize, from the winter evening, the expiring smoky days, the scraps of dried-up leaves and rubbishy bits of discarded newspapers, right down to the squalling flashes of rain beating down. The first sign of active, self-motivated life in this dismal scene is, again, the horse—not a human volition, but an animal volition, and not a cheerful or a hopeful activity, but only a self-protective, reactive activity. It is not much, but it is enough to give us what sign of human activity, and human aspiration perhaps, the poet wants to permit, namely "the lighting of the lamps" along these gray, dim, drizzly city streets.

And that much human activity then permits, in the first line of the second section, at least an implicit, meta-phorical human "consciousness" to appear in the poem.

> The morning comes to consciousness
> Of faint stale smells of beer
> From the sawdust-trampled street . . .

Like the "winter evening" at the start of the first section, this "morning" is a personification. It is a generalized rather than a particularized morning, it is not linked to any one human being. There is, however, a fairly clear suggestion that the reader of the poem has been moved a bit closer to some sort of living consciousness. The evening "settles down," the morning "comes [up] to consciousness. . . ." And though the "smell of steaks in passageways" is neither more nor less *attractive* than the "faint stale smells of beer," there is at least some sense of motion, of things preparing, perhaps, to be focused, pointed, possibly even explained. The street, for example, is "sawdust-trampled": we are not shown the actively moving feet which have done the trampling, but they are pretty clearly evoked, both in this line and in the "muddy feet" of line 4. These feet, further, "press" toward an indisputably human activity, the drinking of coffee at "early coffee stands." In poetic terms, more than the morning is waking up. The poet has deliberately kept us from any active human consciousness or movement in the first section of the poem, but here we are shown such distinctly human matters that we begin to anticipate more focused evidence:

> With the other masquerades
> That time resumes,
> One thinks of all the hands
> That are raising dingy shades
> In a thousand furnished rooms.

And the sense of anticipation is partly fulfilled, in these concluding lines of the second section. The "masquerades / That time resumes" starts things off; it is a personification of an inescapably human and personal sort. An evening, or a day, or a morning can all exist without any human linkage. Plainly, a "masquerade" cannot. (The third of the personifications which have preceded this one, that of the awakening morning, is the most human-related of the three. And that too helps build the reader's sense of approaching focus.)

And though the notion of a "masquerade" is to some

extent generalized, and even in part abstracted, by its immediate link to "time," the very next line resumes what can only be seen as a fairly steady march toward the particular, the human, the intimate and affecting. "One thinks of all the hands. . . ." The entirely passive observer of the first section has now become an actively ruminating, involved observer. And what the observer meditates upon is specifically human activity, focused upon the "raising [of] dingy shades / In a thousand furnished rooms." Again, the focus remains on the lower levels of society, the poor and the near-poor, the transient, the working classes. And the hands, here, are exhibited to us in an act which is one of consummate weariness, even futility, for all furnished rooms are by implication very much like all other furnished rooms. And yet this act requires of us both sympathy and understanding, even pity, though that is not as yet fully clear.

Eliot, however, makes it a good deal clearer at the start of the third section:

> You tossed a blanket from the bed,
> You lay upon your back, and waited;
> You dozed, and watched the night revealing
> The thousand sordid images
> Of which your soul was constituted . . .

It is too easy to see "sordid images" as disdainful and condemnatory. Not only is there much in other poems of this period, especially "Morning at the Window" (which I have at times jokingly called the fifth poem in the "Preludes" sequence), to indicate the exact opposite of any such stance, but there is much in later parts of "Preludes" to indicate that "sordid" is neither disdainful nor condemnatory but, rather, saddened and sympathetically rather than nastily critical.[4] Indeed, all that a reasonably objective reader ought to be able to conclude, at this point in

"Preludes," is that the greater intimacy, the increased closeness exhibited in the five lines just quoted point heavily toward sympathy and toward a positive rather than a negative approach. Four second-person pronouns in the space of five lines is, plainly, a vast heightening—in the context of the sequence to this point.

What after all does the newly visualized persona do? His (or her) actions are sleep-connected, in part semi-automatic, in part *self*-critical. The reader needs to ask, accordingly, not whether the persona is correct to be critical, but only whether the poem's presentation of the self-criticism is apt to make us respectful or disrespectful of the persona. As a poem so often does, this one answers any such query in the lines which follow. After displaying the "thousand sordid images," metaphorically, flickering "against the ceiling," and after taking the persona through the long, unhappy night to the dawn, "when all the world came back / And the light *crept up* between the shutters" (italics added), the poem focuses more intensely, more intimately than ever on the human—all-too-human—persona:

> You had such a vision of the street
> As the street hardly understands;
> Sitting along the bed's edge, where
> You curled the papers from your hair,
> Or clasped the yellow soles of feet
> In the palms of both soiled hands.

Throughout the poem the persona has been carefully kept from sexual specificity, carefully kept *either* male, *or* female, or possibly both. The one specifically oriented detail is, of course, the papers in "your hair," and this is without question female. But not only are none of the other details specifically oriented, clasping "the yellow soles of feet / In the palms of both soiled hands" is, if

anything, rather more male than female. And it fits with
the development and progression of the poem that these
trivial, intimate details are designedly omni-sexual: it
would make little sense for the persona here to be overtly
and exclusively female, since Eliot's indictment, like his
imagery, is universally intended. (Note the first words of
the poem's fourth section: "His soul . . .") Neither the
"sordid images / Of which your soul was constituted," nor
the "vision of the street," is in any way sexually condi-
tioned.

And all these details, however "sordid," are given to
us with a clearly affective quality. The feet may be "yellow," and the hands may be "soiled," but *clasping* is far
too powerful and positive a verb to be ignored. And this
conclusion of the third section begins with an absolutely
unequivocal endorsement of the persona, granted "such a
vision of the street / As the street hardly understands."
That is, the poem's persona, for all his / her "sordid"
human nature, and for all the sordid existence he / she
leads, is profoundly perceptive—and the self-criticism
stems, equally plainly, from a broad and far-reaching comprehension. All we have been shown, thus far, is the background for this judgment ("vision") of urban life ("the
street"), coupled with the unremarkable assertion that it
is not a judgment of which many city dwellers are likely
to be capable. But both the structural progressions of the
poem (its movement from neutral and unpopulated scenes
to intimate and humanized ones), and its metaphors and
image materials, point toward the conclusions about to be
offered us, in the sequence's fourth and final section.

The first six lines of this fourth section, interestingly,
retreat from the "sordid" intensity of the previous section,
giving us what seem to be bland observations about working-class life in the metropolis. The "feet" in line 3 of this
section are "insistent," just as the time indicators are set

at four, five, and six o'clock, because these are the hours
working people return home. The skies "fade behind a city
block," much as the winter evening settled down and the
"smoky days" were presented to us with their "burnt-out
ends." But this is, in fact, a delicate and craftsmanlike
tightening of structure—and just as in the musical ana-
logues evoked by the poem's title, the poet / composer
slackens the reins only to whip things even higher.

The "eyes" of these working urbanites, we are assured, are locked into their "certain certainties"—that is,
not "certain" as meaning "some," but "certain" as a kind
of ironic and tautological heightening. We move swiftly to
a street that is no longer simply "sawdust-trampled" but
is now "blackened," a visual image that is even more
morally and spiritually expressive. Eliot emphasizes this
moral and spiritual thrust by making it the "conscience"
of this "blackened street" which is "impatient to assume
the world." This tends, I think, to evoke the powerful
notion of Christ assuming the sins of that world. In the
lines which immediately follow, the first four lines are
separated by a stanza space, which to be sure is hardly a
remarkable poetic device, but up to this point there has
been no such stanza space employed in the poem—and
that makes it, surely, of much greater significance. But
Eliot goes a good deal further than that. He starts this
segment with the only first person pronoun used, anywhere in the entire poem. And the reactions and conclusions which follow are as *un*-neutral as could possibly be.
The whole movement of the poem, from its carefully controlled neutrality at the beginning to its greater and greater involvement and intimacy and its sudden burst of
intense sympathy, heightens the force of these lines. And
heightens, too, their pain:

    I am moved by fancies that are curled

Around these images, and cling:
The notion of some infinitely gentle
Infinitely suffering thing.[5]

The positive thrust of the earlier verb, "clasped," is here carried forward by "curled," which is both a more instinctual movement and also, in the context, a more powerful one. That is, the "I" of the poem is "moved" *toward* the action expressed by "curled." He no longer just sits "along the bed's edge" and, on the whole rather passively, clasps his feet in his hands. And he is moved, furthermore, toward "fancies"—that is, toward notions which are, if not exactly flighty, yet unrealistic. There is no need to return to Coleridge or to older eighteenth-century ideas of "fancy" versus "imagination." The common desk dictionary will do, here. The noun "fancy" is defined as "imagination, especially as exercised in a capricious or desultory manner." Exactly: the affective nature of the persona's reaction is as clear as the hopeless nature of that affection and concern.

But the movement toward, the affective, hopeless movement toward these images of working-class life in the great city, is still more positive. The persona's fancies not only curl "around these images," but they "cling" to them. Clearly, the emotion involved is a large and a powerful one: no one clings to something without some such motivation. And Eliot does not leave us in doubt. "Cling" is followed by a colon, and the motivation is pretty plainly stated: "The notion of some infinitely gentle / Infinitely suffering thing." What is this "infinitely gentle" and "infinitely suffering thing" if not the same lost souls dealt with throughout the poem, souls who are potentially great in the eyes of God but, as Eliot puts it in "Morning at the Window," in fact only "damp souls of housemaids / sprouting despondently at area gates"?[6] "The simple soul," as Eliot later put it in "Animula," one of the "Ariel" poems, "issues from the hand of God . . . to a flat world." The "growing soul" is weighted down with a "heavy burden"—and all one can do, asserts that poem's final line, is "Pray for us now and at the hour of our birth." Given still greater reason for despair, these intensely sympathetic reactions may come to seem, as in "Gerontion," "thoughts of a dry brain in a dry season." The world may come to seem, as in "The Hollow Men," "the dead land . . . [the] cactus land," and the men in it "not as lost / Violent souls, but only / As the hollow men / The stuffed men." But in the earlier poems, and for the earlier Eliot, one could at least toy with the notion, beautifully dandled and then destroyed in "Prufrock," of forcing "the moment to its crisis." One could wonder, fatuously, as the speaker in "Portrait of a Lady" does, if "Perhaps it is not too late." One could savagely mourn, as at the end of "Rhapsody on a Windy Night," that mundane notions of preparing "for life" are in reality "The last twist of the knife." One could even, as in "Sweeney Erect," recall that "The lengthened shadow of a man / Is history, said Emerson"—and then insist, with what I take to be bitter irony, that Emerson "had not seen the silhouette / Of Sweeney straddled in the sun." One can lash out at the world, as Eliot did in many of his early poems; one can turn one's back on the world, as in a sense Eliot does at the end of "The Waste Land," "with the arid plain behind me," wondering, "Shall I at least set *my* lands in order?" (italics added).

Yet what "Preludes" points to is equally plainly established. It is a mistake to see Eliot as indifferent to or contemptuous of the world. It is a mistake to underestimate his involvement—which involvement, indeed, helps explain the intensity of his withdrawal, and the intensity of his negative reaction to the barren, inadequate, dangerously empty world in which, willy-nilly, he, and in his

18   *T. S. Eliot*

view, all of us find ourselves. Eliot starts, in short, as a
distinctly social poet, just as he ends, in his plays, in his
social criticism, and to a large extent in his "Four Quartets," as a social poet and writer. And he ends "Preludes,"
after the helpless assertion of affection for the "infinitely
gentle / Infinitely suffering thing," with still another small
segment set off, and highlighted, by a stanza space:

> Wipe your hand across your mouth, and laugh;
> The worlds revolve like ancient women
> Gathering fuel in vacant lots.

One can be moved, but one cannot do anything. It is a
bitter "laugh," devoid of humor. It is perhaps a melodramatic laugh, as the gesture of wiping your hand
"across your mouth" is surely somewhat melodramatic,
belonging indeed to a frustrated romantic idealist, deeply,
painfully persuaded of his helplessness. In context I am
not sure that the melodrama hurts the sequence in any
significant way, especially considering its elaborately, frig-
idly neutral opening. And the "ancient women" of the
penultimate line refers, not to women out of ancient times,
but to women of great age and decrepitude, obliged by
poverty to stagger about ("revolve") in vacant lots, hunting what "grimy scraps" they can scratch out of largely
barren ground. This then is the world's rationality, the
carefully articulated social structure of the universe, as
"Preludes" sees it, and as Eliot in poem after poem insist-
ed he too saw it. But, again, this is specifically social
criticism, and even more importantly, it is founded in
affection, not in contempt. Readers of Eliot's later poetry
forget these facts, I think, at their peril.[7]

2

From St. Louis to London: Prufrock *to* "Gerontion"

In his late, small book, *Notes towards the Definition of Culture*, Eliot wrote that "The primary channel of transmission of culture is the family: no man wholly escapes from the kind, or wholly surpasses the degree, of culture which he acquired from his early environment."[1] There is a great deal about Eliot's "early environment" which we do not know; much of what documentation may eventually be available is still under lock and key. Eliot himself did not "wish my executors to facilitate or countenance the writing of any biography."[2] There is likely to be more than one biographical study, eventually, of a completeness now impossible; there will surely be editions of Eliot's letters, though none has as yet appeared.[3]

But a good deal is already known and in public print. Eliot's family had migrated from England to New England. He is related to Sir Thomas Elyot (1499–1546), author of *The Governour*. Among his ancestors was the famous missionary preacher, John Eliot (1604–90) and among his latter-day relatives was Charles William Eliot (1834–1926), president of Harvard from 1869–1909 and editor of *The Harvard Classics*. Eliot's paternal grandfather, William Greenleaf Eliot (1801–87), a Unitarian minister, was trained, like his more famous grandson, at Harvard. He migrated west, founding a Unitarian mission in St. Louis and helping to found what became Washington University (of which he became the third chancellor in 1872). He was without doubt a man of high principles and immense energy. "A business enterpriser once said that if [Eliot's grandfather] had been his partner, 'we should have made most of the money west of the Alleghanies.' But he lent his strength wholly to ideal enthusiasms."[4] William Greenleaf Eliot's oldest son, Thomas Lamb Eliot, became a crusading Unitarian minister, moving still farther west to Portland, Oregon. Henry Ware Eliot, the second son,

disappointed his father by becoming a very successful
brick-maker. "He had had enough of church and Sunday
school obligations in twenty years of a preacher's home."[5]
Another son, Edward Cranch Eliot, became a successful
lawyer, again in St. Louis.

William Greenleaf Eliot remained a potent influence
in all his children's and his grandchildren's lives. Thomas
Stearns Eliot (Stearns was his mother's maiden name; her
father was Thomas Stearns, Jr.) grew up in his grandfather's shadow. His mother "revered her father-in-law
and brought up her children to observe two of his laws in
particular, those of self-denial and public service. T. S.
Eliot acknowledged that his early training in self-denial
left him permanently scarred by an inability to enjoy even
harmless pleasures. . . . Even as a boy, said one cousin,
'Tom had a great sense of mission'."[6] His mother was also
a poet, but one who "assumed that poetry is a high, virtu-
ous vocation, which teaches and encourages its readers."
Plainly, she "thought of her poetry and her religion
together."[7] Equally plainly, she thought very little of
"conventional femininity . . . [Her] bed faced a mant-
lepiece draped with a velvet cloth on which rested a paint-
ing of the madonna and child [and on] her wall there hung
an engraving of Theodosius and St. Ambrose, illustrating
the triumph of holy over temporal power."[8] Nor did she
think much of conventional sports and games. "Tom was
the last of seven children, . . . had few playmates and spent
most of his time reading. He had a congenital double
hernia and [his mother], afraid it would rupture, forbade
football and strenuous sports."[9] There is clear evidence,
too, that "disappointed that her poems had gone almost
unrecognized, Mrs. Eliot took comfort from her youngest
son's literary promise."[10] Though the evidence is less
clear, it seems that his mother, and indeed most of his
family, regarded him as "special" from the very start.[11]

Whether his father shared this feeling is not clear; later evidence might suggest that he did not, since both toward the end of his life (he died in 1919) and even in his will, Henry Ware Eliot registered disapproval of his son's career, his son's marriage, his son's choice of residence.[12]

The Eliot family had both familial and residential links to New England. "In 1896 Eliot's father built a large, solid house for his family at Eastern Point, near Gloucester [, Massachusetts]." Spending summers in this house, which was near Cape Ann, Eliot "became a proficient sailor."[13] He explored the beaches and acquired a considerable fund of lore about the sea. Formally educated at Smith Academy, a conservative private school in St. Louis, Eliot moved on to Harvard in 1906. He had started Latin at age twelve at Smith, and Greek at age thirteen; at Harvard his studies were similar, though more advanced and more varied. He took his B.A. in 1909, an M.A. in English literature in 1910, spent 1910–11 at the Sorbonne, and then in 1911–14, back at Harvard, he studied and taught philosophy and got within one final notch of the Ph.D. degree. His doctoral thesis, *Knowledge and Experience in the Philosophy of F.H. Bradley,*[14] was completed and accepted, but World War One, which broke out while he was in England, kept him from returning for the defense of his thesis. When the war ended, Eliot was married and had decided to remain in England, determined to live a life outside of the university.

It is hard to tell, without documentation not yet available, just how Eliot's marriage came about. What is certain is that it was hasty (he had known the lady for two months), it was in some sense knowingly in defiance of his parents (who had supported him for twenty-six years but cut him off, at once, after his marriage), and it was in virtually every sense a disaster. Vivienne Haigh-Wood was slightly older than Eliot and very much more flamboyant;

her flamboyance quickly deteriorated into shrillness and, before long, into obvious instability. "One Friday evening at dinner," writes Lyndall Gordon, "Vivienne Eliot told Bertrand Russell that she had married her husband to stimulate him, but found she could not do it. . . . [But] Vivienne misrepresented their relationship to Russell . . . her nervous, hysterical, unsympathetic nature contributed substantially to their unhappiness."[15] The marriage quickly became what it remained until, in 1933, Eliot left her; Vivienne died in a mental home in 1947, and ten years later Eliot married his former secretary. Stephen Spender believes "that while Vivien[ne]'s health may have made a normal marriage relationship difficult, she was totally and irrevocably dedicated to him."[16] Much of the restrained, but fairly obvious, sexual torment in Eliot's poetry may well be linked to "this misalliance."[17]

And not only did Henry Ware Eliot cut off support for his wayward son. He also "made arrangements that any property left to Eliot would in the event of his death revert to the family trust and not go to" his wife.[18] Eliot at once sought employment, first as a school teacher, then as a junior-level banker, and then as an editor, especially of *The Criterion* magazine, and in 1925, at what later became Faber and Faber, the distinguished publishing house. He was a director of Faber and Faber until his death in 1965. But in the early years he also did extension lecturing, and seems to have taken virtually any paid journalism which came his way: from 1915 to the early 1920s he worked himself to "the verge of a nervous breakdown."[19] This, too, is of clear significance in much of Eliot's poetry of the period, most especially *The Waste Land.*[20]

The chief early volumes, *Prufrock and Other Observations* (1917) and *Poems, 1920,* also entitled in a slightly earlier version *Ara Vos Prec* (being the first words of a

poem by the Provencal poet, Arnaut Daniel: "Now I pray
you"), made a small but not insignificant impact. "Even
by 1925 Eliot's reputation as a literary man had not spread
very far."[21] On the other hand, the poet Kathleen Raine
declares flatly that "For my generation T. S. Eliot's early
poetry, more than the work of any other poet, has enabled
us to know our world imaginatively."[22] Or as a German
observer put it, "Around 1920 Eliot was discovered by the
English literary avant-garde. He was propagated by the
highbrows, ignored by the Establishment."[23]

There are twelve poems in the *Prufrock* volume, including the famous title poem, and twelve in *Poems, 1920,*
which is led off in its turn by the almost equally well-
known "Gerontion" (which Eliot had intended to incorporate into *The Waste Land;* he was dissuaded, in this as
in so much else, by Ezra Pound—but more of that at a
later point). To understand the nature and extent of Eliot's
achievements and innovations, we need to examine many
of these poems, though not in the same detail with which
we examined "Preludes."

"The Love Song of J. Alfred Prufrock," composed
over the period 1909–11 and finally finished in August of
the latter year in Munich, Germany, is very much a parallel piece to "Preludes." "Prufrock," however, is both more
pointed as a poem, and less pointed as social criticism.
Unlike the anonymous and omni-sexual persona of "Preludes," "Prufrock" is built around the arid, timid, conventional persona of a man sexual enough to admit desire, but
insufficiently sexual to do anything about it. Still, at one
point, the two poems virtually intersect. Having asked
three times, "how should I presume," the persona of "Prufrock" steps back, in a three-line section carefully separated off by a line of spaced-out periods, and wonders:

Shall I say, I have gone at dusk through narrow streets

> And watched the smoke that rises from the pipes
> Of lonely men in shirt-sleeves, leaning out of windows?

The echo of "short square fingers stuffing pipes, / And
evening newspapers, and eyes / Assured of certain certainties," from "Preludes," is clear. And the significance of
lines like this becomes still plainer when we read, in Lyndall Gordon's biographical study, that "Failing to find life
amongst his own class Eliot sought out the slum areas."[24]
Nor was exploration of lower-class urban areas a merely
transient phase, practiced while Eliot was an undergraduate at Harvard. "He paced the streets of Paris," too;
"slumming, for Eliot, was no pastime: he took it too seriously."[25] It was the same thing when he moved to London: "As Eliot had sought depravity in Montparnasse in
1911, he sought it again in disreputable suburbs in South
London."[26]

But was it really "depravity" Eliot was hunting, in
life and in his poems? Was he seeking thrills, or disgust—
or was he, in fact, trying to understand a side of the world
from which his upper-class upbringing had barred him?
And did he look at it with horror or, rather, with remorse
and a very deep sorrow? "Despite his solitary nature, Eliot
did not find it easy to reject society. . . . It seemed to many
of Eliot's contemporaries that he willfully averted his eyes
from social problems between the wars and took refuge in
obsolete institutions."[27] It is I think profoundly true that
"Eliot was not against liberalism or democracy *per se;* he
simply feared that they would not work. . . . [He] saw the
children of the early twentieth century as an alien people
clutching cheap gods . . . [and] tried to give back to the
early twentieth century a world in which men lived by
. . . moral dimensions."[28]

And these "moral dimensions" add to rather than
detract from the weight and force of "Prufrock," which is,

I think, pretty well agreed to be the greatest of Eliot's poems before *The Waste Land.* "And where in modern poetry," asked F. O. Matthiessen as long ago as 1935, "are there characters realized with such convincing definiteness as Prufrock and Sweeney?"[29] Eliot's focused, taut approach makes Prufrock (the name is casually appropriated from Prufrock-Littau, furniture wholesalers, a firm which advertised "in St. Louis, Missouri, in the first decade of the present century . . ."[30]) more than simply alive. He becomes the object of intense pity and intense scorn: the student editors of a university newspaper, of which I was once faculty advisor, not only named their dog Prufrock, but also put his name on the masthead.

Eliot draws us into the poem at once: "Let us go then, you and I . . ." The invitation is powerful, if not entirely welcome. And the tremor of unpleasantness to come is immediately confirmed: ". . . When the evening is *spread out* against the sky . . ." (italics added). It does not sound much like a cheerful stroll, but neither does it sound like an invitation we can successfully resist. Eliot follows the harsh, helpless, perhaps brutal "spread out" with the famous third line, again brutal and transfixing. ". . . Like a patient etherised upon a table."[31] The combination of lyricism and brutality, of soft words and harsh ideas, is deeply established in these first three lines; it continues with variations in the rest of the poem. If we have "restless nights in one-night cheap hotels," on the one hand, we soon enough find ourselves confronted, to balance matters, with "tedious argument[s] / Of insidious intent. . . ." If we have the cat-like "yellow fog," that soon enough leads us to the apparently equally lyrical "There will be time, there will be time," which invocation immediately becomes, "There will be time to murder and create. . . ." If there is seriousness in the presentation of the "hundred indecisions," the "hundred visions and revisions," it is promptly undercut with the intense triviality of "Before the taking of a toast and tea." It is, in short, a passionately ironic poem, committed to showing us at one and the same time the human potential of sterile socialites like Prufrock, but also the immutably helpless nature of that sterility. It is an affecting, even an achingly affecting fact that he can hear "the mermaids singing, each to each." But it remains conclusively true that "they will [not] sing to me." He can wonder, but he cannot dare. He can, in the style of John the Baptist, weep and pray, but "I am no prophet—and here's no great matter."

Eliot's techniques, in this and similar poems, are both exceedingly deft and exceedingly diverse. He owed much, as all artists do, in many directions.[32] But too much can be made of those debts: what Ezra Pound wrote to Harriet Monroe, then editor of *Poetry* magazine, on September 30, 1914, is I think perhaps the most important single comment ever made about the influences on the young Eliot:

> He is the only American I know of who has made what I can call adequate preparation for writing. He has actually trained himself *and* modernized himself *on his own.* The rest of the *promising young* have done one or the other but never both. . . . It is such a comfort to meet a man and not have to tell him to wash his face, wipe his feet, and remember the date (1914) on the calendar.[33]

Eliot's use of rhyme, for example, is both immensely varied and immensely ingenious. It can be sharply out of phase (that is, employed in lines of very different metrical length), as in / *I, sky* / in lines 1 and 2, or as in / *argument, intent* / in lines 8 and 9. Used this way it has a kind of off-key sound, neither quite traditional nor quite mocking. In the repeated couplet, almost but not quite the balanced iambic pentameter couplet of Alexander Pope (the second line having only four instead of five feet), "In the room the

women come and go / Talking of Michelangelo," the
rhyme is so distinctly overemphasized that it is clearly an
undercutting or mocking feature. Eliot uses other sorts of
rhyme too, part-rhyme (as in / table, hotel / in lines 3 and
6), spaced-out rhyme (as in / leap, asleep / in lines 20 and
22), multisyllabic rhyme (as in / indecisions, revisions / in
lines 32 and 33), insistent over-rhyme (as in / dare, stair,
hair / in lines 38–40 and / thin, chin, pin, thin / in lines
41–44), or slant rhyme (as in claws at the end of line 73
and floors in the middle of line 74).

Like his rhyming techniques, and the metrical diversity he manipulates so effectively, Eliot's rhetorical and
metaphorical devices are untraditional. The clanging
together of dissimilarities, as in the key metaphor of lines
2 and 3 ("When the evening is spread out against the sky
/ Like a patient etherised upon a table"), helps explain his
lifelong affection for and championing of John Donne and
the other Metaphysical poets, who of course employed
very similar metaphorical devices. Shock is, to be sure, a
basic feature of poetry like "Prufrock," and as we have
already seen, Eliot does not use it without clear purpose.
Nor does he overuse it: indeed, he blends it with "soft"
passages like the eight lines about the yellow fog, and the
nine-line passage about "Prince Hamlet," as if to heighten
the shock effect when it does come. His rhetoric can be as
straightforward as "certain half-deserted streets, / The
muttering retreats / Of restless nights in one-night cheap
hotels . . ." or as elaborately high-toned as "I have seen
them riding seaward on the waves / Combing the white
hair of the waves blown back / When the wind blows the
water white and black."

And to audiences, even literate audiences, unused to
such sharp-edged mixtures of rhetorical levels, and such
wide-ranging and untraditional poetic techniques, "Prufrock" can, and did, seem disturbingly new. Again, Ezra

Pound's fierce and trenchant criticism of Harriet Monroe, in a letter to her dated January 31, 1915, is of much more than mere historical interest:

"Mr. Prufrock" does not "go off at the end." It is a portrait of failure, or of a character which fails, and it would be false art to make it end on a note of triumph. I dislike the paragraph about Hamlet, but it is an early and cherished bit and T. E. won't give it up, and as it is the only portion of the poem that most readers will like at first reading, I don't see that it will do much harm.

For the rest: a portrait satire on futility can't end by turning that quintessence of futility, Mr. P. into a reformed character breathing out fire and ozone.[34]

That Miss Monroe was seriously disturbed, incidentally, is emphasized by Pound's sharp reproof to her, in a letter dated November 9, 1914. "No, most emphatically I will not ask Eliot to write down to any audience whatsoever. . . . Neither will I send you Eliot's address in order that he may be insulted."[35] Sixty-five years after the poem's first appearance in print (and almost seventy years after its composition), we are considerably more accustomed to such "modern" approaches—but it was Eliot as much as any man who made them acceptable.

Perhaps the most difficult aspect of "Prufrock," and a continuing difficulty in all of Eliot's poetry to the end of his life, is what might be called its "indeterminacy." That is, Eliot is constantly making two basic and exceedingly important kinds of assumptions as to his readership: (1) that his readers can and do understand his allusions, his references to people and to literary works, and in time to other things as well; and (2) that his readers can readily reconstruct an entire skeleton, as it were, though presented only with, say, a metatarsal bone or a chunk of a skull. Eliot's allusions are not much of a problem, in "Prufrock," though they become a matter of some importance later on in his work. Let me therefore focus briefly on the second variety of "indeterminacy."

Perhaps the most famous example in "Prufrock" is the couplet toward the end, "I grow old . . . I grow old . . . / I shall wear the bottoms of my trousers rolled." We can read, in the ingenious pages of Eliot's many scholarly explicators, that this refers to "stylish trousers with cuffs."[36] Over-ingenuity can create, and in the past it has, fantastic and profound (but also profoundly irrelevant) significance for such minor matters. And it is true that Eliot has not troubled to give us all the information we need. But is it true that he has not given us *enough* information (as in other and later poems I think he sometimes has not)? We know that Prufrock is a socialite; we have heard him tell us, proudly, of "My morning coat, my collar mounting firmly to the chin, / My necktie rich and modest, but asserted by a simple pin." Just after the lines at issue he worries, "Shall I part my hair behind?" and goes on to proclaim that he will "wear white flannel trousers, and walk upon the beach." And with so full a presentation of Prufrock's sartorial nature, do we really need more details about his trouser cuffs? Or, to put it differently, is it not enough to leave some minor indeterminacies, when the main outlines are so firmly sketched in? (One might invoke the "impressionism" of Cézanne and other modern painters, even the "pointillisme" of Georges Seurat, whose canvases seem incomprehensible when viewed too closely, but fall into pretty clear shape when viewed from an optically correct distance. Eliot is of course the contemporary of such painters, and more than probably knew their work.)

The poet needs, of course, to draw a fine but basic line between confusing and illuminating the reader. Indeterminacy can be bewildering if not kept under control. Even in "Prufrock," readers have for years been troubled by the "overwhelming question," which is never expressly formulated. It is one thing, such readers have argued, to shock us into comprehension with indeterminate metaphors like, "I have measured out my life with coffee spoons," metaphors which we do not and cannot take literally but which forcefully oblige us to see the intense triviality of Prufrock's well-bred existence. But how, they insist, are we to deal with what seems much more specific —an "overwhelming question"—yet is in the end only infuriatingly obscure? One response to such objections might be that we simply do not need to know. The fact that Prufrock never asks an "overwhelming" question, that he is not, indeed, capable of asking it, is arguably enough information. But I think it is not difficult, using the larger context of the poem as a whole, to see that the overwhelming question which Prufrock "dares not ask [is]: What is the meaning of this life? He realizes the sterile monotony of his 'works and days,' and he senses that a more fruitful and meaningful life must exist."[37] If this is not precise enough, I do not know what is. Nor is it drawn from external (or esoteric) sources: the poem itself gives us all we need, if we read it closely enough.

And Eliot plainly expects, even requires, such close reading. We do not personally know, nor can we possibly know, "our dear deplorable friend, Miss X, the *precieuse ridicule* to end all preciosity, serving tea so exquisitely among her bric-a-brac, . . . [and] pinned like a butterfly to a page in *Portrait of a Lady.*"[38] But once again, as in "Prufrock," "Portrait of a Lady" (1909–10) opens with lines that oblige the reader to fix his attention, and fix it carefully. "Among the smoke and fog of a December afternoon / You have the scene arrange itself—as it will seem to do— / With 'I have saved this afternoon for you'. . . ." There is not the same depth of perception in this poem as there is in "Prufrock," and most especially there is not the same sympathy. Even the male persona, who more than a little resembles Prufrock, is not treated with anything like the same warmth. "I mount the strairs and turn the handle of the door / And feel as if I had mounted on my hands and knees." Nor are the ideas of the poem more than a kind of echo of "Prufrock," with the sexual polarities reversed. "Recalling things that other people have desired," the persona at once asks, Prufrock-style, "Are these ideas right or wrong?" The final two verse paragraphs attain to a somewhat more passionate intensity, but it is not enough, and it is on the whole too late. The poem is, I believe, slighter than its reputation and need not unduly detain us here.[39]

"Rhapsody on a Windy Night" (1910–11) and "La Figlia che Piange" (1911–14) are still further variations on themes already familiar. "Rhapsody" is the lesser of the two, more a youthful experiment than successfully realized poetry. The last three lines, though they strongly echo "Preludes" and "Prufrock," are much too melodramatic to have the force of either. "The bed is open; the toothbrush hangs on the wall, / Put your shoes at the door, sleep, prepare for life. // The last twist of the knife." The first verse paragraph, with its "lunar synthesis, / Whispering lunar incantations," is simply pretentious, while the second verse paragraph, which gives us the street-lamp's night thoughts, is arch and rather strained. But the third verse paragraph suggests some of the shape of things to come. "The memory throws up high and dry / A crowd of twisted things; / A twisted branch upon the beach / Eaten smooth, and polished / As if the world gave up / The secret of its skeleton, / Stiff and white. / A broken spring in a factory yard, / Rust that clings to the form that the strength has left / Hard and curled and ready to snap." Eliot here prefigures his later push toward abstraction of the physical world, so marked from "Gerontion" on, and perhaps especially so in "The Hollow Men" (1925) and in *Ash-Wednesday* (1930). Significantly, there are to be no broken springs in factory yards, in that later poetry. Eliot's slum tours seem to have been replaced late in the 1920s by parish-visiting and other quasi-ecclesiastical occupations. And the world, once rejected, is not easily readmitted—as we shall see much later on, when we come to "Four Quartets" (1935–42). But that this is, at least, the physical world of "Preludes" and "Prufrock," there can be no doubt. Eliot emphasizes that fact with yet another "reminiscence," toward the poem's close, a memory "Of sunless geraniums / And dust in crevices, / Smells of chestnuts in the streets, / And female smells in shuttered rooms, / And cigarettes in corridors / And cocktail smells in bars." It is the physical world of "Preludes," but there is very little of that poem's power and force. The images are too scattered here, and the effect is too thin. There is, interestingly, a very similar passage in "Portrait of a Lady," where it does not fit entirely well: "Let us take the air, in a tobacco trance, / Admire the monuments, / Discuss the late events, / Correct our watches by the public clocks. / Then sit for half an hour and drink our bocks." There is insufficient context for this sort of thing in "Portrait of a Lady." There is rather more context in "Rhapsody," but still not enough to turn indeterminacy into powerful, embodied verse.

"La Figlia che Piange" (Weeping Girl) is both shorter and tighter in structure; still, the absence of a solid context leaches some of the poem's potential effect. The Latin epigraph, which is from Virgil's *Aeneid,* does not help much: "Maiden, by what name shall I know you?" There is real drama in her "pained surprise," in her flinging her flowers to the ground. But though "Weave, weave the sunlight in your hair" is a very beautiful line, it is not fully meaningful. (Young poets are addicted to such lines.)

Without knowing why she has been rejected, we cannot know *how* her lover has left her, "As the soul leaves the body torn and bruised, / As the mind deserts the body it has used." That is, the two strands of the metaphor do not fully coalesce, absent more information. The soul / body / mind categories are, of course, fully familiar to us, as abstractions—but how are they to be embodied, here? She is the "body," plainly, in both the lines just quoted, and he is both the "soul" and the "mind." But what does that really tell us, except, perhaps, that Eliot might well be what we are apt to call today a male chauvinist? And the ironic self-consciousness at the end—"Sometimes these cogitations still amaze / The troubled midnight and the noon's repose"—seems oddly out of place without the larger context the poem does not give us. Rather than justified irony, these lines seem, at least partly, a pose, an unearned mask, though just what is behind the mask I do not think anyone can say.

The three pleasantly satirical poems about New Englanders, "The *Boston Evening Transcript,*" "Aunt Helen," and "Cousin Nancy," all dating, like "Morning at the Window," from 1915, are charming and need no long explication. In the first poem, there is a nice echo of "Prufrock." "When evening quickens faintly in the street, / Wakening the appetites of life in some / And to others bringing the *Boston Evening Transcript.*" And in the second poem, there is an anticipation of the religious satires shortly to be written, "Now when she died there was silence in heaven / And silence at her end of the street." The attack on New England in the third poem is the weakest, the least well-focused of these satires, but it is no less pleasant than the others. "Conversation Galante" (1909–10) is purely and simply a pastiche based on the assorted French poets who were then influencing Eliot, most especially Jules Laforgue.

Which leaves us, of the poems in Eliot's first volume
of poetry, only "Mr. Apollinax" (1915), which is by common consent a portrait of Bertrand Russell as a visiting
professor at Harvard, and "Hysteria" (1915), a prose
poem, which I suspect might be about Eliot's future wife,
Vivienne Haigh-Wood. Bertrand Russell as Priapus is all-
in-all an inspired association, as are the names of the staid
and uncomprehending Bostonians, "Mrs. Phlaccus" (flac-
cid) and "Professor Channing-Cheetah." There is great
delicacy in the first five lines and real passion in "I heard
the beat of centaur's hoofs over the hard turf / As his dry
and passionate talk devoured the afternoon." The movement from that often violent mythical half man, half
horse, the centaur, across "hard turf"—a beautifully restrained image—to the classically "dry and passionate
talk" of Bertrand Russell, is deftly managed. The phrase
"devoured the afternoon," too, leads directly into the final
dismissing of the Bostonians. "Of dowager Mrs. Phlaccus,
and Professor and Mrs. Cheetah / I remember a slice of
lemon, and a bitten macaroon." But the second half of the
first verse paragraph, beginning with the fetal image in line
7 and continuing through the overlong and underfocused
sea images which follow in lines 8–12, does not hold up
well under close examination. How did those "coral is-
lands" get into the poem? And those drowned bodies?
What have we actually been told when we are informed
that "His laughter was submarine and profound"? And
the implicit personification in "fingers of surf " is totally
irrelevant to anything in the poem, so far as I can see. The
sea imagery at the beginning of the second verse paragraph, Russell's head "rolling under a chair . . . With
seaweed in its hair," is a great deal more pointed, and
mercifully shorter as well.

"Hysteria" is Eliot's only prose poem, and therefore
only one among many paths untaken for this perpetually

experimenting, perpetually restless poet. (The poem needs, I suggest, to be read aloud in order to be fully appreciated, and until the waiter speaks it should I think be read with increasing rapidity; the last sentence should be spoken in one breath and pretty much in a monotone.) Most critics ignore "Hysteria"; it has been asserted, I think without justification, that "the whole religious perspective is mocked by the woman" in this poem,[40] and Grover Smith is sure, though I am not sure why, that "It is he [the persona / speaker], not the lady, who is hysterical."[41] It seems to me that the lady's mad laughter is distinctly hysterical; something about it, or about some episode not given to us in the poem, has also made the waiter hysterical, as both his actions and his speech indicate with absolute clarity. The persona, on the other hand, is capable of both decision and action based on that decision; he seems also to be rather objectively perceptive about the effect of the lady's laughter on him. "I was aware of being involved. . . ." The implicit eroticism is beautifully whisked to the surface in the final sentence: ". . . if the shaking of her breasts could be stopped, some of the fragments of the afternoon might be collected . . ." And the timid, rational, hopeful seducer, concentrating his "attention with careful subtlety," is neatly counterpointed by that final sentence against the dark inner worlds evoked earlier in the poem, worlds which are largely governed not by poets but by Messers. Jung, Freud, and Co. "Hysteria" is too different from Eliot's other works for us to be able to make any larger claims. What he might have made of the prose poem—his prose style was, as we shall see, masterful—it is quite impossible to say. But I think it says something important about Eliot as a poet, both that he tried the form and that, in this single instance, he made as much out of it as he did. It is an impressive performance, if not exactly a typical one.

* * *

Four of the poems in *Poems, 1920* are in French. Of those in English, seven are in the quatrain form which preoccupied Eliot at this period, and one, the volume's major effort, "Gerontion," is in lines of variable length but without the rhyme used in "Prufrock."[42] The satirical quatrains deserve some attention; the French poems deserve less; and "Gerontion" obviously deserves most.

The title of this poem, drawn from the Greek word for old man, is a coinage much like that used in the title of Edward Elgar's tone poem, "The Dream of Gerontius," or in the word we have invented to describe the science that treats the decline of life, namely gerontology. The three-line epigraph comes from Shakespeare's *Measure for Measure,* where it is part of a speech by the duke, delivered to convince a condemned man that after all life is not worth hanging on to. These extremely visible signs of erudition definitely presage the future for Eliot, as also do the increasing signs of impersonality and the increased level of abstraction. "Prufrock" was, whatever indeterminacy his poem may contain, still a full-fledged human being, with a full if unusual name. Gerontion is simply, as the first line tells us, "an old man in a dry month." He has neither name, in the usual sense, nor identity and background. He is much like what Henry James called a *ficelle* —that is, a character designed "to swell a progress, start a scene," but not to become full-fleshed, and above all not to become literarily dominant. The *ficelle* cannot be permitted to assume any sort of dramatic prominence—and Gerontion does not assume it. He remains, from start to finish, a half-real persona, designed to raise questions on the poet's behalf. It is a perfectly legitimate approach; I do not mean to denigrate but only to describe it. It is, however, a large shift from the approach taken in poems like "Prufrock," which are dramatic monologues of a sort

Eliot will not again attempt. And the shift is both deliberate and, in and of itself, of considerable significance.

"Gerontion," then, is what might be called the first fully "intellectual" poem by one of the most intellectual of poets. The very last line, not coincidentally, sums it all up as *"thoughts* of a dry brain in a dry season." (Italics added). And what seems to me the key line announcing the central thrust of the poem, is "After such knowledge, what forgiveness?"[43] That is, given the opportunities mankind has had, given the knowledge it has been given and the knowledge it has won for itself, how can its present lack of fundamental understanding be forgiven? That understanding, as we have begun to see in Eliot's earlier poems, is both a secular and a religious matter—secular in the sense that we are obliged to deal with the world we dwell in, and religious in the sense that ultimate reliance seems clearly misplaced when rested on mankind alone. Something more is needed; we humans are too plainly unreliable and, in the spiritual sense, too unsuccessful. "In the juvescence [youth] of the year / Came Christ the tiger," writes Eliot, indicating what ought to be, but still is not, the answer. From the beginning, he means to say, we have had the knowledge of Christ. But it has been "The word within a word, unable to speak a word"—at least, unable to speak a word to the like of us, who refuse to listen.

The opening verse paragraph gives us a partial sense of Gerontion the character. It is, however, largely a sense of (a) his age, (b) the unadventuresomeness of his existence, then and now, and (c) the rot of so-called Christian society, one significant result of which is that "any large number of free-thinking Jews [is] undesirable."[44] "My house is a decayed house," Gerontion tells us, speaking both literally and in some not entirely apparent larger sense. His house is a house; it is also his "home" in a spiritual sense. And since the house is "owned" by a Jew who "squats on the window sill," the decay is plainly to be ascribed to the Jew, "spawned in some estaminet [public-house, saloon] of Antwerp, / Blistered [disgraced, shamed] in Brussels, patched and peeled in London." The anti-Semitism is obvious, and we shall meet with it again in even more virulent forms in other poems in this volume. It is no excuse to note that Eliot was by no means alone, even among literary figures, in his mistrust of and contempt for Jews. Ezra Pound was similarly inclined, as was E. E. Cummings; and there were others. Anti-Semitism has a long history in European and American history. Further, the persona is "peevish"; his surroundings are essentially barren, "rocks, moss, stonecrop, iron, merds"; and he is, finally, "a dull head among windy spaces." That is about all the physical reality Gerontion is permitted to have in this poem of spiritual realities.

"Signs are taken for wonders," the next paragraph begins. Human beings are content with vulgarizations, with inadequate representations of the true. Christ's arrival in this world of decay occurs "in depraved May." That is, even the calendar succumbs to the rot, though the "dogwood and chestnut" bloom on in their innocence— joined, significantly, by the "flowering judas," which according to legend is the tree upon which Christ's legendary betrayer is supposed to have hanged himself. The disembodied names, like those toward the end of the poem, are not intended to have even as much physical reality as does Gerontion. They are symbols, though whether of Gerontion's own past or of European and even Asian humanity generally the poem does not tell us. And by suggesting, at least in part, some specific realities, which it refuses to embody for us, the poem is to some extent weakened, as later poems will also be weakened.

The key paragraph is that which begins with "After

such knowledge, what forgiveness?" The lessons imparted here revolve around the fact that secular knowledge is insufficient; human "history" deceives rather than enlightens, using ambition, vanity, confusion, lack of belief, bad timing, fear, and even courage as its tools. And humankind is astray in its "many cunning passages, contrived corridors." Even whatever may be given comes to us "with such supple confusions / That the giving famishes the craving." Accordingly, the "tiger" who leaps out at us, "in the new year," is Christ the tiger, invoked earlier in the poem. And Christ comes, now, not to be eaten, but to eat: "Us he devours"—for we have not profited from what has remained, for us, "swaddled with darkness."

Gerontion is, he tells us, not content to say that all is over; he is still alive, there is still the possibility of redemption, of change, while he is "stiffen[ing] in a rented house." He seems to assure Christ (though Christ is not named) that there is nothing demonic or evil in his admissions, or in his state of mind. "I that was near your heart was removed therefrom"—and he seems to suggest that old age is to blame. "I have lost my sight, smell, hearing, taste and touch . . ." One has the sense, however, that for Eliot old age is simply emblematic, even symbolic, of the general decay of Western civilization. He will write, in *Ash-Wednesday,* "Why should the agèd eagle stretch his wings?" and the line ought not to be taken literally (Eliot was 42 when *Ash-Wednesday* appeared).[45] But death, whether merely physical or spiritual as well, does not wait. "Will the spider . . . suspend its operations . . ."? Plainly it will not. We all (the names, as I have said, are not personal) will be "whirled . . . in[to] fractured atoms," just as in Eliot's sense of things, we are all, like Gerontion, "tenants of the house."

The poem has been criticized as imperfectly focused. I think, however, it is fairer to say, with Elizabeth Drew, that it "is one of Eliot's most powerful, and one of his most obscure" poems.[46] "Gerontion" must also be understood, not only as a transitional poem pointing toward much that came after it, but as a not entirely successful attempt to deal with the new forces, the new ideas, and the new people affecting the poet himself. Eliot's marriage had gone from bad to worse. "The qualities of patience and forbearance which her [Vivienne's] hysteria brought out in him may not have been the best thing for either of them."[47] Ezra Pound had come into Eliot's life in 1914, and for a number of years was part literary mentor, part friend and educator, part bully to his younger fellow exile. Pound was a totally dedicated writer, a learned man (though also a crank), something of a dandy, and something too of a bohemian. Eliot was an equally dedicated writer, an equally learned man, something of a dandy himself, and not at all a bohemian; indeed, he was reserved and conservative in most things social and personal. Their meeting and their friendship, which was relatively brief (less than a decade saw them drifting into polite respect, without much contact or warmth), brought Eliot more than an extraordinarily generous and well-connected literary friend. It put him face to face with a host of new ideas in literature and in larger matters. It is no exaggeration to say that in good part Eliot defined himself in these years from 1915 to the early 1920s by reference to Pound— sometimes in opposition to Pound. It was through Pound, for example, that Eliot met Wyndham Lewis, Harriet Weaver, the poet H. D., and Richard Aldington, and in the company of these and other luminaries of the London literary life, he also came into contact with Ford Madox Ford and Arthur Waley and Amy Lowell—and more.

Eliot entered the London literary world both as a writer and as a working editor. He was literary editor of a magazine, *The Egoist,* from 1917–19; after 1922, and until its demise in 1939, he was editor-in-chief of *The Criterion.* Neither journal had a large circulation, but both journals were active combatants on the literary, and in the case of *The Criterion,* the social, philosophical, religious, and even political battlefields of the day. "By 1922 he had written nearly a hundred book reviews and occasional essays for various periodicals,"[48] including work for both the International Journal of Ethics and "two highly technical articles on Leibniz and Bradley in *The Monist* . . ."[49] From 1917 to 1925, Eliot worked in the foreign department at Lloyds Bank, and when in 1925 he joined the Faber publishing firm, "he had good qualifications for a man of business, and it was as a man of business . . . that he was taken on."[50]

Eliot was, after all, a foreigner, not yet a British subject and in some important ways never anything but an American resident in London. "The consensus," says one well-known literary Briton, "is that Eliot knew England and the English very imperfectly, after thirty years."[51] He was a witty and urbane man, confronting with increasing concern matters that wit alone could not deal with. "If T. S. Eliot were not a famous poet," writes Clive Bell, Virginia Woolf's brother-in-law, "he would be known as a remarkably clever man."[52] How was he to square his wit and his humor—it must not be forgotten that Eliot wrote nonsense verse and funny poems all his life, publishing *Old Possum's Book of Practical Cats* in 1939 (Possum was one of his lifelong nicknames)—with the seriousness of his social and spiritual preoccupations? How was he to define himself, as husband, as poet, as citizen, as literary critic, as teacher and journalist? "Even after he abandoned the classroom, Eliot remained an educator."[53] The "wilderness of mirrors" which we find in "Gerontion," as well as the whirling winds and "fractured atoms," are in an important way reflective of Eliot's inner life at the time he wrote this and the other work in *Poems, 1920.* And those other poems, quite as well as "Gerontion," show how he struggled to come to terms with at least some of the many and varied and sometimes jangling strands of his new life in England.

The two Sweeney poems, and "The Hippopotamus," are generally and correctly taken as the best of the seven quatrain-poems, all satirical. As I have already indicated, "The Hippopotamus," written in 1917, was understood as savagely anti-clerical. As late as 1964, Genesius Jones, a Roman Catholic priest, could record that "I have heard Mr. Eliot damned out of hand by the orthodox because of 'The Hippopotamus'."[54] The poem's two epigraphs might have alerted readers to Eliot's seriousness. The first and longest reads, in translation, "In like manner, let all reverence the Deacons as Jesus Christ, and the Bishop as the Father, and the Presbyters as the council of God, and the assembly of the Apostles. Without these there is no Church. Concerning all which I am persuaded that you think after the same manner." The second epigraph adds that "when this epistle [read: "poem"] is read among you, cause that it be read also in the church of the Laodiceans," who were notoriously the most lukewarm and indifferent of the early Christians. Some of the satire is indeed pretty savage, especially the comparisons between the rejoicing choice and the mating hippo, and that between the sleeping animal and the Church, which somehow is able to "sleep and feed at once." If there is any ecclesiastical "error," it is precisely in the extremes to which Eliot pushes his satire. This may be (as of course it is) concerned criticism, but it is not "insider" work. On the other hand, these same excesses point, for our purposes here, at the still deeply unsettled attitudes of the poet, attracted and repelled by "this, and so much more," all at the same time. It is an unusually straightforward poem, and without

question an enduring one, which derives much of its
power from the forces contending within the poet.

The Sweeney poems, "Sweeney Among the Nightingales," written in 1918, and "Sweeney Erect," written in
1919, to which we should add, "Mr. Eliot's Sunday Morning Service," written in 1918 (it invokes Sweeney in the
last quatrain), are considerably less straightforward. They
are also much more akin to "Gerontion," technically,
especially in their shows of erudition and their insistence
on the indeterminate and the abstract. And finally, though
all three poems achieve moments of power, they are on the
whole less successful than "The Hippopotamus," much as
"Gerontion" is for all its power less successful on the
whole than is "Prufrock." "Apeneck Sweeney spreads his
knees / Letting his arms hang down to laugh," begins the
first of these three poems, at once contradicting the literal
sense of the title and asserting the harsh indeterminacy of
approach we are to find throughout. That is, Eliot is not
functioning here as the sort of dramatic monologuist he
was in "Prufrock." We are not to know Sweeney, but only
to despise him; he is not a person (nor even quite human),
but a lower-class, Irish "ape." We are a long way, too,
from the intense social sympathies of "Preludes." Eliot
has had half a dozen more years of experience with the
world, and it has not been terribly pleasant. "I have *lived*
through material for a score of long poems in the last six
months," he wrote to Conrad Aiken, January 10, 1916,
and on September 6, 1916, he added in a letter to his
brother Henry Eliot, "The present year has been, in some
respects, the most awful nightmare of anxiety that the
mind of man could conceive, but at least it is not dull, and
it has its compensations."[55] One of those compensations,
perhaps, was the satisfaction of hammering away at the
Sweeney-brutes of the world—not simply apelike, but

given "zebra" stripes and a "maculate [stained, spotted] giraffe" style jaw.

"Sweeney Among the Nightingales" takes place in a public house—i.e., in American terms, a bar, though lines like the following obscure the locale:

> The circles of the stormy moon
> Slide westward toward the River Plate,
> Death and the Raven drift above
> And Sweeney guards the hornèd gate.

"In plot, setting, and characters this poem is opacity itself."[56] It has been suggested that Sweeney may be asleep, here, since "the hornèd gate" is the aperture through which, in the ancient view of things, dreams escape from the underworld in order to rise and come into human heads. This is reinforced, some say, by the poem's epigraph, which has (in Greek) Agamemnon exclaiming, as he does in Aeschylus' play, *Agamemnon*, "Ay me! I am struck with a mortal stroke." And Agamemnon was asleep in his bath when he was murdered by his vengeful wife, Clytemnestra. (And say others, since Sweeney is taking a bath himself, in "Mr. Eliot's Sunday Morning Service," the link is even stronger!). But, "In any case, the lines are weak, . . . and why must we stand on our heads about it? I prefer to point out that Eliot has, after a fashion, stood on his."[57] Since the "raven" of line 7 is a reference to the constellation of Corvus, and given the vaguely ominous, even portentous tone of the quatrain, it may well be the poem here "uses astronomical symbols to suggest the time, place, and portent of the situation."[58] But though this explanation makes a kind of sense of the moon and the Raven, what sense is there to make of the River Plate—fairly clearly altered from its proper form, River Plata, in order to accommodate the rhyme with "gate." True, the hunter Orion, also astronomical, will appear in the next quatrain, he who pursued the Pleiades and was put to death by Artemis for that lecherous pursuit. But who is Sweeney pursuing? He seems in this next quatrain to be very much more pursued rather than pursuer. "The person in the Spanish cape / Tries to sit on Sweeney's knees." In short, we can readily tie ourselves into knots, unless we assume, and hold to the assumption, that the difficulties here are not poetically legitimate, and that Eliot must be held responsible for them.

Beginning with line 11 the poem drops its erudition and concentrates, though still with a high degree of indeterminacy, on varieties of dramatic action. We may not know why "the silent man in mocha brown" is either silent or in mocha brown, but we do know that he "sprawls at the window-sill and gapes" at the drunken slovenliness taking place. The almost obligatory nastiness about Jews, "Rachel *née* Rabinovitch," who "tears at the grapes with murderous paws," may not fit any logical schema, but it makes a kind of imprecise sense. We do not know if "the man with heavy eyes" is or is not Sweeney. I happen to think he is, but it does not much matter, for what we are told of him is that, faced with the "suspect" females, "thought to be in league" (though we do not know about what), he "declines the gambit" and goes outside, reappearing "Outside the window, leaning in." Does he have "a golden grin" because his mouth is full of dentist's gold? ("Do I dare to eat a peach?") No matter, as also it does not matter who the "someone indistinct" is or is not. What does matter, clearly, is that somewhere, presumably close by,

> The nightingales are singing near
> The Convent of the Sacred Heart,
>
> And sang within the bloody wood
> When Agamemnon cried aloud,

And let their liquid siftings fall
To stain the stiff dishonoured shroud.

Again, whether we are supposed to link these nightingales
with the nightingale in Ovid's bloody, sadistic, and lecherous "Tereus and Procne" tale, as has been argued, does
not seem important, for the poem no more establishes this
than it does the astronomical imagery, earlier. What the
poem does accomplish here is first a link between the birds
and a religious house, and second the fact that the inno-
cent birds sing now as they did in the past, when "their
liquid siftings"—bluntly, bird shit—stained the ancient,
fallen hero's shroud. Perhaps even more importantly, the
marvelous lyricism of these final lines persuades us, as the
esoteric pomposities earlier on cannot, that Eliot *feels* the
dishonoring. Is the point, then, that the modern-day
"hero" has turned from the fallen grandeur of Agamemnon to the never-risen depravity and brutality of Sweeney?
Perhaps. The poem does not nail the point down, and it
is to that extent only partially successful, its power intermittent and to a significant degree blunted.

"Sweeney Erect," too, begins with an excess of erudition and, after ten lines (and a four-line epigraph from
Beaumont and Fletcher's drama, "The Maid's Tragedy"),
becomes a distinctly straightforward narrative. The
woman in the bed, compared to an orang-outang as
Sweeney was compared to an ape, is having an epileptic
attack; Sweeney ignores her. The other women in the
house (of prostitution, obviously) are disturbed, but one of
them, Doris, brings the epileptic some "sal volatile / And
a glass of brandy neat." The narrative is neither remarkable nor even interesting. What is of interest, apart from
the expert handling of the quatrain form, is the seventh
quatrain, which is the obvious core and point of the entire
poem. "(The lengthened shadow of a man / Is history,

said Emerson / Who had not seen the silhouette / Of Sweeney straddled in the sun.)" It is nasty, but not I think vastly illuminating; nor is it particularly amusing. There is indeed a kind of snide, petty nastiness about the whole poem, which also I do not find amusing. Nor do I think the pseudo-Homeric opening lines are (a) connected to the rest of the poem in any meaningful way or (b) particularly interesting in and of themselves. The poem shows consistency of techniques; it has the single striking quatrain I have noted; and it exhibits Eliot's social criticism at its pettiest, shallowest, and least admirable level. Eliot had his reasons for lashing out. As he later said of *The Waste Land,* "To me it was only the relief of a personal and wholly insignificant grouse against life; it is just a piece of rhythmical grumbling."[59] On the other hand, Eliot also said of the Sweeney poems generally (including "Burbank with a Baedeker: Bleistein with a Cigar" as one of those poems, though Sweeney is not mentioned in it) that they "are intensely serious . . ."[60] He was offended that "even here [i.e., London] I am considered by the ordinary newspaper critic as a wit or satirist, and in America I suppose I shall be thought merely disgusting."

"Mr. Eliot's Sunday Morning Service" carries things, as Hugh Kenner nicely puts it, "to a further extreme . . ."[61] After a careful dissection of those extremes, Smith concludes: "Unhappily, the poem is obscure, precious, and bombastic."[62] Bernard Bergonzi, much kinder to the quatrain poems as a whole, notes that they are not particularly "substantial compositions. In places, undoubtedly, they sink beneath their own unassimilated erudition."[63] What saves any and all of the quatrain poems, of course—and it is just as well to say this straight out—is that "Eliot has so obviously *enjoyed* the exercise . . ."[64] David Ward seems to me sensitively accurate. "The underlying debate is, I believe, entirely serious, but it is expressed in this poem, as in all the other quatrain poems, in a game of ideas: the kind of over-clever play which often is the signal of a delicate and very active mind driven close to desperation by unresolved conflicts."[65] Stephen Spender finds most of the quatrain poems "stiff, rigid, static . . . The quatrains do not come naturally to Eliot."[66] "Sweeney Among the Nightingales" he labels "a violent cartoon," and goes on to discuss, as I already have, "the hatred for life in some of these poems . . ."[67] (This is even truer, I believe, of the four poems in French, which I will not discuss. The French critic, Georges Cattaui, says of them, very accurately, that they "are in a particularly sardonic vein, and seem to lack the essential charm of his English verse."[68]) And one of the most encyclopedic and sensitive of all the many critics who have written about modern British and American poetry, David Perkins, says of these poems that "they stare at man's emptiness, egoism, psychological fragmentation, and animality, their emotion barely controlled by ironic distance and strict form."[69] And what, indeed, is there to say of a poem which begins, like this one:

> Polyphiloprogenitive
> The sapient sutlers of the Lord
> Drift across the window-panes.
> In the beginning was the Word.

Shall we say, with Ernst Curtius, that "Eliot is an Alexandrian poet in the strictest sense of the word . . . He is first of all an erudite poet"[70]? We can agree with virtually all of the critics that the concerns of "Mr. Eliot's Sunday Morning Service," like the concerns of "The Hippopotamus," are ecclesiastical. We can agree, too, that it is critical, even nasty, as it contemplates clerics unworthy of their name or office.[71] But it seems to me a modish, immature poem that tells us rather more about Mr. Eliot's state of mind than we likely want to know.

The "Burbank" poem, though Eliot himself considered it (along with "Sweeney Among the Nightingales") "among the best that I have ever done,"[72] does not add much to our discussion. It is fearfully erudite, fearfully nasty, savagely anti-Semitic ("The rats are underneath the piles. / The jew is underneath the lot"), and whatever force or value it may once have seemed to have, it seems by now both dated and inert. As is also "Whispers of Immortality" (1918), a poem which is divided for no observable reason into four quatrains about the Jacobean poets Webster and Donne, and four about Sweeney-type females and the men who frequent them. ". . . Our lot crawls between dry ribs / To keep our metaphysics warm." There is little that is erudite, little that is dramatic, and little that is worth remembering, finally, in "A Cooking Egg," probably written in 1919. It is not the equal of the other quatrain poems even in nastiness. And what appears to be the child-oriented wistfulness of the final lines—"Over buttered scones and crumpets / Weeping, weeping multitudes / Droop in a hundred A.B.C.'s"— dissolves when one learns that the letters do not stand for the letters of the alphabet, but for the tea-room chain, the Aerated Bread Company.[73]

I want to end this perhaps overlong chapter with some words of Eliot's, written in 1949 about his friend and contemporary, James Joyce, but to my mind wonderfully true of Eliot himself:

Joyce's writings form a whole; we can neither reject the early work as stages, of no intrinsic interest, of his progress towards the latter, nor reject the later work as the outcome of decline. As with Shakespeare, *his later work must be understood through the earlier,* and the first through the last; it is the whole journey, not any one stage of it, that assures him his place among the great.[74] (Italics added).

When John D. Margolis, in *T.S. Eliot's Intellectual Development,* examines Eliot's work, he inevitably finds the poet's "many articles, like his lectures, . . . considerably more revealing . . . [than] his early poetry." The latter, given Margolis' purposes, "is of limited value in illuminating the intellectual concerns that were exercising Eliot during the first years of his career."[75] I'm not sure I would agree, even in Margolis' own terms. But in my terms, which place the poetry first, and the literary criticism second, Margolis' emphasis is skewed.

The early Eliot, the Eliot before *The Waste Land,* is all too frequently understood as "of limited value." But the truth is that it is impossible to truly understand the later Eliot without a solid grounding in the early poetry. It is in a sense like trying to judge the last hundred yards of a great discus toss, without any consideration of the arm which gave the instrument its aim, and the body which gave the arm its power. Almost nothing in life is truly inevitable. I do not mean to argue that Eliot's path, after *Poems, 1920,* was marked out and inescapable. Nothing, let me emphasize, is so neatly determined, and poetry least of all. But I do mean that the marks of Eliot's early poetry and early poetic concerns continue in the rest of his work, and that the direction of that later work becomes more meaningful and more readily comprehensible when the early work is kept in mind. I think the examination of the later poems, together with this discussion of the early ones, will more than prove the point.

The Waste Land,
in two versions and
two handwritings

There are two versions of *The Waste Land.* The version published in 1922 was the final version; it was also long thought to be the only surviving version, a much longer manuscript having been given to a New York collector, John Quinn, and thereafter lost sight of. But the longer manuscript surfaced unexpectedly in 1968, and in 1971 the poet's widow, Valerie Eliot, edited a facsimile, adding helpful notes, commentary and assorted poems that were at some point part of the plan for what became *The Waste Land.* (Eliot's early title, drawn from Charles Dickens, "He Do the Police in Different Voices," refers to a character, Sloppy, who in *Our Mutual Friend* is described as reading from the newspaper police reports, and doing them extremely well in "different voices.")

The second handwriting on the original manuscript version is that of Ezra Pound, whose work as unofficial editor had long been known, though the precise extent did not become clear until 1971. "Early in January [1922] Eliot returned to London, after spending a few days in Paris, where he submitted the manuscript of *The Waste Land* to Pound's maieutic [Socrates-like] skill."[1] The book appeared with a dedication, "For Ezra Pound, *il miglior fabbro,*" "the better workman." The evidence in support of this dedication includes a letter from Eliot to Pound, January 1922, asking among other things, "Do you advise printing 'Gerontion' as a prelude in book or pamphlet form?" To which Pound replied, "I do *not* advise printing 'Gerontion' as preface [to *The Waste Land*]. One don't miss it *at* all as the thing now stands. To be more lucid still, let me say that I advise you NOT to print 'Gerontion' as prelude."[2] Eliot had earlier suggested that he might print Pound's marginal comments along with the poem, to which Pound replied, December 24, 1921, "My squibs are now a bloody impertinence. I send 'em as requested; but

54

don't use 'em with *Waste Land.*" In the same letter, Pound also observed, with typical ferocity, "The thing now runs from 'april . . .' to 'shantih' without a break. That is 19 pages, and let us say the longest poem in the English langwidge. Don't try to bust all records by prolonging it three pages further." And he added, "Complimenti, you bitch. I am wracked by the seven jealousies . . ."[3] He also added a mock poem, "Sage Homme" [Male Midwife], which begins, "These are the poems of Eliot / By the Uranian Muse begot; / A Man their Mother was, / A Muse their Sire," and goes on to explain to the "diligent Reader / That on each Occasion / Ezra performed the Caesarian Operation."[4] Eliot wanted to print this, too, with *The Waste Land.*

Pound's editorial work was on the whole beneficial, but study of the final version and the original manuscript version lends, I think, considerable support to Donald Gallup's qualification on that judgment:

. . . Pound's major deletions in the central poem seem to reflect a lack of sympathy with some of the experiments that Eliot was trying to carry out. The poem which resulted from the Eliot-Pound collaboration was in some respects quite different from that which Eliot had in mind.[5]

Pound was able to say, on July 9, 1922, writing to his old teacher at the University of Pennsylvania, Felix E. Schelling, "Eliot's *Waste Land* is I think the justification of the 'movement,' of our modern experiment, since 1900."[6] And though Eliot himself, looking back on the "Caesarian Operation" in 1959, said that Pound "was a marvellous critic because he didn't try to turn you into an imitation of himself,"[7] the statement is not entirely true. That "Caesarian Operation" was, as Gallup observes, very much "the high point in the relationship . . ."[8] And Gallup adds: "It is ironic that Pound's editorial comments on the origi-

nal draft of *The Waste Land* were almost certainly a factor
in the suppression of the more earthy side of Eliot's
creativity . . . [which] less exalted side of Eliot's imagination had from the beginning received Pound's hearty approval and encouragement."[9] And since that "earthy
side" and its "suppression" have been a major concern in
this book, let me proceed now to amplify Gallup's view,
with which I emphatically agree, and then to discuss the
second and better-known (and certainly poetically superi-
or) *Waste Land.*

First, however, partly in order to establish the basic
principle from which I want to operate, let me cite and
briefly discuss a poem by a Romantic for whom Eliot
himself had only qualified sympathy, William Blake.[10] In
Blake's most famous poem, "The Tyger," stanzas three
and (in part) four read as follows:

> And what shoulder, & what art,
> Could twist the sinews of thy heart?
> And when thy heart began to beat,
> What dread hand? & what dread feet?

> What the hammer? what the chain?
> In what furnace was thy brain?
> What the anvil? . . .

The conclusion of stanza three is syntactically broken.
"And what dread feet" is obviously deliberate, and we
need to hypothesize either that Blake knew it was ungrammatical and did not care, or that he felt that the gains
outweighed the losses and, though ungrammatical, he
would use it anyway. The manuscript evidence is fortu-
nately very clear on all of these matters. In the first draft
of the poem, the third stanza ended and the fourth began
as follows: "And when thy heart began to beat / What
dread hand & what dread feet // Could fetch it from the
furnace deep . . ." That is, at the earliest stages of composi-

tion, Blake did not give any ungrammatical aspect to the
lines in question. The second draft is quite different. "And
when thy heart began to beat / What dread hand? & what
dread feet? // When the stars threw down their spears.
. . ." Blake had already, in this second draft, switched to
the ungrammatical syntax we have noted, though the
poem as a whole was not yet in its final form. But there
is no doubt that Blake was consciously balancing this
ungrammaticality against the staccato, even percussive
effect he wanted, for in yet another manuscript copy, this
time of the final version, he altered the last line of stanza
three to "What dread hand Form'd thy dread feet?" This
version was grammatical, but he plainly decided against it,
and we have ever since read the poem with the syntactical
break.[11]

Eliot had to make a similar decision, indeed a whole
series of similar decisions, in trying to reduce *The Waste
Land* to manageable and coherent proportions. Those
decisions reflect the sort of conscious weighing of alterna-
tives operating in Blake's various versions of "The Tyger."
But the editing of *The Waste Land* also reflects, importantly, the hand of a differently oriented poet, Ezra Pound,
who was partly in sympathy with and partly out of sympathy with Eliot's concerns. I think it will help us to understand the final version of *The Waste Land,* and both the
effect it had and the frequently contentious disputes that
have been waged about it, if we approach that final version
through the morass of the original version, noting especially which deletions and alterations emanated from
Pound and which from Eliot.

"He Do the Police in Different Voices" is a far more
socially, even novelistically, oriented title than *The Waste
Land.* And though the first section of the draft poem has
the same subtitle as the first section of the final version,
"The Burial of the Dead," in the draft there are fifty-four

lines which preceded what is now the beginning of the first
section, namely "April is the cruellest month. . . ." These
fifty-four lines have been much revised; they were ultimately cancelled by Eliot himself, lightly and in pencil,
though there is no way of knowing how and under exactly
what circumstances the cancellation took place. "It has
been difficult," writes Valerie Eliot, "to decide who canceled certain lines, especially when both Eliot and Pound
have worked on them together."[12] How large a hand
Pound had, or did not have, in Eliot's canceling the lines,
it is impossible to know. But it does seem clear, from what
is known of Pound, and his stated principles, and of Eliot's
uncertainties, that in these 54 lines, as elsewhere in the
draft poem, something distinctly un-Poundian was being
attempted and that it meant something to Eliot, though
not enough to defend it against attack.

The draft poem begins in a slangy, distinctly prosey
vein; it is full of such jazz-age phrases as "a couple of
fellers," "boiled to the eyes," and "a bottle of fizz." Eliot's
characters, most of them male, are boozers and womaniz-
ers, and above all are pretty thoroughly middle-class
urban American. The females in this long passage, which
for copyright reasons cannot be here reproduced, are
whores and madames. Instructed to "get me a woman,"
for example, a madame-like figure refuses, calmly asserting that the man is "too drunk." She puts him up, feeds
him the next morning, and then orders him out to "go get
a shave." Later on, the central character in the passage is
about to be arrested for committing public nuisances of a
drunken variety, and the dialogue between him and the
arresting policeman is, again, both realistic and not in the
usual sense poetic. The lines have no great intensity, nor
any of the poetic goals cultivated so passionately by
Pound. But there is a careful social texture, woven with
a deft sense of the speech rhythms and the empty, sordid

natures involved. Again, this was important to Eliot, though obviously, in the final analysis, it was not crucial to him; it was just as obviously of no interest to Pound. And it was removed from the poem, lock, stock and barrel.

But there is more to be said about this passage, and passages like it. Considering the puritanical, repressed background from which Eliot came, his long nocturnal prowlings in any number of urban centers on both sides of the Atlantic are pretty clearly sexually connected. There is no evidence that Eliot experimented with any of the prostitutes he encountered on these slumming expeditions. And there is considerable evidence that he saw a good deal more than nocturnal sex and the commercial "infrastructure" which always surrounds it—bars, hotels, pimps, and so on. All the same, there is a constant sexual undercurrent in a great deal of his early poetry, an undercurrent I have not commented on because it could be distracting, before we encounter *The Waste Land*. Certainly, it is not all there is to those early poems and it has proved easier for critics to deal with the sexual theme than with the social one. It is women, after all, which bedevil J. Alfred Prufrock. "Is it perfume from a dress / That makes me so digress?" It is Prufrock's inability to assert himself as a man, and as a man among women, which symbolizes his spiritual sterility. But he is sterile sexually, as are the characters in "Portrait of a Lady," as is the character in "Rhapsody on a Windy Night" (tempted by "that woman / Who hesitates toward you in the light of the door . . ."), and it is a kind of stifled sterility which afflicts the characters in poems like "Aunt Helen" and "Cousin Nancy." Not to mention the sensual emptiness depicted in "Whispers of Immortality," in which the persona is helplessly drawn to Grishkin, who "is nice: her Russian eye / Is underlined for emphasis; / Uncorseted,

her friendly bust / Gives promise of pneumatic bliss." As
we shall see, there is a good deal of similarly sexual material in the final version of *The Waste Land*. The point to
be underlined here is that as Eliot tried, unsuccessfully, to
articulate the poem, it originally contained a great deal
more of sexual material, in the social context in which
"illicit" sex exists. "Tease, Squeeze, lovin & wooin / Say
Kid what're y'doin'," reads one of the additions Eliot
made to his original typescript. It is hard to argue with
that perceptive reader of twentieth-century poetry, Helen
Vendler, who says flatly that *"The Waste Land* is obsessed
with sex. . . ."[13] It is indeed—and was even more obsessed
with it as Eliot had tried to write the poem.

The next large section of canceled material occurs in
part three, "The Fire Sermon," where Eliot wrote approx-
imately seventy lines of end-stopped iambic pentameter
couplets, clearly in the style of Alexander Pope. "Pope has
done this so well," Pound objected, "that you cannot do
it better; and if you mean this as a burlesque, you had
better suppress it, for you cannot parody Pope unless you
can write better verse than Pope—and you can't."[14] The
passage is both satirical and, again, sexually obsessive;
significant rhymes include, for example, "gapes" and
"rapes," "itch" and "bitch," and "dull" and "trull." In
one more or less Swiftian couplet, the rhyme is, revealingly, "French" and "stench." Swift's anti-female attitudes,
and his verse to match, are of course legendary in English
literature. Eliot does not show quite the scatological (ex-
crement-linked) tastes of Swift, but the negative, fearful
attitude toward women is much the same. In one ten-line
passage we find the words "bitch," "cat," "slattern," and
"trull," none of them complimentary. Lines like these
make one see how accurately Randall Jarrell perceived
Eliot, and how inaccurately all too many of his other
critics have perceived him:

Won't the future say to us in helpless astonishment: 'But did you actually believe that all those things about objective correlatives, classicism, the tradition, applied to *his* poetry? Surely you must have seen that he was one of the most subjective and daemonic poets who ever lived, the victim and helpless beneficiary of his own inexorable compulsions, obsessions. From a psychoanalytical point of view he was far and away the most interesting poet of your century'.[15]

Again, Ezra Pound's editorial intervention resulted in a poem that was better but also very different. Removal of what Gallup calls the "earthy" side of Eliot's draft swings the thrust of the poem sharply and definitively away from social presentation and into a more generalized argument. Much is gained, but something is lost, too. These roughly seventy lines are neither as good poetry as the final version of the *Waste Land* or *The Rape of the Lock,* on which they are based. But not only is the context of the poem changed by the deletions, a good deal of the underpinning for what has remained in the poem is also removed. The neurasthenic Fresca (the name occurs also in "Gerontion," 9 lines from the end of that poem) is more than casually linked with Eliot's neurasthenic first wife. Indeed, a *Criterion* piece in 1924, anonymously printed but in fact by Vivienne Eliot, included doctored versions of part of this couplet sequence.[16] And it has long been suspected that much of the neurasthenia exhibited by women in Eliot's poetry, in *The Waste Land* and elsewhere, was more or less directly inspired by Vivienne Eliot. "Not quite an adult, and still less a child," as one line puts it. "The Russians thrilled her to hysteric fits," says another line—and in short there is more than biography and autobiography in the canceled lines. There is, for better and for worse, psychological authenticity, and the final version of the poem, as I shall note later in this chapter, is somewhat deficient in that respect.

There is much, in this long pseudo-Pope passage, which reinforces the sense of Eliot's deep and continuing preoccupation with the world as it actually was, the world he saw about him, the world in which, willy-nilly, he and his readers were obliged to live. The inner world which one might (or might not) bring to pass, commonly taken as the central theme of *The Waste Land,* was—at least in this early version of the poem—clearly not Eliot's sole preoccupation. There are references to horse-racing sets, and boxing sets, and to the adulation of movie stars by the "rabble," unable to distinguish between a "goddess" and a "star." The heroic couplet was not Eliot's natural metier; Pound was quite right. Much of the verse, and most of the irony, is heavy-footed. But the social dimension remains important—for, whether in the end deleted or not, it was present at the beginning, and criticism of the poem as it finally appeared in print must I think take cognizance of that fact.

I would have liked to reproduce, here, the next sequence, a fifteen-line passage deleted in Pound's handwriting; again, copyright restrictions make that impossible. It says in very plain terms that London, whose inhabitants are compared to bees ("swarming"), both spawns and kills off its people (referred to as "huddled" between the cement city and the sky overhead). Londoners have no knowledge of thought, or of feeling; they are "gnomes," except that they dig in "brick and stone and steel." A repeated line asserts, not in very good poetry, but in very plain English, that this metropolitan folk is "bound upon the wheel." And at the end of the passage, not accidentally, the vocabulary flickers back to "Preludes," speaking of secret messages potentially "curled within" what is, no matter how "faint," nevertheless palpably something which has "movement" and even light. Nor is it accidental, having said this, that Eliot first inserts a dividing space, and then appends a line which makes it plain that, if there is to any sort of good emerging from a monstrous site like modern London, it will not be in this but in "another world."

Mrs. Eliot writes of this last line: "Appalled by his vision of the 'Unreal City,' Eliot may be alluding to the passage [in Plato's *Republic*] . . . which inspired the idea of the City of God among Stoics and Christians, and found its finest exponent in St. Augustine."[17] Mrs. Eliot is more than probably correct. But what is perhaps of more interest, especially when juxtaposed against Eliot's obviously passionate concern—"appalled" is certainly not too strong a word—is Pound's comment, written in the margin, opposite two lines beginning "Some minds, aberrant . . ." Writes Pound, with savage distaste: "Palmer Cox's brownies." Mrs. Eliot's note explains the reference. "Palmer Cox (1840–1924) worked in America as an illustrator and author of children's books. His popular 'Brownie' series portrayed in verse and pictures the activities of a group of benevolent elves."[18] At the very least, if this is what "phantasmal gnomes"—the phrase which probably triggered Pound's comment—meant to *il miglior fabbro,* Eliot might in some ways have been more accurate to refer to his informal editor as *il different fabbro,* "the different workman," rather than, as in Eliot's printed dedication, "the better workman."[19]

Lines 292–299 of the final version of *The Waste Land,* interestingly, are represented in the manuscript by two and perhaps three different versions. Pound has marked the shorter of these two versions, the one that finally saw print, as "O.K., echt [genuine]," and has written next to the longer version, which did not see print, "Type out this *anyhow.*" Eliot was obviously uncertain how to handle the material, at this point, and his first instinct was to present a full social background for the female character being portrayed. We are informed, that is, that she played in Highbury Park, was the daughter of people who were both "humble" and "conservative," and that her father scraped out a living as the proprietor of a small business, one that did neither badly nor well. The lines peter out, after this bare beginning of a background has been rather loosely traced. There is a second attempt, still more fragmentary. And finally, that too being abandoned, Eliot began a third attempt, and from the evidence was still unsure of himself: the passage is much worked over. But it is plainly the direct progenitor of the passage printed in *The Waste Land.* As before, from a narrowly esthetic viewpoint, the lines are not in fact very good; as a critic, Pound was without doubt correct in canceling the passage. But for all that, the social concern is evident, and significant—and surely *some* of these passages could have been left in had Pound been of broader sympathies and concerns himself?[20]

The next long deletion occurs in part four of the poem, "Death by Water." Some eighty-three lines have been deleted; next to the start of the passage Pound has written: "Bad—but cant attack until I get typescript." The judgment needs some examination. Eliot begins with three rhymed quatrains. Though the facsimile shows us a handwritten manuscript rather than the more usual typescript for more finished poems of the period, it is written in ink rather than in pencil and Mrs. Eliot's note points out that "the writing," which is obviously careful transcription rather than original composition, "suggests that Eliot may have been copying from an unpreserved draft."[21]

The three quatrains are, indeed, poetically interesting; essentially, they are stanzas in praise of sailors. Metrically a bit irregular, they are fully rhymed—that is, all the lines employ end-rhyme, in the pattern A B A B. And, set off as they are, as the introduction to an even longer section on the sea, 81 lines in something approximating blank verse, I would have thought Pound might have judged them effective and left them in. He did not, reducing the twelve lines in quatrain form and also the 81 lines that follow, to a ten-line passage (which is, in truth, really eight lines of Eliot expanded, by changed lineation, into ten lines). Hugh Kenner is surely right when he asserts—and without benefit, at the time, of the manuscript version now in print—that *The Waste Land* "was conceived as a somewhat loose medley, as the relief of more diffuse impulses than those to which its present compacted form corresponds." But is it equally clear that what Pound's editing unearthed was a "wholeness, not at first foreseen by the author, which the greater part of *The Waste Land* at length assumed"? Kenner goes on:

That wholeness, *since it never did incorporate everything the author wanted it to,* was to some extent a compromise, gotten by permuting with another's assistance materials he no longer had it in him to rethink . . . Pound, by simply eliminating everything not of the first intensity, had revealed an unexpected corporate substantiality in what survived. . . . .[22] (Emphasis added).

But what does it mean to say that the poem "never did incorporate everything the author wanted it to"? An author usually compromises with himself. In *The Waste Land* Eliot has compromised with (more accurately, has succumbed to) Ezra Pound. What does it mean to say that Eliot "no longer had it in him to rethink" the materials which compose the poem? Eliot had not been well; he had been advised some years earlier to do no writing except what was required by his employer, advice which Eliot had, however, completely ignored—and he had gone on to write much brilliant poetry and equally brilliant prose.[23] To say, therefore, that he "no longer had it in him" must refer to the ordering of the poem and not to Eliot's abilities

at the time. And what that means, I suggest, is that in
Kenner's view, Eliot *could* not write his own poem; he had
to have Pound's help. And that, in turn, makes the poem
not entirely Eliot's. Eliot had to get "used to the poem in
its final form," Kenner adds.[24] Indeed—for Pound was
more than Caesarian Operator, more than midwife, he
was in some good part parent, too. It is not a matter of
"simple" elimination, of taking out everything not of "the
first intensity." Nor is it clear just whose "unexpected
corporate substantiality" we have in front of us when we
read the printed version. Opinions will of course remain
divided on this. Kenner did not have the manuscript to
consult; Spender, who did, remains convinced that "What
Pound did essentially was to release the energy of the
poem and suppress what was distracting, superfluous,
slovenly, or rhythmically or imagistically obstructive in
it."[25] A very much less penetrating critic than Spender,
Robert Sencourt, but one on the whole closer to Eliot the
man, writes that Eliot "came round to the view that
[Pound's alterations and deletions] had immensely
strengthened the poem's impact; but whether Pound's
judgment was competent I [i.e., Sencourt] would strongly
question."[26] The truth, it seems to me, lies somewhere
between these two poles. Essentially, Pound did indeed
help the poem, especially considering *The Waste Land* as
a narrowly literary production. But he significantly
changed it as well, and as a social and a psychological
document, *The Waste Land* as printed is a somewhat
weakened, somewhat confused affair.

Let me return, briefly, to the lines eliminated from
"Death by Water." What remains in the printed version
(rewritten, let me note, from the concluding lines of one
of Eliot's 1916–17 French poems, "Dans le Restaurant"),
is verse of the first intensity. Although I cannot reproduce
the lines which at one time preceded the surviving short

passage, it is, after the opening 12 line quatrain sequence, poetry of a fine and moving nature. Pound thought it, "bad"; Kenner is sure it must not have been of the first intensity; and Spender concludes, flatly, that "It is possible to regret the omission of some lines, but of remarkably few."[27] I am not at all so sure: the largest part of this omitted section, it seems to me, is a singularly fine portrayal of unease at sea, mutating deftly and gradually into something a good deal more than unease. After references to the everyday details of a sailor's existence—sleep, and coffee, and keeping watch—there is an admittedly rather vague reference to a "horror" somehow perceived, by all the sailors, in the entire world about them. The narrator begins to have visions and he wishes, no matter how fearful, that he could simply wake up and the dream would be over. So much of the passage is neither first-rate nor obnoxiously poor, as poetry. But then we proceed into eleven lines which seem to me without question of the first intensity, lines that deal with "a different darkness," which turns out to be, beautifully described, a barrier of floating ice, against which the boat is doomed to destroy itself. These eleven lines end with a moving statement, by the narrator, that he knows only that, now, "there is no more noise." And after this, preceded by a row of asterisks, come the lines which we know, now, as part four of the poem, "Death by Water." I would argue that, though Pound may have been right that these eleven lines and those that precede them in the canceled passage, would distract from the focus of the poem as he saw it, he may also have been wrong. I would argue that he was, in fact, wrong, at least in terms of his judgment of the whole passage: it is simply not "bad" as he labeled it. It is, of course, futile to speculate, but I tend to think *The Waste Land* as a whole, and "Death by Water" in particular, would be improved had these lines been allowed to remain. It does not seem to me even arguable to conclude, further, that the social content of the poem would have been both stronger and much, much clearer. Eliot wanted it to be clear, but he could not get it to come clear. Pound, I must say, pretty plainly did not want it to be clear, and he made sure that it was not. He did not simply dictate to Eliot, let me emphasize; indeed, Pound himself typed out this long passage,[28] and then worked it over in pencil, trying to make it do what he wanted it to do. But when he could not, he made sure it was cancelled: his marginal comment following the "Death by Water" lines which were retained, says forthrightly, "OK from here on *I think.*"

The remaining deletions, which in their diversity more than justify Kenner's characterization of the manuscript *Waste Land* as "a somewhat loose medley," are of an exceedingly miscellaneous nature. It would unduly prolong the discussion to look at all of these passages in detail, but some indication of their content and approach is necessary to complete the picture. (It is worth noting, first, that Eliot in two letters to Ford Madox Ford, written August 14, 1923 and October 4, 1923, said, "There are, *I* think about thirty *good* lines in *The Waste Land*. . . . The rest is ephemeral." He then explained that "As for the lines I mention, you need not scratch your head over them. They are the twenty-nine lines of the water-dripping song in the last part."[29] That is, lines 331–359 of the printed version.)

"The Death of St. Narcissus," in a first draft and then in a fair copy, is a thirty-nine-line poem, probably written in 1915. "In August of that year Pound submitted it to *Poetry* [magazine]; it was set up in type, though never published," Eliot having withdrawn it.[30] The first five lines became lines 26–29, revised, of the printed *Waste Land*. The poem describes a saint who "could not live mens' ways, but became a dancer before God." Imagining himself a tree, and then a fish, and then "a young girl / Caught in the woods by a drunken old man," the saint "danced on the hot sand / Until the arrows came." He embraces the arrows, presumably dies, "satisfied," and in the last two lines is "green, dry and stained / With the shadow in his mouth." The "somewhat loose medley" could perhaps have accommodated this poem, too. It is interesting, if rather indeterminate. The focus which would make it deeply powerful is lacking, but at times it is hauntingly suggestive of pathways not to be explored by Eliot. The later religious poetry does not much resemble "The Death of St. Narcissus."

"Song," published pseudonymously in 1921, found its way, in part, into the poem now entitled, "The wind sprang up at four o'clock." "The song has only two lines which you can use in the body of the poem," declared Pound.[31] In a marginal note he labeled the line, "Perhaps it does not come to very much," as "georgian"—i.e., tame and bland like the so-called Georgian poets, Rupert Brooke, Walter de la Mare, and so on. "Song" seems to concern Eliot's first wife. The last fragmentary lines of the draft, heavily scored out, read: "Waiting that touch / After thirty years." Pound's "georgian" label does not seem to me to apply. The full passage in question reads, "Perhaps it does not come to very much / This thought this ghost this pendulum in the head / Swinging from life to death / Bleeding between two lives." It is yet another path not taken, but it suggests fascinating possibilities. I do not think this is negligible poetry—far from it. What Eliot might have made of it, had he continued to work this vein, it is obviously impossible to say. But I find an odd power in even this minor fragment. It is not, perhaps, the same power as resides in either version of *The Waste Land,* but it reminds me, all the same, of much of the

poetry written thirty years or so later by the poets of the
so-called "Confessional" school, Robert Lowell, Sylvia
Plath, Anne Sexton, and others.

"Exequy" [Funeral Rite] is an elaborately formal exercise in closely rhymed stanzas of seven lines, but it is not
to my mind at all focused. Pound wrote in the margin, at
one point, "This is Laforgue . . .," and in a letter dated
December 24, 1921, asserted that the poem "doesn't hold
with the rest."[32] A glance at the poem in Mrs. Eliot's
edition of the early *Waste Land* indicates, simply enough,
that here Pound was entirely correct.

"The Death of the Duchess," just over seventy lines
long, is remarkably *Prufrock*-like. As Pound wrote, speaking perhaps of this fragment, it "does not advance on
earlier stuff."[33] Eliot quarried a few lines from this material for the printed version; most of it went unpublished.
At one point, indeed, "The Death of the Duchess" seems
to consciously parody "Prufrock." There is satire, but
without any great bite; there is, from lines 25–34, a strong
suggestion of the neurasthenic women in the printed
Waste Land, with an oddly effective set of bird-images
superimposed. Pound's marginalia twice refer to the Pru-
frockian echoes; he is plainly right. I could wish, for all
that, Eliot had been able to make more of the tormented
love themes here rather fumblingly expressed.

The thirteen-line fragment from which Eliot drew
line 322 of the published version, "After the torchlight red
on sweaty faces," ends with three interesting lines, reminding us of the last lines of "The Hollow Men." Rather
than with a "whimper," Eliot here has the world destroyed in something like picnic style. What seems to me
oddly worth noting is how clearly Eliot was in fact thinking, as he struggled to put the pieces of the poem together,
in exactly the large, even cosmological terms which he

spent years denying had been his purpose in *The Waste Land.*

Of the remaining fragments, other than "Dirge," nothing substantially different can be said. Probably written in 1921, "Dirge" is frankly one of the most repulsive things Eliot ever wrote.[34] Violently and vilely anti-Semitic, the lines attempt a sort of "comic" grotesquerie which simply does not come off. It is a style which Eliot returns to, in somewhat more controlled form, in "Sweeney Agonistes"—but that is four or five years in the distance. It is time we proceeded to that poem of which we have as yet said little, Eliot's most famous and to some his greatest poem, namely the published, Pounded version of *The Waste Land.*

It appeared in 1922, in the October issue (indeed, the very first issue) of Eliot's magazine, *The Criterion,* and the next month, in the United States, in *The Dial.* Responses on both sides of the Atlantic were predictably mixed. The poet Amy Lowell said, "I think it is a piece of tripe"[35]; John Middleton Murry thought it a poem destined for the rubbish heap; and the *Times Literary Supplement*'s anonymous reviewer found it a sort of parody "without taste or skill."[36] But Robert Langbaum speaks of "the first stunned, admiring critics,"[37] and Richard Ellmann sums it up as follows: "Lloyds' most famous bank clerk revalued the poetic currency fifty years ago. As Joyce said, *The Waste Land* ended the idea of poetry for ladies. Whether admired or detested, it became, like [Wordsworth's] *Lyrical Ballads* in 1798, a traffic signal."[38] Eliot "has always resented the description of 'The Waste Land' as a poem expressing the attitude of its generation,"[39] but, in fact, that was in good part how the poem was received. Even publication in book form, with a passle of excessively erudite notes that may or may not have been a joke of

sorts, or merely a necessary space filler to eke out enough
pages to justify charging book prices for a less-than-book-
length work,[40] did not change that essential fact. *"The
Waste Land* had a unique influence on the development of
modern poetry . . . no previous poem gave so vivid an
impression of the contemporary, urban metropolis. In
some sequences *The Waste Land* resembled an avant-
garde documentary film . . . *The Waste Land* broke the
fixed association between verse and the agreeable, the
beautiful, or the ideal . . . ."[41] Or as Helen Vendler quietly,
and correctly, puts it, *The Waste Land* is "the most famous of modern poems."[42] "It enchanted and devastated
a whole generation."[43]

It was, and remains, a difficult poem; as I have already indicated, the sources of that difficulty lie partly in
Eliot's inability to fully master his materials and partly in
Pound's rather different vision of what the poem was
about. "In *The Waste Land,*" Eliot once said, "I wasn't
even bothering whether I understood what I was
saying."[44] But Pound, as we have seen, had small doubt—
and in his own slightly earlier *Hugh Selwyn Mauberley,*
written between 1915 and 1920, he spoke savagely of "an
old bitch gone in the teeth, . . . a botched civilization," and
summed that botched civilization up, bitterly, as "two
gross of broken statues . . . [and] a few thousand battered
books."[45]

The Waste Land is 433 lines long, divided into five
parts of unequal size and nature. Let us take these parts
one by one, though in fairly brief style. Part one, "The
Burial of the Dead," opens with the famous inversion of
Chaucer's bright and happy invocation of April "with his
shoures soote" revivifying the world:

> April is the cruellest month, breeding
> Lilacs out of the dead land, mixing

> Memory and desire, stirring
> Dull roots with spring rain.
> Winter kept us warm, covering
> Earth in forgetful snow, feeding
> A little life with dried tubers.

The five sections of the poem, like the five "movements" in each of the *Four Quartets,* are in some sense analogous to musical movements. (Igor Stravinsky's titanic, savage, and immensely powerful *Le Sacre du Printemps* [Rites of Spring], heard in 1921, plainly had much to do with the writing of *The Waste Land.*[46]) And these seven lines have much the same sort of rhythmic propulsion as one finds in modern music. Note especially how each of the lines, except those which end with a period, concludes with a single verb in *-ing* form, thus establishing one of those insistent rhythms of which Eliot's best poetry is always composed. And though Pound may have understood the symbolization, here—life as death—as a bitter rejection, Eliot understood it in the terms of his original epigraph, a passage from Joseph Conrad's *Heart of Darkness* which ended, "The horror! the horror!" "Pound should not have dismissed this epigraph for, as Eliot modestly protested, it is 'somewhat elucidative'."[47]

The tightly consecutive opening lines are broken, in line eight, by eleven lines without context, lines which come at us, in a sense, rather than to us.[48] Their function, despite the absence of context, is clear. "I read, much of the night, and go south in the winter." The character is female, wealthy, and utterly aimless, and is meant to represent the sterile rich as a whole. The poem breaks, abruptly, into an obviously religious, quasi-prophetic tone, marked for us by a physical break (i.e., a space) between lines eighteen and nineteen. "What are the roots that . . . grow out of this stony rubbish?" And who are we to even "guess" at an answer, we who "know only / A heap of broken images"? We need to know something first, something which the threateningly inviting persona promises to show us, "under the shadow of this red rock," namely, "fear in a handful of dust." ("Water," here, represents salvation and knowledge, and dryness represents, logically enough in this schema partly suggested by the anthropological writing fashionable at the time—James Frazer, Jessie Weston—sterility and ignorance.)

The quatrain from Richard Wagner's opera *Tristan und Isolde,* where it is sung by the homesick steersman, comes to us both without context and without translation. I have never believed, and I do not now believe, that this is poetically legitimate, much less comprehensible. "Expecting the reader, even if he were able, to instantly transport himself to the opera house, to the precise moment of these lines, and to recapture the feeling he had then, seems to me a fantastic demand."[49] On the other hand, it is also true that, whether successful or not, the passage remains interstitial: it is only four lines, and one can more or less glide past it, into the famous "hyacinth" passage. The first snippet from Wagner's *Tristan* is meant to prepare us, somehow, for this more specific (though still somewhat indeterminate) presentation of the inevitable "death" that is associated with love—or as Wagner explicitly labels it, in the famous conclusion to *Tristan, Liebestod,* "love death." Because it is secular and uninformed with the necessary spirituality, it is like being "neither / Living nor dead." *Oed' und leer das Meer,* says the final quotation from *Tristan,* "the sea is barren and empty." The suggestion, clearly, is that this is how it has always been and how, inevitably, it must always be. Neither love nor other humans can be enough, and the sole answer is (though Eliot does not expressly say so) God.[50]

There is immense power in these first forty-two lines.
We do not always see precisely where Eliot is going, or
what he means to do when he gets there; we do not always
understand why he travels a particular path. But the taut,
tight rhythms, the stripped diction, and the intense passion, disguised as a kind of objectivity but constantly push-
ing through at the reader, all combine to make this
tremendously gripping.[51] Lines 43–59, however, are, I'm
afraid, poetically barren. This is a kind of realism, though
heavily tinctured with esoterica like the Tarot pack and so
on. But it is not only flat realism, without either context
or power, it is also very different from the earlier attempts
to deal with the external world, as for example in "Preludes." It is true, as Robert Langbaum says, that " 'Preludes' gives us a world where people live alone in
furnished rooms . . . [and] *The Waste Land* gives us a
world in which people do not communicate."[52] This is
precisely the power of all the unfocused "dialogues" in the
poem, which are never truly dialogues, since the speakers
are invariably speaking across and above and around rather than directly to another human being. Actual contact
is never established. In that sense, indeed, "the structure
of 'Preludes' anticipates that of *The Waste Land.*" But it
seems to me wrong to explain the link between the two
poems by saying, in explanation, that "Both present separate vignettes of city life; yet the vignettes are unified by
the central consciousness which must be understood as
perceiving or imagining them all."[53] There is, unfortunately, no such "central consciousness" in *The Waste
Land:* what lawyers and philosophers call the "weasel"
word, here, is "must." Simply because we are dealing with
a great poet, and with a poem of great effect and power,
does not mean that we are obliged to see what is not shown
to us. Whatever *The Waste Land* might have been, with
this or that contextual passage reinserted, we *are* obliged,

for better or worse, to take it as Eliot himself put it in print.

But it is too fine a poem, whatever its lapses, not to return to its central and powerfully embodied thrust, the "collage of symbolic urban and desert settings, each of which reveals one or more aspects of the sickness of man's soul in this modern Inferno."[54] And we see, once more, the death-in-life motif of the opening lines ("April is the cruellest month . . ."), to which in a structural sense these final seventeen lines of the poem's first section are a balance, almost (in musical terms) a development and restatement. That is, the city is real, for all cities are real. But it is here introduced to us as "unreal," and the signification of that unreality is urged upon us by the portrayal of "a crowd" flowing over London Bridge, who are alive and yet, in the poem's sense of the word (and of the world), dead. "I had not thought death had undone so many." These are people on their way to work; the church bells, pointedly, mark off their time of arrival by "a dead sound on the final stroke of nine." Whether we know or care who "Stetson" might be, we know he is a modern-day human, and even if we do not know that the Roman naval victory over Carthage in the First Punic War took place in 260 B.C., we more than likely know that "Mylae" was not a battle fought yesterday or even the day before that. There has been preparation for the disarmingly casual query, "That corpse you planted last year in your garden, / Has it begun to sprout? Will it bloom this year?" Indeed, when real cities are unreal, when "April is the cruellest month," when the living are dead, why should corpses *not* bloom? I suppose one can say, as Cleanth Brooks once did, that the "Dog" in line seventy-four "is Humanitarianism and the related philosophies which in their concern for men extirpate the supernatural."[55] I prefer to note that the lines are taken almost verbatim from the Elizabethan playwright John Webster (*The White Devil,* V, iv, 113), of whom Eliot was fond and about whom he wrote a fine essay. Eliot has altered "wolf" to "dog," surely to lower the tone of the excerpt, and has inverted "foe" to "friend," more than likely because (a) we are now dealing with a dog and (b) because in this entire death-in-life stance everything which is stated to be black is white, and vice versa. Whatever the "Dog" is fancied to "represent," I think we are entitled, by what we can legitimately find in the poem, to go no farther than Hugh Kenner's apt characterization of this as "a sinister dialogue." Planting a corpse and digging "it up again" cannot be anything but sinister. For anyone who knows Baudelaire, the final line, reproduced directly from "Au Lecteur" (To the Reader), contains precisely the kind of ironical inversion in which Eliot has been dealing throughout this first part of the poem. The reader, says Baudelaire, is "mon semblable," my likeness or counterpart; he is "mon frère," my brother; but he is also a hypocrite. For anyone who does not know Baudelaire (and knowing Baudelaire is perhaps a shade more legitimate an expectation, at least for the reader of a modern poem, than knowing the work of Richard Wagner—or knowing, say, Sanskrit), the line retreats into the kind of obscurity which, like it or not, haunts this and so many other poems of the twentieth century,

The second part of *The Waste Land,* "A Game of Chess," is structurally an amplification and reinforcement of part one of the poem. We see, first, a woman in a scene of immense but artificial opulence; the intricate description, beautifully sustained, ends with a reference to Ovid's tale in his *Metamorphoses,* of Tereus and Procne and Philomela. It is a tale of rape and murder and revenge, of sadism and brutality. And Eliot's delicately overelaborate scene-painting ends with "Jug Jug" sung, now, not to distant figures out of the classical past, but to contemporary "dirty ears." And having reached that revelation, Eliot at once drops the elaborate formality. "And other withered stumps of time / Were told upon the walls. . . ." We are back with a woman very like Marie, in the opening section, who reads "much of the night, and go[es] south in the winter."[57] We may not know precisely—but then, who does know anything precisely in a "waste land"?—what "rats' alley" means, but plainly it means nothing good. And it is a place where "the dead men lost their bones." What there is is, largely, "Nothing again nothing."

And from this compressed, powerfully evocative first scene, we are swung, as always abruptly, into a marvelously counterpointed flapperism. "O O O O that Shakespeherian Rag— / It's so elegant / So intelligent."[58] Robert M. Adams' comment about this line, which Eliot lifted almost verbatim from an old song (the / h / is Eliot's nicely tuned addition), is brilliantly persuasive. Its power to say "something in brief compass about a complicated state of consciousness . . ." lies, says Adams, not in "the content of the line, or its implications, or its tone, even; it is the very fact that Eliot felt free to incorporate it, as an *objet trouvé* [found object], in his poem, that gives the line its contemporary sense. . . . It was a phrase beyond Eliot's power to discover or create, [as it was] beyond the power of any of his translators . . . to render."[59] Exactly: the swing into the jazz age follows, after all, on the elaborate Jacobeanism of the opening lines, and on the elaborately sterile one-sided conversation. And when that is followed by " 'What shall I do now? What shall I do?' " the frantic hysteria is very fully realized.

> 'What shall we ever do?'
>   The hot water at ten.
> And if it rains, a closed car at four.

> And we shall play a game of chess,
> Pressing lidless eyes and waiting for a knock upon the
> door.

The "lidless eyes" evoke sleepless nights ("I read, much of the night"); the "knock upon the door" may well be harmless, but it is presented with a delicately threatening casualness.

And the third and final portion of this part of the poem, lines 139–172, are without question "the nearest in the poem to the Ur-*Waste Land* [i.e., the manuscript version] scenes from modern life."[60] Having perceived this not very obscure truth, Stephen Spender goes on to dismiss the lines as "little more than programmatic." This seems to me deeply mistaken. Helen Vendler, in contrast, after pointing out that the Cockney dialogue is modeled on a maid then employed by the Eliots, observes tartly, and accurately, that "Half the poets in England at that point probably had maids; Eliot's genius was to listen to what his maid said, write it down, and make it poetry."[61] And by enlarging the social boundaries of his poem to admit a scene depicting a lower-class life that is no less (and no more) sterile than the upper-class scenes previously presented, Eliot has in my view deeply, and very importantly, strengthened his poem. Commentators do not need to do much more here than point out how, at the legally proscribed closing time for British pubs, the proprietor will call out, "Hurry up, please. It's time." (Licenses can be lost if drinks are served past the stipulated hour.) But absence of esoteric content and erudite allusions do not make fine and illuminating passages like this "little more than programmatic." I have in my possession a privately recorded reading of *The Waste Land,* in which Eliot does not (as he does in the commercially available recording, based on a much later and very much stiffer reading) hold back in realizing these lines. He lets them rip and roar: this is a key passage, and one which adds precisely that humanity and compassion which Pound could not or would not see. This is not snobbishness, any more than earlier passages are anti-aristocratic or "The Hippopotamus" is anticlerical.[62] It fits the overall thrust of the poem—and makes sense, too, of some passages later on in *The Waste Land,* which like this one deal with nonaristocratic characters.

Part three, "The Fire Sermon," is the longest, most allusive, and in some ways least successful of the poem's five parts. "It would be sheer simple-mindedness to pretend that being able to spot the allusions in *The Waste Land* guarantees anything about anybody."[63] There is a portentousness in even the opening of "The Fire Sermon." "The river's tent is broken: the last fingers of leaf / Clutch and sink into the wet bank." Many critics have noted the inadequacy of lines cut out of the poem by Pound, but what of lines like this, which Pound did not cut? No reference to "Miss Jessie L. Weston's book on the Grail legend: *From Ritual to Romance,*" or assertion that "Anyone who is acquainted with [Frazer's *The Golden Bough*] will immediately recognize . . . certain references to vegetation ceremonies,"[64] can I think make portentousness less portentous. Again, though "The Fire Sermon" is in its present form perhaps overextended, it still preserves, largely, the force and bite of the rest of the poem. The use of Edmund Spenser's beautiful line, "Sweet Thames, run softly, till I end my song," is one of Eliot's most inspired borrowings. The "gashouse," behind which the persona sits "Musing upon the king my brother's wreck / And on the king my father's death before him," on the other hand, has rather too much oversolemn indeterminacy about it, too much heavy-handed allusiveness—and allusions to matters the reader cannot be expected to know. Sweeney and Mrs. Porter restore the momentum, but the line from Paul Verlaine's sonnet, "Parsifal," "*Et, O ces voix d'enfants, chantant dans la coupole*" [And oh, those children's voices, singing in the cupola (or "dome")], cannot to my mind redirect the reader's attention to the Grail legend. The technique becomes, at such moments, far too much like forcing the reader to hunt for the proverbial needle in the haystack. Nor does the reevocation of Philomela, transformed into a nightingale after her rape and confrontation with her brother-in-law, Tereus, who was the rapist, make a great deal of sense. "But the blackguardly intentions of Sweeney, now the quester, have overcome the abstinent spirit of Parsifal, . . . and Philomel is ravished, though her song is heard once more with the phrase from 'A Game of Chess,' 'so rudely forc'd'."[65] If such passages make sense in the critic's pages but not in the poem's, I think we are forc'd to ignore the critic's explanations.[66]

Lines 207–214, which deal off-handedly with "Mr. Eugenides, the Smyrna merchant," probably stem from Eliot's banking experience. They seem to me essentially pointless, as does, I'm afraid, most of the intrusion into the poem of the double-sexed Tiresias ". . . the land is dead, and it is dead because Tiresias, the Fisher King, has been wounded and has not achieved, in the person of the quester, the goal of the quest. . . . The action of the poem [is] as Tiresias recounts it. . . ."[67] But where do we learn that Tiresias recounts the poem or that Tiresias is the Fisher King? Not, it seems clear, in *The Waste Land*. The long seduction scene, between the typist, female, and the "small house agent's clerk," male, is extremely well done. It needs, I would argue, none of the sometimes incredible explication given to this poem by some critics. And it not only makes sense in and of itself in *The Waste Land*'s larger structure, but it makes a kind of sense of the Tiresias reference in lines 243–246. Both parties to the

seduction are lowered, shamed, made less worthy by what
each has done. To give the recognition of that fact to a
character—the one character in human history—who has
been of both sexes, is appropriate.

The lines devoted to Queen Elizabeth and her one-
time lover, the Earl of Leicester, whose royal barges are
counterpointed to modern day barges with their "oil and
tar," is comprehensible though not terribly effective. Especially in the first of the two short-lined verse strophes, we
have more indeterminacy than we can deal with. "Red
sails / Wide / To leeward, swing on the heavy spar," for
example, strongly suggests and requires the support of a
kind and a degree of specificity which the poem does not
contain. The Rhine Maiden reference, too, drawn again
from Wagnerian opera, is distinctly misconceived. What
indeed is the reader to make of "Weialala leia / Wallala
leialala"? The middle-class seduction which follows, lines
292–305, is as effective as the lower-class one. Like the first
seduction scene, it requires no elucidation and does what
it is meant to do in amplifying the poem's overall thrust.
I do not think that knowledge of St. Augustine is either
necessary or indeed suggested by the final lines of this
third part; the notion of "burning" is more than sufficient-
ly well understood in the context of illicit sex, so that these
lines as a kind of summary, from the viewpoint of religion,
are fairly readily comprehensible. And Eliot's verse
rhythms, propulsive, even jagged, help make the point
clear.

Part four, "Death by Water," seems to me terribly
slight. It seems, now that the original and much longer
section has been rediscovered and put into print, even
slighter than it did before, but in my judgment this small
lyric, though unified and well wrought as far as it goes, is
too slender to hold up any significant part of *The Waste
Land*'s overall structure. We are told that death is inevita-

ble, and assured that one "Phlebas," not mentioned before in the poem, and not mentioned again, has been a merchant, has been at sea, and has died. He was "once handsome and tall as you," and like him you too will die. But can it possibly be true that "the Phoenician sailor and the merchant" (I had thought they were one and the same, but I will not stop to argue) ". . . are symbols of the initiates of the mystery religions, going back to the fertility cults with their ritual of consigning the effigy of the god to the sea and welcoming it as reborn at the end of its journey, carried by a predictable current"?[68] Surely this is scholarship run away with itself, and totally illegitimate as commentary on what is, after all, a poem rather than an anthropological treatise. Nor can I see Phlebas as, in Kenner's terms, one of "two images of asceticism."[69] If one has the learning to spot the reference to St. Augustine—and I do not think the poet has the right to expect it—one can see in that reference a distinctly ascetic meaning. But Phlebas? On what conceivable ground does Kenner postulate, even hypothetically, that Phlebas is "a trader sailing perhaps to Britain"? Nothing in the poem lends that supposition the slightest support. Nothing. I do not think that we help the poem by burdening it with our own free associations.

Part five, "What the Thunder Said," does what the final part of a long poem must do, namely draw together in intensified and dramatic form the disparate threads that have been woven. The religious references, which are many and which indeed start off this final part, were for the most part ignored, initially. Very few of its early readers considered *The Waste Land* a religious poem. The "agony in stony places," however, is, of course, Christ's agony, as lines 322–330 all deal with the crucifixion and death of Jesus. "He who was living," namely Christ, "is now dead," and—in a neat rephrasing of the death-in-life motif—"We who were living are now dying / With a little patience." (One can hear, suddenly, anticipatory echoes of Eliot's next major work, "The Hollow Men.") The water-as-salvation motif, similarly, reemerges and is intensified in lines 331–358, ending with what seems to be utter despair. "But there is no water." The seven-line section which immediately follows, however, suggests that in spite of everything, even in our modern waste land, there is someone (Christ) "who walks always beside you . . . I do not know whether a man or a woman / —But who is that on the other side of you?" This possibility of succor is not, the poem immediately assures us, something to be found anywhere in the "falling towers" of the secular world, for all of them, whether in "Jerusalem Athens Alexandria / Vienna London," are "unreal." Their "cracks and reforms and bursts in the violet air" add up to nothing.

Valerie Eliot cites Conrad Aiken's recollection of having seen "poems or part-poems" containing what became lines 377–384, presumably at some point earlier than 1922.[70] I can make no sense of this passage, aside from the water-as-salvation reference in the last line. "The 'lady of situations' fiddles lullabies on her hair to 'bats with baby faces,' adding frustration to maternal lamentation. . . ."[71] Line fifty, in part one, does indeed refer to "the lady of situations," but how we get from there to here is quite simply beyond me. If "frustration" is, indeed, all that these lines are about, Eliot would have done well, and Pound still better, to omit them—for the following passage, lines 385–394 and beyond, fits extremely well with the passage rejecting the various capitals of the world. The "empty chapel, only the wind's home," may stand in a "decayed hole," it may have "no windows, and the door swings," but here and only here, Eliot now insists, is to be found the possibility of water, the possibility of salvation. The road to Christ, that is, who is salvation, is through the

church. Period. And the water / rain which is salvation
says, though we would not know it without Eliot's note,
that we must "Give, sympathize, control": "Datta.
Dayadhvam. Damyata."[72] But "what have we given?"
Lines 402 straight to the end of the poem at line 433, are
in effect an exposition of (a) how hard it is to give, (b) how
important it is to give, and (c) what joy there is in giving.
What Eliot means by "give," of course, is the giving of
oneself to Christ. The key passage, here, is lines 418–425:

> . . . The boat responded
> Gaily, to the hand expert with sail and oar
> The sea was calm, your heart would have responded
> Gaily, when invited, beating obedient
> To controlling hands.
>
> I sat upon the shore
> Fishing, with the arid plain behind me
> Shall I at least set my lands in order?

The "awful daring of a moment's surrender," postulated
in line 403, which then modulates into the key which turns
"in the door once and turn[s] once only," now modulates
into a somewhat indeterminate but not in any way esoteric
symbolization. The notion of boat-as-human-traveler-
along-the-spiritual-road, that is, is neither expressly formulated nor fully prepared for. But in the context which
the poem *has* created—an enormous number of water
images—it is not hard to understand what Eliot is talking
about. Just as "the hand expert with sail and oar" can
make a sailing craft respond "gaily," so too does the heart
respond, when its owner and proprietor invites it to respond, "obedient / To controlling hands." Significantly,
even the sea itself responds in this symbolic picture. It
becomes "calm," as all things are to become calm, when
under proper religious restraint, when controlled and
guided from above by a power higher than anything

merely human. The space after line 422 highlights and emphasizes the point. "The arid plain," clearly the "endless plains" of line 369, "cracked earth / Ringed by the flat horizon only," is now "behind me"—once, that is, the decision to risk that "awful daring of a moment's surrender" has been, at long last, decisively made. "We have existed," Eliot has declared, "By this, and this only." And though the "falling towers" will go on falling out there on those "endless plains," once that decisive step inward and upward has been established, and once the "arid plain [is] behind me," one can finally decide to "at least set my lands in order."[73] That is, one can recognize that we are "each in his prison" only so long as we refuse to take the risk of religious surrender. Once we venture, we also gain. Having turned away from the fruitless quest for social salvation, and in giving up on the unreality of "Jerusalem Athens Alexandria / Vienna London," we will have found, "at least," the possibility of personal redemption.

Eliot once more highlights and emphasizes the drama of this turning point by the use of a space—and line 426, which follows, clearly shows that the world, once abandoned, demonstrates its unreality in vivid style. "London Bridge is falling down falling down falling down." The echoes of childhood, inevitably evoked by the all-familiar nursery rhyme, simply reinforce the emptiness of what has been abandoned. And in lines 427–431 Eliot indeed seems to permit the whole secular structure to blow itself up in a whirl and jumble of mad fragments. Echoes of Dante, and of the French poet Gerard de Nerval, and of the Elizabethan dramatist Thomas Kyd's *Spanish Tragedy,* all go flying past, concluding with, first, a repetition of the "Give. Sympathize. Control." formula in Sanskrit, and then terminated, as the poem is terminated, with a threefold repetition of "Shantih," which, says Eliot's note, is something like "The Peace which passeth understanding."

* * *

The Waste Land is not, plainly, an easy poem. But neither is it anywhere near so fearsome or so esoteric as its reputation would sometimes make it appear. If it is not entirely Eliot's poem, neither is it anyone else's: Pound is responsible for much of the structure, for better and for worse, but he is emphatically not responsible for (as surely he could not have been in sympathy with) the religious content. David Ward's summary seems to me richly worth quoting, as I end this long chapter:

... on one level the poem is the expression of an emotional mess, and it is characteristic of certain kinds of emotional muddle that the sufferer projects his own troubles on to everybody else. But, paradoxically, the emotional inadequacies of the poem add to its persuasive power: *The Waste Land* catches at and exploits a self-hatred which too often distorts the human spirit, and did so at a time when, though man was no more prone to bestiality and hypocrisy than before or since, had reason to be more acutely conscious of these failings than at any previous time. In this way, at least, *The Waste Land* richly deserves its classic status, that it expresses a certain kind of civilized morbidity more powerfully than it has ever been expressed. And what is more important, it expresses that morbidity directly, by action in words, not through a series of poses and conventional gestures as, for instance, Byron was apt to express the morbidity of the Romantic temperament.[74]

4

The road to religion:
England and
its Church embraced;
"The Hollow Men"
and
Ash-Wednesday

The impulse that produced *The Waste Land* continued for some years, certainly through "The Hollow Men," published in 1925 as a complete poem. Arguably, that same impulse persisted in a very different form even in *Ash-Wednesday,* published in 1930. The so-called "Ariel Poems" (which in later editions incorporate *The Cultivation of Christmas Trees,* published as a small volume in 1954), are of a somewhat different nature and deserve separate discussion. *Sweeney Agonistes,* an unfinished poem whose two parts were published in 1926 and 1927, must also be noted, as should some of the so-called "Minor Poems," which date from 1924, 1933, and 1934–35. Plainly, in the period which followed *The Waste Land* and preceded the first of the *Four Quartets*—"Burnt Norton," published in 1936—Eliot was as active as a poet as he had ever been. That fact becomes significant: after 1942, when "Little Gidding," the last of the *Four Quartets,* appeared, Eliot still had over two decades to live, but he did not write any poetry worth talking about. He won the Nobel Prize in 1948 for his poetry, but his poetry had effectively come to an end half a dozen years earlier, when he was only fifty-four. It is an early ending for a poet's work, and one that deserves discussion.

"I have been led to contemplate, for many moments," Eliot wrote in an essay for the *Dial,* published in April of 1922, "the nature of the particular torpor or deadness which strikes a denizen of London on his return."[1] On the other hand, as Jay Martin nicely puts it, "Unquestionably, Eliot draws in *The Waste Land* upon recollections of an actual London, and in large part accurately provides a literal geography for his poem. But it is the geography of mind and imagination in which he is really interested. . . ."[2] If there must remain some uncertainty as to how much of the "literal geography" was removed because Pound, rather than Eliot, did not want it to appear, nevertheless by the time of "The Hollow Men" Eliot had, in his poetry at least, shut the door on both "literal geography" and the world from which any such geography could be drawn. *The Waste Land* had established his position as a poet, and it had directly and indirectly brought him a measure of financial relief, including a $2,000 prize from the *Dial* and the generous assistance of the New York lawyer and collector, John Quinn.[3] But nothing could, would, or in fact did slow his despair of the secular world, and his almost desperate turn toward the only salvation he could contemplate.[4]

> We are the hollow men
> We are the stuffed men
> Leaning together
> Headpiece filled with straw. . . .

The symbolization process here is not in the least esoteric, and needs no more explication than do, a few lines farther along, the references to "wind in dry grass" or to "rats' feet over broken glass / In our dry cellar." Perhaps the most difficult note in this first part of "The Hollow Men," though it is not, in fact, difficult, is the reference to "death's other Kingdom." Eliot means, of course, a simple extension of the theme of *The Waste Land,* namely that our death-in-life existence requires us to call death by some other name, since we are as good as dead.[5]

But since the mainspring in Eliot's poetry was the tension between a reaching toward, and a movement away from, the secular world, the flattening out of that world in "The Hollow Men," no matter how effective, was bound to have important consequences. If one places "Preludes" at one end of a scale (though no such literal precision is possible), then "The Hollow Men" stands at the other end. "You tossed a blanket from the bed, / You lay upon your back, and waited," may not be "literal geography," but plainly it is solidly connected to the external world. "Shape without form, shade without color, / Paralysed force, gesture without motion"—this is "the geography of mind" with a vengeance. Ideational abstractions are not indeterminant, but simply abstract. The external world persists, even in *The Waste Land* as edited by Ezra Pound. It does not really exist in "The Hollow Men."

And though "The Hollow Men" is a powerful poem, it does not have the power of either "Preludes" or "Prufrock," on the one hand, or of *The Waste Land,* on the other. Where the earlier poems have sharp-edged observation, or bitter regret, or "a vision of the [world that] the [world] hardly understands," Eliot has now progressed to a kind of seamless rejection, a renunciation not so much bitter as resigned. "The Hollow Men" is by no means passionless, but its passion is of an essentially static sort. If not exactly flat, the poem is at least as two-dimensional as fine poetry can be. We are not "lost / Violent souls, but only / . . . hollow men / . . . stuffed men." From a technical standpoint, indeed, Eliot has done virtually everything that can be done to heighten and intensify both the beat and the rhetoric of the poem. The short lines marked by intermittent rhyme (grass / glass; crossed / lost), and dry precision of lexicon are joined to a burnished pallor of rhetoric, as smooth and as cold as the few material objects permitted to enter these lines, "broken glass . . . dry cellar . . . broken column . . . crossed staves . . . dead land . . . cactus land." Against so crushed and drained a background, even the restrained allusion, drawn from Dante (*Paradiso,* 31–32), to "the perpetual star / Multifoliate rose / Of death's twilight kingdom" takes on something of a glow. And that background allows Eliot, in the fifth and last part of the poem, to counterpoint both Biblical

and nursery-song fragments. The effect is remarkably pul-
sating, especially when we stop to consider that in this
same section, there is not a single real object, not a single
thing of the external world. (Unless, that is, we count the
"prickly pear" of the nursery rhyme as a real object, or the
"world" itself in the final quatrain.) Technically, "The
Hollow Men" is a masterful, even a virtuosic performance.
Antagonistic critics who have argued that Eliot was some
sort of bumbling fashionmonger, largely devoid of poetic
skill, seem not to have bothered reading the poetry.

It is impossible to say how much of the poem was
meant, at one time or another, to be included in *The Waste
Land.* "Song to the Opherian," published pseudonymously in 1921, suggests a possible link to the verse of the later
"Confessional" school and also a very clear link to Eliot's
relationship with his first wife. Separation by a river,
which is described as "blackened" in "Song" but "tumid"
in "The Hollow Men," and the movement of the wind as
virtually the only sign of life, show the cross-connections
and linkages. But in noting these ties, one must at the same
time see how, by 1925 when "The Hollow Men" appeared,
Eliot had taken a decisive swing away from these Robert
Lowell-like "Confessional" turnings. "As for *The Waste
Land,*" Eliot wrote to Richard Aldington, November 15,
1922, "that is a thing of the past so far as I am concerned
and I am now feeling toward a new form and style."[6]

> Is it like this
> In death's other kingdom
> Waking alone
> At the hour when we are
> Trembling with tenderness
> Lips that would kiss
> Form prayers to broken stone.

It *is* a new form, and a new style. But how far could it take

him, how much resonance was left in a world so thoroughly wrung out, a world in which, emphatically, "Between
the idea / And the reality / . . . Falls the Shadow"? Once
blown up, "Not with a bang but a whimper," how is the
poet to readmit the world to his poetry? And if, as I have
been arguing all along, one or another relationship to that
external world is at the heart of Eliot's best work, the
swing toward theological matters could not possibly satisfy the needs of his poetry, however much it might have
satisfied him personally. Because it did not satisfy the
poetic needs, in pretty direct consequence the poetry
began to dry up, and all too soon died away entirely.

It was not, however, an immediate turning. Lyndall
Gordon, who is convinced that Eliot was far more religious than I think the evidence demonstrates, and who is
convinced that he was thus religious almost from the start,
is nevertheless puzzled that he did "not make any serious
religious commitment in 1914." She finds herself explaining, uncomfortably, but I think correctly, that "Despite
his solitary nature, Eliot did not find it easy to reject
society. There was always the side . . . that felt keenly its
attractions."[7] "In 1914 Eliot might have become a Christian in a mood of passionate assent," she goes on; "by 1927
[when he was in fact formally received into the Church of
England] he had hesitated too long for such a mood to be
possible. What he needed now was essentially a haven.
. . ."[8] And she includes in her careful book a good deal of
evidence demonstrating how much of a wrench conversion was for Eliot, how deeply willed rather than innocent-
ly and passionately felt this turning was. She tells, for
example, the following brief story. "When Eliot visited
Rome in 1926 he suddenly fell on his knees before Michelangelo's *Pietà,* to the surprise of his brother and sister-
in-law who were with him."[9] The need to make so public,
not to say so violent a display of religious feeling, is hardly

the gesture of someone deeply convinced or deeply sure. Eliot's conversion came hard, and came painfully, and as I have indicated, and will shortly demonstrate, it came only in part, and that part was largely intellectual rather than passionate or poetic.

But for a while at least the urgencies exhibited by "The Hollow Men" persisted. *Sweeney Agonistes,* drafted in 1924, is described as "Fragments of an Aristophanic Melodrama," but it owes more to the stylized Noh drama of Japan and to music-hall burlesques and jazz-age music. It is not possible to say, on the basis of the fragmentary evidence left to us, what the entire work, had it been completed, might have looked like. ". . . All attempts, however ingenious, to reconstruct the plot from internal data are necessarily disappointing."[10] "*Sweeney Agonistes* was never completed," argues Carol Smith, "for [Eliot] realized the inadequacy of both dramatic realism and the current types of poetic drama for the expression of his dramatic ideals, and he was aware of the enormity of the task facing anyone who attempted a one-man theater movement along new lines."[11] I doubt that Eliot realized or was aware of anything of the sort. The "new form and style" that he wanted after *The Waste Land* was a style which he groped toward rather than one he formulated as a fully conscious decision. As Arnold Bennett reports in his *Journal,* under the date of September 10, 1924:

T.S. Eliot came to see me. . . . I said I couldn't see the point of [*The Waste Land*]. He said he didn't mind what I said as he had definitely given up that form of writing, and was now centred on dramatic writing. He wanted to write a drama of modern life (furnished flat sort of people) in a rhythmic prose 'perhaps with certain things in it accentuated by drum-beats.' And he wanted my advice. We arranged that he should do the scenario and some sample pages of dialogue.[12]

This hardly sounds like a man who knew precisely what he was up to. And for Eliot to consult Bennett, a solid, popular writer of no great range or depth—on January 29, 1926, Bennett records an attempt to read Eliot's magazine, the *Criterion*, "in which are some weird things," especially some Gertrude Stein, "out of which I could make nothing," an essay by Eliot, of which he could make "not much," and a story by Aldous Huxley, which "had absolutely no plot, and is really only a sketch"[13]—indicates to my mind something like desperate uncertainty. It seems clear that Eliot did not finish *Sweeney Agonistes* because, simply stated, he could not. He did not know exactly what he wanted, he did not know how to do what he thought he wanted, and after producing the two fragments (and presumably being told by Bennett that they would not work well on the commercial stage, as indeed they would not) he gave it up and never returned to it or to anything like it.

All the same, what he produced is in its way very fine. "The fragments present a picture of the boredom and emptiness of modern life with its evasion of fundamental realities," writes David E. Jones,[14] to which Helen Gardner adds that "*Sweeney Agonistes* appears a rather sterile appendix" to *The Waste Land*.[15] The sterility is both deliberate and extremely well-handled.

> Birth, and copulation, and death.
> That's all, that's all, that's all, that's all,
> Birth, and copulation, and death. . . .
> I've been born, and once is enough.
> You don't remember, but I remember,
> Once is enough.

If there is virtually no drama in *Sweeney Agonistes*, nor much of what is usually called characterization, there is a curiously lively presentation of "boredom and emptiness." As he has done before, and will do again, Eliot parodies a popular song in his own song "Under the bamboo / Bamboo bamboo / Under the bamboo tree." And so expert is the aping of lower-class slang and lower-class speech generally, that it is hardly surprising to find that an alternative title for the unfinished play, indeed the title under which Eliot first published the two fragments, was *Wanna Go Home, Baby?*[16] There are obvious links to earlier poems, not only in the use of the name Sweeney, but also, more than likely, in the character Doris, and in the reference to Mrs. Porter (who in *The Waste Land,* along with her daughter, washed her "feet in soda water"). But it is the flat, almost marionettelike characters, jerking out their flat, urban banalities in staccato rhythms, which give the fragments their life. Almost fifteen years later, in his "Five Points on Dramatic Writing," written very much tongue-in-cheek, Eliot showed that he had not lost these knacks, and could very well have created more Sweenies, had he wanted to:

1. You got to keep the audience's attention all the time.
2. If you lose it you got to get it back QUICK.
3. Everything about plot and character and all else what Aristotle and others say is secondary to the forgoin.
4. But IF you can keep the bloody audience's attention engaged, then you can perform any monkey tricks you like when they ain't looking, and it's what you do behind the audience's back so to speak that makes your play IMMORTAL for a while.

If the audience gets its strip tease it will swallow the poetry.

5. If you write a play in verse, then the verse
ought to be a medium to look THROUGH and
not a pretty decoration to look AT.[17]

There was only one *Sweeney Agonistes,* and a very fragmentary one at that, for yet another reason. In all his later
dramatic work, from the collaborative *The Rock* in 1934
to *The Elder Statesman* in 1958, Eliot was a conscious
propagandist—by which I mean nothing derogatory: art
as instruction and as polemic is as ancient a phenomenon
as is art itself—for the Christian religion.[18] In 1924, however, he was still caught up in that motion away from,
indeed that revulsion from, the secular world which is
exhibited in both *The Waste Land* and, roughly contem-
poraneous with *Sweeney Agonistes,* in "The Hollow Men."
A man who is trying as hard as he knows how, and perhaps harder even than that, to break his connections with
what has been of enormous importance to him is not a
man in any position to create large new structures of a
positive order. *The Waste Land* is of course, though large,
not more than peripherally positive; "The Hollow Men"
is not positive at all—and neither is *Sweeney Agonistes.*

It was in 1928, the year after his religious conversion,
that Eliot made his famous declaration to the effect that
his "general point of view" was "classicist in literature,
royalist in politics, and anglo-catholic in religion."[19] It
was in 1927 that he became a British citizen. And in 1927,
1928, 1929, and 1930 he wrote, for use in an annual series
put out by his publishing house (the series was called
"Ariel Poems" and was for contemporary writers), "Journey of the Magi," "A Song for Simeon," "Animula" [little
soul], and "Marina," the only one of the original Ariel
poems which postdates *Ash-Wednesday.* I want to discuss
the first three of the Ariel poems here and leave "Marina,"
which needs no large commentary, until after I have dis-

cussed the larger and more important poem to which, in my judgment, it is in fact something of a pendant.

"Journey of the Magi" has somewhat embarrassed Eliot's critics. Many readers, however, treasure this (and also the others of the original Ariel poems) as one of the noblest and most meaningful of all Eliot's verse. Hugh Kenner introduces his discussion of the Ariel poems with a comment about "the torpor of his muse," and largely talks around rather than about the poems themselves.[20] Bernard Bergonzi, while conceding that "Considered as poetic structures, they are dramatic monologues of a more straightforward kind than anything Eliot had previously produced," adds at once that the Ariel poems are "rhythmically less interesting than all Eliot's previous poetry, and read like summaries of experience rather than enactments of it."[21] Critics like Helen Gardner and Elizabeth Drew, who are enthusiasts of Eliot's religious poetry, tend to regard the more religiously affirmative "Marina" as the most impressive of the lot; critics like Stephen Spender, who prefer the starker and more obviously secular poems, tend to pass over all of the Ariel poems as rapidly as possible. Grover Smith, who like George Williamson can see the transitional function of the poems in Eliot's overall career, and who can even see good things in some of the poems, finds "Animula" in particular "prosaic in tone and traditional in meter. The rhyming pentameter is monotonously regular; the diction flat. One is dismayed to see in Eliot so cheap a phrase as 'fragrant brilliance' . . . ."[22] The reference to what is "traditional" as that which is blatantly bad is I think significant, telling us perhaps more about the critic than about the poem in question.

It seems to me that such criticisms have missed the merits and the place in Eliot's poetic development of the Ariel poems in general and of "Journey of the Magi," which I take to be the best of them, in particular. I find

it hard to describe any of Eliot's published poems, even
those I do not consider of major importance, as rhythmically uninteresting or monotonous. One could argue that
rhythm, indeed, is of all the elements of poetic technique
Eliot's strongest and most enduring trait. One of the most
sensitive commentators on such matters, Harvey Gross,
puts it like this:

Eliot has given us unforgettable rhythms—rhythms which echo
and re-echo in the mind's ear. We need only go to our memories
for prosodical touchstones: lines grasped long ago by the "audi-
tory imagination" and never lost. They recover an emotion from
personal and racial origins, recall some shuddering gesture of the
spirit, or catch the flat intonation of a bored voice. It is the heard
rhythms which animate these lines. [Citations omitted]. Eliot's
rhythms, capable of such variety in movement and sonority,
return us to the musical function of prosody. No modern poet
has so effectively used rhythm to evoke a "knowledge of how
feelings go"; no rhythms have shown such power to summon
emotion to the forefront of consciousness.[23]

And Virginia Woolf, no very charitable commentator (especially when dealing with other writers), has left us more
than one account of Eliot's impressive performances, in
private company, of his own verse. On June 23, 1922, for
example, she writes in her diary:

Eliot dined last Sunday & read his poem [*The Waste Land*]. He
sang it & chanted it and rhythmed it. It has great beauty & force
of phrase: symmetry; & tensity. What connects it together, I'm
not so sure. But he read it till he had to rush . . . & discussion
was thus curtailed. One was left, however, with some strong
emotion. The Waste Land, it is called . . .[24]

The rhythms of the Ariel poems are not the rhythms
of *The Waste Land;* the poet is, however, very much the
same, and Eliot as author of the Ariel poems is separated
from himself as author of *The Waste Land* by no great

distance in time. We would do well, it seems to me, to read the poems, and "Journey of the Magi" especially, with open minds—and ears.

> 'A cold coming we had of it,
> Just the worst time of the year
> For a journey, and such a long journey:
> The ways deep and the weather sharp,
> The very dead of winter.'

These opening lines are in quotes not only because they are interior monologue, but principally because they are a subtle reworking of a passage from one of the sermons of Bishop Lancelot Andrewes (1555–1626):

It was no summer progress. A cold coming they had of it at this time of the year, just the worst time of the year to take a journey, and specially a long journey in. The ways deep, the weather sharp, the days short, the sun farthest off, *in solstitio brumali,* "the very dead of winter."[25]

In his essay on Andrewes, written in 1926, Eliot had said that "his sermons are too well built to be readily quotable; they stick too closely to the point to be entertaining. . . . [Andrewes] assimilates his material and advances by means of it. His quotation is not decoration or irrelevance, but the matter in which he expresses what he wants to say. . . . Andrewes takes a word and derives the world from it. . . ."[26] Eliot is of course trying to do exactly the same thing. It is not surprising that he goes on to claim for Andrewes that his "emotion is purely contemplative; it is not personal, it is wholly evoked by the object of contemplation, to which it is adequate; his emotions wholly contained in and explained by its object."[27] This is Eliot's own ideal; how far his poetry achieves it, or can usefully be measured against it, is another matter entirely. But is Eliot responding, here, simply and straightforwardly to An-

drewes' "matter"? Or as Matthiessen once put it, has the
prose "started cadences in Eliot's mind that were ultimately transformed into new patterns"?[28] It seems clear
that, whatever the similarities in content, even in the use
of identical words and phrases, Eliot's five lines are rhythmically entirely different from Andrewes' three prose sentences. And this effect is not achieved by simple
elimination or by the arrangement of the lines in standard
poetic form. What Eliot has done varies from dropping
whole sentences, to pronoun shifts, to structural rewriting
("just the worst time of the year to take a journey, and
specially a long journey in," becomes "Just the worst time
of the year / For a journey, and such a long journey"), to
linkage variations ("the ways deep, the weather sharp,"
becomes "The ways deep and the weather sharp"). Andrewes is without any doubt the source of the passage, and
the general resemblance is close enough so that quotation
marks are justified. But the *poetry* is entirely Eliot's. Andrewes' prose has been, in effect, translated, almost as if
from another language, into a tight, rhythmically altered
pattern which is Eliot's, and is poetic.

    The proof, to my mind, is that after leaving An-
drewes' prose behind him, Eliot moves forward in exactly
the same rhythms and exactly the same diction. "And the
camels galled, sore-footed, refractory, / Lying down in the
melting snow. / There were times we regretted / The
summer palaces on slopes, the terraces, / And the silken
girls bringing sherbet." This is not the matter nor is it the
manner of "Prufrock" or of "Preludes"; it is neither the
matter nor the manner of *The Waste Land* or of "The
Hollow Men." But the poetic voice, it seems to me, is
unmistakeably Eliot's. And though the poetic goals are
different, most of the poetic techniques are clearly related
to techniques he has used before. I suspect that a critic
who objects to a phrase like "fragrant brilliance" should

object about equally to one like "silken girls"—but the objection would be beside the point, because Eliot is quite simply trying to do something he has not done before. He is trying to write more or less public poetry, that is, poetry capable of being read fairly widely and by people who do not subscribe either to the *Criterion* or to the Gospels according to Ezra Pound. He is trying to make his poem consecutive, and narrative, and non-esoteric. He wants the rhythmic movement to be smoother and considerably less jagged at all points; he wants also to suggest substantive (i.e., religious) possibilities that he has not wanted to suggest before. And he succeeds, it seems to me, extraordinarily well. The first strophe of "Journey of the Magi" works some fine variations on what has become, to that point, a rhythmic pattern: "the voices singing in our ears, saying / That this was all folly" has, to my ear, something of the broken rhythm of parts of *The Waste Land.* When, therefore, Eliot immediately breaks that strophe off and begins the next one with a long, lyrical and descriptive and swinging verse line, he sets both strophes off against each other and thrusts his poem forward nicely. The descriptive lines are remarkably fine, at times almost oriental in their sparse and yet colorful detail: "a running stream and a water-mill," "three trees on the low sky," "six hands at an open door," and so on. The risky modulation of the last line of the second strophe—"it was (you may say) satisfactory"—is hardly the sort of torpidity ascribed to this and to the other Ariel poems. And the risk is on the whole well taken, for in strophe three Eliot once again shifts rhythmic gears, this time moving into a more strongly propulsive pattern, one at times reminiscent not only of *The Waste Land* but also of *Sweeney Agonistes:*

> . . . And I would do it again, but set down
> This set down

> This: were we led all that way for
> Birth or Death?

Note too that the highly specific diction has, without any more warning and any stronger transition than that parenthetical "you may say," become far more abstract. The visual has become, abruptly, ideational; the sense of consecutive motion has given way to doubt and uncertainty, expressed both rhythmically and in the diction. And then the diction and the rhythm change once more, as the persona chews, hard and long, on what he now has to deal with:

> . . . There was a Birth, certainly.
> We had evidence and no doubt. I had seen birth and
>   death,
> But had thought they were different; this Birth was
> Hard and bitter agony for us, like Death, our death.
> . . .

The poetic devices are beautifully matched to the substantive content: it would be hard to write more expert poetry. And the restrained but only partial sense of relief afforded by the ending, spoken in the midst of "an alien people clutching their gods," dovetails equally well with what Eliot means to say. "I should be glad of another death." But it simply is not that easy, not even for one of the Magi, and certainly not for anyone in Western civilization in the 1920s. From the choice of tense, the carefully conditional "should," to the carefully unspecific reference to "another death" (with a lower case initial letter to set this death off from Christ's), this dry concluding line does exactly what it is meant to do.

"Journey of the Magi" cannot be ranked with Eliot's major poetry. It lacks the sweep and the power; it is perhaps too well-balanced, and contains too perfectly the attitudes and ideas Eliot wants it to convey. But if it is small, it is also genuine. Eliot has managed here to deal with deeply religious material in a consistent, effective, and to my mind, moving fashion. I think he does not display such abilities either in "Marina," the last of the original Ariel poems, or in *Ash-Wednesday,* the first of what are usually considered the major religious poems of his last decade as a practicing poet. Those two poems will be discussed shortly. For the moment, let me say only that I think the success of "Journey of the Magi" is the result of a number of contributing factors: (a) its scope is limited; (b) it is content to report in a fairly objective style, rather than to preach or debate; (c) it is essentially narrative, and, therefore, externalized, rather than an interior, meditative dramatization; and (d) if not exactly uncertain, religiously, it is nevertheless not one-sided; it can and does present and deal with both doubt and uncertainty, and it thereby builds into the poem's structure a quiet but important tension.

These distinctions may become clearer if I show them at work in somewhat different and less successful poetic form in "A Song for Simeon" and "Animula," and then turn to *Ash-Wednesday,* which goes off in new and, in my judgment, unsuccessful directions. ("Marina," as I have said, tails along behind this initial monument to Eliot's conversion.) It does no good to speculate about what might have happened had Eliot been able to continue in the directions marked out by "Journey of the Magi" and the next two Ariel poems. As I shall try to make clear, Eliot's conversion had poetic consequences which he could neither anticipate nor, at least in part, control.

And, behold, there was a man in Jerusalem, whose name was Simeon; and the same man was just and devout, waiting for the consolation of Israel: and the Holy Ghost was upon him. And

it was revealed unto him by the Holy Ghost, that he should not
see death, before he had seen the Lord's Christ.[29]

Jesus' parents bring him to the temple, Simeon sees
Jesus, and declares: "Lord, now lettest thou thy servant
depart in peace, according to thy word: For mine eyes
have seen thy salvation." This is the brief Biblical tale on
which the poem is based. Eliot begins his poem with lines,
and with procedures, very reminiscent of "Journey of the
Magi." "Lord, the Roman hyacinths are blooming in
bowls and / The winter sun creeps by the snow hills." For
all the reasons cited, a moment ago, this is a promising
start. But the focus is not well-maintained. Indeed, a sort
of bifurcation of both purpose and technique begins to set
in as early as line 3: "The stubborn season has made
stand." The adjective, "stubborn," is distinctly indeterminant—why is the season "stubborn"? is the season or the
people or the city being described?—and the firm, limited,
narrative approach of the first two lines is undermined. A
clash of techniques results, and the consequences of that
clash are not dissipated, but are in fact worsened by what
follows.

> My life is light, waiting for the death wind,
> Like a feather on the back of my hand.
> Dust in sunlight and memory in corners
> Wait for the wind that chills toward the dead land.

The first two lines are lighter in tone than the verse of
"Gerontion," but very reminiscent of that quite different
poem. The next line, too, echoes "Gerontion," but the
fourth of these lines takes on both the movement and the
rhetoric of "The Hollow Men." And the entire small passage flirts with exactly the internalized or meditative material which, on the whole, "Journey of the Magi"
eschews. That is, in this first seven-line strophe we are
presented with three different and unreconciled (and per-

haps unreconcilable) poetic approaches. The poem cannot help but suffer.

The second strophe, attempting perhaps to recapture the directness and simplicity of the first of the Ariel poems, goes too far in the direction, becoming flat and dull, rather than simple and direct: "I have walked many years in this city, / Kept faith and fast, provided for the poor, / Have given and taken honour and ease." The verse does not, in truth, dramatize anything. It merely states facts—and facts do not build poetic tension, or poems. The "goat's path" and "the fox's home," images which follow these prosaic recitations, are similarly flat, derivative, and, therefore, without dramatic power. In a poet less gifted, one might call such secondhand images "push-button" poetry. In Eliot, one is obliged to call them confused.

But the third strophe demonstrates that the confusion is by no means total. From the first line we sense the verse tightened into place, the ideas embodied, the dramatic scene recaptured: "Before the time of cords and scourges and lamentation. . . ." What Eliot has done, to revive his flagging poem, is exceedingly simple. He has dropped both the internalized material and the derivative images, and has returned to stating, in language dramatically appropriate to his persona-narrator, what seem to be objective realities. His control of this approach, drawn of course from "Journey of the Magi," flickers a bit. "Now at this birth season of decease" is about as clumsy a line as Eliot ever wrote, and "the mountain of desolation" has slightly uncomfortable echoes of John Bunyan's *Pilgrim's Progress,* one of the theological hits of 1678. The fourth and final strophe: "Not for me the martyrdom, the ecstasy of thought and prayer, / Not for me the ultimate vision," begins to stray toward the manner of *Ash-Wednesday.* But the final lines hold to the objective drama:

> I am tired with my own life and the lives of those after
>   me,
> I am dying in my own death and the deaths of those
>   after me.
> Let thy servant depart,
> Having seen thy salvation.

Note how in the last two lines Eliot has done with the
Bible's words exactly what he did earlier with Lancelot
Andrewes. It works, I think, equally well.

"Animula"—again, the title means "a little soul"—is
a word choice meant, in all probability, to evoke memories
of Publius Aelius Hadrianus (the Emperor Hadrian, pro-
claimed emperor in A.D. 117), addressing his soul as
"Animula vagula blandula. . . ." In the famous translation
of Hadrian's poem by Lord Byron: "Ah! gentle, fleeting,
wav'ring sprite, / Friend and associate of this clay! / To
what unknown region borne / Wilt thou now wing thy
distant flight? / No more with wonted humour gay, / But
pallid, cheerless, and forlorn." The quotation marks in the
first line, however, indicate a borrowing not from Hadrian
but from Dante, Purgatorio 16: 85–88, "Esce di mano a
lui, che la vagheggia / prima che sia, a guisa di fanciulla
/ che piangendo e ridendo pargoleggia, / l'anima sem-
plicetta. . . ." ("From his hands who fondly loves her ere
she is / in being, there issues, after the fashion of a little
/ child that sports, now weeping, now laughing, / the
simple tender soul. . . .") But as Mario Praz nicely says,
in discussing "T.S. Eliot and Dante," "such passages need
not detain us for long: one can find similar deft insertions
in dozens of other poets."[30] What matters is the poem
which follows after the quotation—and that poem has
evoked strikingly dissimilar reactions, ranging from the
assertion that, aside from "The Hollow Men," it "is Eliot's
most pessimistic poem,"[31] to Father Genesius Jones' judgment that "*Animula* provides a picture of the growing soul

which is the antithesis of the Lord's growing in wisdom and age and grace; but it contains an element of hope. . . ."[32]

It is a much more consistent poem than "A Song for Simeon," and on the whole much closer to "Journey of the Magi" in technique—though, except for the final six lines, it is written in a loose iambic pentameter blank verse. From the biographical evidence now available to us, further, it seems to be a portrait drawn directly, or very closely, from Eliot's own childhood, over-protected, rather sterilely prosperous, "taking pleasure . . . in the wind, the sunlight and the sea," but on the whole obliged to "curl up . . . in the window seat / Behind the *Encyclopaedia Britannica*," rather than being permitted much time or opportunity for the out-of-doors. Until the end of the first long strophe, there is relatively little that strays beyond the approach of "Journey of the Magi." The poem deals in "a flat world of changing lights and noise," leading by slow stages to "the pain of living and the drug of dreams." Rather more Johnsonesque in tone than the crisper and more vivid "Journey of the Magi" (see especially Johnson's "Vanity of Human Wishes," published in 1749), "Animula" is still a consistent performance. If one objects to "fragrant brilliance," I think one would be bound to object also to "drug of dreams" or to "grasping at kisses and toys," or even to the statemental reference to "the growing burden of the growing soul." But these and similar phrases are, I believe, deeply integral to the poem's rhetoric and purpose; they could not be removed or altered without changing that fabric. One may wish the fabric were different, but that is quite another matter.

And the curious, Villonesque *envoi* [a short stanza concluding a poem, as a postscript may conclude a letter], six lines long, is deftly counterpointed against the faintly drab regularity of the bulk of the poem. It is not in blank

verse, as the rest of the poem is, nor is its diction drawn
from any sort of "flat world." "Pray for Guiterriez, avid
of speed and power, / For Boudin, blown to pieces.
. . ." This is surely deliberately reminiscent of both the
brawling François Villon and the fine (if occasionally
somewhat too literary) imitations of Villon written by
Ezra Pound. Father Genesius Jones adds, perceptively,
that such references as "Pray for Floret, by the boarhound
slain between the yew trees," are anything but casual.
". . . In the new life Eros returns with all the other meanings which attach to the fertility symbol in a purified form.
This is the significance of the request in *Animula* to [pray
for Floret. . . .]. This death will be followed by a rebirth
(as in the Attis myth associated with the boarhound).
. . ."[33] The invocation in the final line, "Pray for us now
and at the hour of our birth," which is from the Church
of England prayerbook, accordingly closes the poem in a
distinctly hopeful vein. It may not be pleasant to read of
the child issuing "from the hand of time . . . irresolute and
selfish, misshapen, lame," but as Eliot has long since
pointed out, "there is a difference . . . between philosophical *belief* and poetic *assent*. . . . You are not called upon
to believe what [the poet] believed . . . but you are called
upon more and more to understand it."[34]

        ". . . I have had a most shameful and distressing
interview with poor dear Tom Eliot, who may be called
dead to us all from this day forward," wrote Virginia
Woolf to her sister Vanessa, February 11, 1928. "He has
become an Anglo-Catholic, believes in God and immortality, and goes to church. I was really shocked. A corpse
would seem to me more credible than he is."[35] The arch
style—she had previously reported to her sister's husband
that "I've been talking for two hours to Tom Eliot about
God,"[36] without ill effects or permanent consequences,
and, of course, she and her family and friends continued

to see Eliot socially—pretends to a more serious reaction
than she in fact felt. But the shock was indeed real. As
early as 1928 E. M. Forster wrote, perceptively, that Eliot
"is not a mystic. *For Lancelot Andrewes* contains several
well-turned compliments to religion and Divine Grace,
but no trace of religious emotion. . . . He has not got it;
what he seeks is not revelation, but stability."[37] A British
theologian, Martin Jarrett-Kerr, has noted that "most"
reactions to Eliot's religious conversion took on "the tone
of 'high hopes disappointed'."[38] As Edmund Wilson
wrote in 1931, "We feel in contemporary writers like Eliot
a desire to believe in religious revelation, a belief that it
would be a good thing to believe, rather than a genuine
belief. The faith of the modern convert seems to burn only
with a low blue flame. . . . From such a faith, uninspired
by hope, unequipped with zeal or force, what guidance for
the future can we expect?"[39] And in the same year
Thomas McGreevy observed briskly that Eliot "may
become a Catholic, a universal, poet, a royal poet, a classical poet. But he should spare us the 'isms'. They are the
business of other men than poets."[40] R. P. Blackmur
seems to me to sum it up, noting that Eliot's "is the last
mind which, in this century, one would have expected to
enter the Church in a lay capacity. . . . [But] however that
may be, within the Church or not, Mr. Eliot's mind has
preserved its worldly qualities."[41]

Ash-Wednesday, the first three parts of which were
published, separately, in 1928, 1927, and 1929, respective-
ly, appeared in April of 1930 as a whole poem. What
might be called the literalist reading labels it "a poem at
once religious in feeling and contemporary in intention: at
once thoroughly personal and without concession to senti-
ment."[42] What might be called the fellow-traveler (i.e.,
fellow religious) reading declares that "*Ash-Wednesday*
certainly belongs to the world of high dream. . . ."[43] The

more professional religious reading (i.e., by a priest) explains that "The feelings and emotions which attend the process of illumination (or purification) are objectified in *Ash-Wednesday*."[44] An essentially secular reading concludes, after a slightly uncomfortable and rather brief discussion, that "The poet is, then, still struggling with his unbelief in *Ash-Wednesday*."[45]

I should like to approach the poem rather differently from any of these dissimilar tacks. It needs to be said, first, that it is dangerous to confuse intention and execution. Whatever Eliot may have meant to accomplish in *Ash-Wednesday*, no matter how interesting, and even no matter how illuminating as to Eliot's then state of mind, is vastly less important in evaluating the poem than what he did in fact accomplish. Similarly, it is dangerous to confuse Eliot's critical formulations with his poem. That is, though the criticism and the poem are written by the same man, and come ultimately from the same sources and the same background, their relationship to that man, Thomas Stearns Eliot, is necessarily different. I will make this clearer when we discuss Eliot's criticism. I want simply to emphasize here that, although I do not think it either possible or advisable to separate any aspect of a writer's work from other aspects of that same oeuvre, I also insist on dealing with each such aspect in its own terms. Poems do not come from exactly the same place as do critical essays (or plays, or social commentary); they do not involve exactly the same components of a writer's personality. What is said in a poem, accordingly, is not said in the same way or with the same effect that it may be said in an essay.

When Eliot "said," therefore, at the time he was beginning to write some parts of what became *Ash-Wednesday*, that he was "anglo-catholic" in religion, it may well be that, after an examination of what the poem itself tells us, we will conclude that the poem "says" something rather different. Without indicating what I think such an examination will prove (though, of course, I have long since indicated in general outline what my views on this matter are), let us turn to the poem. And let us look, most seriously and intently, at the *poem's* furniture, the component parts out of which the poet has built it. No matter what his conscious and intellectual concerns, what he puts in the poem is what he is poetically concerned with. And it is his poetic concerns that here concern us.

We need to consider the poem's furniture, too, both from a positive and from a negative standpoint. That is, we need to look at what Eliot puts in and what he does not put in. By this point we have some idea of what his past poetic concerns have been, and we can most validly measure the poetic concerns of *Ash-Wednesday* in the larger context thus afforded us. And we need not suspend our own critical faculties. What a poet accomplishes fully is in a different relationship to that poet than something which he accomplishes only fitfully, or badly, or fails to accomplish at all. We must, that is, continue to use all the tools of analytical inquiry and not forego those tools at the behest of an authority less compelling than the text of the poem itself.

Part one begins in a rhythm and, in part, in a voice similar to that employed in "The Hollow Men." "Because I do not hope to turn again / Because I do not hope / Because I do not hope to turn. . . ." The bleak negativisms of the earlier poem, however, have yielded to a tentatively hopeful humility. Bluntly, there is no humility in Eliot's poetry before about 1927. Even *The Waste Land,* which talks of "surrender," "obedience," and "control," does not present these concepts in terms of humility so much as it does in terms of risk and eventual satisfaction. "The boat responded gaily . . . your heart would have responded

/ Gaily. . . ." Give this and get that, is the point in *The Waste Land,* not—as Eliot writes later in this first part of *Ash-Wednesday*—"Teach us to care and not to care / Teach us to sit still."

Ideas are, of course, every bit as much and as valid poetic furniture as material objects, and the idea of humility is plainly new to Eliot's poetry. But how forcefully is this new idea presented? And what support is it given by the other poetic techniques of the poem, rhythm, imagery, and so on? For one thing, humility is stated and restated, formulated and reformulated. This is surely not a sign of secure belief. A poet who feels secure about an idea does not feel obliged to insist on it. When at the start of *Paradise Lost,* John Milton tells us that he will "assert Eternal Providence, / And justify the ways of God to men," that is that. He tells us, and then he moves on, considering that he has done what needs to be done simply by making the statement. He believes it, he expects us to believe it, and there's no more to the whole process than that. Or, when Alexander Pope, in *An Essay on Man,* wants to establish a concept, he goes right to it and, in a very few lines, moves on—and does not look back, does not restate and restate. "Of Systems possible, if 'tis confest / That Wisdom infinite must form the best, / Where all must full or not coherent be, / And all that rises, rise in due degree; / Then . . . 'tis plain. . . ."

The chief metaphor of part one, which is designed to embody and to illustrate this new idea of humility, is the notion of an "agèd eagle" which no longer wishes to fly, its wings having become "merely vans to beat the air," and even the air itself having become "now thoroughly small and dry." As I have noted, many readers, especially at the time of the poem's first appearance, were troubled, and many offended by this metaphor. It was frequently taken, with perhaps understandable, but certainly erroneous, literalness. Yet, there is something wrong with the metaphor, whether it be read simply as a metaphor or as some sort of personal declaration (which, again, it is not). To abandon flight is an act of humility for a creature born to fly; that much is plain in what Eliot wants to convey. And to embody that flying creature as an eagle, a bird of great strength and pride, also illustrates those character traits which make humility hard and painful. But, no matter how much validity the metaphor might have had, Eliot feels obliged to force the issue by making his flying creature an "agèd" eagle. The metaphor is at once seriously compromised. What does an "agèd" flying creature give up that is not required of it by the mere fact of its age? That is, in his earnest but uncertain need to sweep away what is still there, in his anxiety to assert what he cannot really credit, Eliot pushes the poem (and the metaphor) too far—and that sense of strain is I think evident throughout *Ash-Wednesday.*

Indeed, where in his earlier work he has struggled to deal with the world, secular and external, in this poem that world has by and large disappeared. It is one thing to analogize men to empty creatures "filled with straw"; it is something different, and less legitimate as well as less convincing, to set up and then knock down poetic straw men. The world in which we stand is very much more difficult to renounce than an abstract world furnished with exotic materials and over-insistent assertions. The only natural objects in part one, for example, are "There, where trees flower, and springs flow." We are told of "the positive hour," and of "the one veritable transitory power"; we are assured of "the blessed face" and "the voice"; and we are given a variety of joy in which we "rejoice, having to construct something / Upon which to rejoice." If, as I have argued, Eliot's poetry draws a large part of its power from the tension between the attraction and repulsion of the secular world, the world of things and people and animals and landscape, then one large source of power has been pulled out of *Ash-Wednesday*. That it was deliberately done, and that it was done for a reason, is once again less important than the plain fact of its having been done.

And when we turn to the remainder of the poem, parts two through five, we find more of what we have found in part one. Part two, for example, begins:

> Lady, three white leopards sat under a juniper-tree
> In the cool of the day, having fed to satiety
> On my legs my heart my liver and that which had been
>   contained
> In the hollow round of my skull. And God said
> Shall these bones live? shall these
> Bones live? And that which had been contained
> In the bones (which were already dry) said chirping:
> Because of the goodness of this Lady
> And because of her loveliness, and because
> She honours the Virgin in meditation,
> We shine with brightness.

We can say at this point that "Eliot's leopards have the same dual function, in what is the essential allegory of this passage, as do the main levels of ambiguity in part one. Being predatory, the leopards may well signify the world, the flesh, and the devil; St. John of the Cross lends a certain weight to such an interpretation by his emphasis in *The Dark Night* upon these three traditional enemies of the soul. Thus they assume the place of the dog in *The Waste Land* or that of the leopard among the three beasts met by Dante. . . ."[46] Or we can say, with more certainty and much more relevance to the text in front of us, that indeterminacy has progressed here to a level of abstraction which is consistent but not satisfying. Who is the Lady? We have no way of knowing. Why are the animals leopards rather than something else? We do not know. Why are they white? We can only guess at some sacral link. Why has the physical existence of the persona been sacrificed to the leopards? Presumably, because this is a poem of humility and renunciation. Fine: the portions of the persona not consumed by the leopards, his bones, are considered for a different and presumably higher form of life. And God ponders their worth for such a level of existence. The already-dry bones themselves assert that "because of the goodness of this Lady / And because of her loveliness, and because / She honours the Virgin in meditation . . .," their worth can indeed be safely asserted. They "shine with brightness," in testimony of that worth. But "the goodness of this Lady" is necessarily a hollow phrase: its content is not clear for us. And why is her "loveliness" relevant? We can only guess. Her honoring "the Virgin in meditation," furthermore, is yet another flat assertion piled on a previous flat assertion: she is "good," she is "lovely," she honors the Virgin. In short, for all the deftness of the verse, for all the excellence of the rhythms and the beautifully controlled diction, this is in some measure a sterile passage—as *Ash-Wednesday* is similarly a sterile poem. "Redeem / The unread vision in the higher dream," the poet intones in part four, "While jewelled unicorns draw by the golded hearse." But how will the "unread vision" ever be perceived, much less "redeemed," so long as it is given an embodiment so intensely artificial and arbitrary? Helen Gardner, herself a believer and also a believer in Eliot's belief, is obliged to admit that "*Ash-Wednesday* is the most obscure of Mr. Eliot's poems, and the most at the mercy of the temperament and beliefs of the individual reader."[47] But is this not to concede, in different terms, that the poem is in large part a failure, an attempt to preach to the already converted—or to identify with the already converted?

The deftness of the poem, let me make clear, is at times dazzling:

> If the lost word is lost, if the spent word is spent
> If the unheard, unspoken
> Word is unspoken, unheard;
> Still is the unspoken word, the Word unheard,
> The Word without a word, the Word within
> The world and for the world;
> And the light shone in darkness and
> Against the Word the unstilled world still whirled
> About the centre of the silent Word.

How many poets were there in the late 1920s who could have equalled that ten-line burst of hand-is-quicker-than-eye magic? The answer, I think, is none, though possibly Wallace Stevens might qualify. Even William Butler Yeats did not have prestidigitational skills of this sort. And yet, boiled down, what is Eliot getting at—and is it as complex as he wants us to think it is, as perhaps he needs us to think it is? "We may not listen to the Christian message, but it remains available to us." Let me paraphrase these lines more fully. It may be that the words of God, as expressed in the Bible and the teachings of the Church, are not sought after ("lost") and are considered useless ("spent"), are neither listened to ("unspoken") nor heard ("unheard"), but even unspoken and unheard, even disregarded ("Word without a word"), God's word remains in ("within") the world and "for the world." Even in darkness there can be light, and the busy ("unstilled") world, whether it knows it or not, still has to reckon with God's word ("against" which it "whirled")—and not only reckon with it in passing, but recognize that the world's business inevitably must confront at its heart ("about the centre") what God has said to and for us. This is serious; it is worth saying. But is it worth quite the weight Eliot seems to be giving it, with his efflorescing verse? Put differently: if any sort of communication were at the "centre" of Eliot's concerns, would he whirl his readers about with such panache and polish, would he make such a brilliant and possibly confusing display? The answer, I think, is clearly negative: he would not. And neither would he juxtapose, against such whirling displays heart-rending cries from the prophets of the Bible, as if prophets like Micah were concerned with appearances and not realities. "O my people, what have I done unto thee," from Micah: 6:3, seems to me distinctly out of place, set in such a mass of verbal fireworks. It is true that in Micah the Lord is crying out to and against His people, demanding their renewed allegiance. "He hath shewed thee, O man, what is good; and what doth the LORD require of thee, but to do justly, and to love mercy, and to walk humbly with thy God?" But neither this, nor the tone of this, is what Eliot is up to. Indeed, immediately after the line from Micah he returns to his dazzling cosmopolitanisms: "Where shall the word be found, where will the word / Resound?" This is fearfully clever; it is not, I'm afraid, particularly just, loving, or humble.

I do not think *Ash-Wednesday* is unserious, or that its ideational content is not serious or worthy. It is not a deceitful poem, nor is it a false poem. But it is a poem so divided against itself that it cannot be seen as an adequate poetic vehicle for the ideas Eliot intended it to embody. It does not embody them, except fitfully; poems are not made up of ideas so much as words, rhythms, images, metaphors, and emotions, all of them elements of human expression, which stem from sources more holistic than the more purely mental source of ideas. "Teach us to sit still / Even among these rocks" is not embodied poetry, nor is it very good poetry. It is not surprising to find that Eliot himself, at about this time, "had doubted . . .

whether he had any more poetry to write." Just then he
had been invited to participate in the pageant entitled *The
Rock,* and had accepted "as an act of conviction and
obligation. In the result his numbed powers were revived
by the exercise, and he was able to proceed to the second
half of his creative life."⁴⁸ Not many critics perceived the
problem, but some, even at the time, were aware of it.
"Mr. T.S. Eliot is a poet of undoubted genius," wrote
Thomas McGreevy in 1931, "but his most recent book of
verse, *Ash-Wednesday,* must be a serious disappointment
. . . the distinct falling off in vigour and vividness, in
pregnancy, suggestiveness of words, in technical adequacy
to the subject, not only from the quality of *The Waste
Land* but from that of the much earlier *Prufrock,* is fairly
disconcerting. The book has virtues, but they are, to use
an inadequate phrase, negative virtues rather than positive."⁴⁹

It is, then, in the light of this analysis that I want to
briefly consider the fourth of the Ariel poems, "Marina,"
published in September of 1930, roughly half a year after
Ash-Wednesday. "The context designated in the title is
that of Pericles' reunion with his daughter Marina in
Shakespeare's *Pericles.*"⁵⁰ The Latin epigraph may be
translated: "What place is this, what land, what quarter
of the globe?" The epigraph is drawn from a play by
Seneca, where it is spoken by Hercules as he returns to
consciousness after a mad fit. But the sense of strain that
one feels in *Ash-Wednesday* is even more acute, in "Marina," and though there are lines of some intensity, the
poem seems almost a pastiche of earlier poems, as if the
poet were—as he himself has said he was—floundering
and unable to see his way as a poet. We are taken from
the sad ecstasy of "O my daughter" directly to the "Hollow Men" abruptness and nastiness of "Those who sharp-
en the tooth of the dog, meaning / Death. . . ." There is

a clear echo of "Gerontion" in "Whispers and small laughter between leaves and hurrying feet," just as there is a clear echo from the unpublished draft *Waste Land* in the brief sea passage which follows. The penultimate strophe is one of the most obviously tired, even drained passages in all of Eliot's poetry: "This form, this face, this life / Living to live in a world of time beyond me; let me / Resign my life for this life, my speech for that unspoken, / The awakened, lips parted, the hope, the new ships." This is a poet at the edge of poetic silence. David Ward's careful, nonjudgmental evaluation of the second strophe ("Those who sharpen the tooth of the dog . . .") speaks, to my mind, to the problems of the entire poem:

In a poem so full of delicate uncertainty this kind of [heavy] emphasis destroys the finely attuned poise so rudely that its dramatic and emotional rightness of purpose must be absolutely secure.

But dramatically it is wrong. . . . And it is emotionally wrong: the assertive negative morality doesn't fit with the air of tentative discovery. And, most important of all, the failure of tone here may seed some doubts about the validity of the rest of the poem.[51]

I do not see how those doubts can be avoided: "Marina" is a largely empty poem, a poem demonstrating the poet's exhaustion rather than the religious truths it struggles to enunciate.

What I have tried to show, in this discussion of Eliot's poetry after *The Waste Land* and before *Four Quartets,* is essentially how Eliot's needs as a man drastically affected his abilities as a poet. His relationship with the physical, secular world had never been a comfortable one, but neither had he, in his earlier work, rejected that world. Indeed, it is more than anything else the tension produced by the pull toward, and at the same time the revulsion away from, that world which drove and informed and made incredibly memorable his poetry. But *The Waste Land* is arguably the last poem to be propelled by that tension. And after *The Waste Land,* as this chapter has attempted to show, Eliot groped for and by and large did not find a satisfactory substitute for what, as a poet, he had always depended on, but what as a man he could no longer tolerate.

5

Last poems and partial poetic recovery: Four Quartets *(with a Postscriptum on Possum)*

"If Eliot is to claim a place in English poetry, it will have to be on the basis of the poems written before 1930."[1] That judgment, written in 1971, might not have been possible earlier, when the sputtering candle of Eliot's poetry had been relit and had produced, one after the other, from 1936 to 1942, the long poems now collected as *Four Quartets.* It is, in fact, an even harsher judgment than it seems. After having noted that "the embarrassments of the plays are beyond comment," Professor Vendler declares flatly, that "The career tailed off more disastrously than any other in living memory, with only sporadic lines reminding a reader of what Eliot had once been."[2] Professor Vendler is neither an eccentric nor (to say the least) a negligible critic—and, in fact, she does not go so far as does F. W. Bateson, who says of *Four Quartets* that "The impression one has is of an essayist in the Lamb or Hazlitt manner eking out material that is subjectively and emotionally decidedly 'thin'."[3] Professor Bateson, whose essay appeared in 1970, is English, as is Donald Davie, who in a 1972 essay manages to defend the *Quartets* as "a substantial achievement" and yet leave us with the uncomfortable feeling that his defense is on essentially extrapoetic grounds. Davie refers, for example, to "heavy stamping up and down on one spot," in a passage from *East Coker;* he speaks of the poems' content as "for long stretches . . . painstakingly discursive, even pedestrian"; he finds "sonorous opalescence" in the verse, but also "a prosaicism so homespun as to be, from time to time, positively 'prosey' "; and he concludes that the cycle of poems makes for "a poem remarkably uneven in tone if not in quality; a poem which has to make a formal virtue out of its own disparities. . . ."[4]

On the other hand, there are many critics who, like Nancy Duvall Hargrove, find that "Artistically, . . . *Four*

Quartets marks the high point in Eliot's poetic style." She refers to his "consummate technical mastery," and calls the cycle one "of the masterpieces of literature," and at the end of a long (over seventy printed pages) and detailed and immensely complimentary analysis concludes that *"Four Quartets* stands as the climax of Eliot's poetic creation both thematically and technically."[5] Helen Gardner is if anything even more complimentary. "I believe *Four Quartets* is Mr. Eliot's masterpiece, and that it contains more fully than any of his earlier works the poetic solution of his peculiar problems as a poet. . . ."[6] Elizabeth Drew, similarly, finds *"Four Quartets* . . . his ripest, most complex and most complete expression of 'the experience of believing a dogma'; of the moments of intuitive apprehension of its truth, and of the relation of these to a view of history and to the general living of life."[7] And B. Rajan, in an essay entitled "The Unity of the Quartets," asserts that "they are great because of a quality which I can only describe as utter and relentless fidelity to the event. . . . Years of thought and of the translation of thought into poetry have intervened to make possible its now complete embodiment. . . . In some of the most moving poetry that English literature has known, [Eliot] speaks with the precision of an ultimate sincerity."[8]

And then, in addition to critics like Ward and Spender, who analyze but do not evaluate *Four Quartets,* there are balanced evaluations like that, for example, of Bergonzi:

Eliot himself thought the *Quartets* his major achievement and so do many of his critics. This is not my own view, although I recognize that sections of them contain some of his finest and most moving poetry; other sections, however, include some of the flattest and least interesting verse that he ever published, and the whole work seems to me to be somewhat less than the sum of its parts.[9]

Or in the terms elaborated by C. K. Stead: "The question which remains to be answered—or at least put—is whether the style of *Four Quartets* carries the burden satisfactorily. In the view of this argument it does not."[10]

Of the three principal reactions—enthusiastic and total approval, strong and total disapproval, and intermittent approval *and* disapproval—I find the last-named the most useful, as well as the most accurate. I can best serve the reader of this book, I think, not by rehashing the overall argument, which can be found in the pages of the critics here quoted (and many others as well), but by explaining how both the particular successes and the particular failures of *Four Quartets* are linked to, and even arise out of, the larger contexts and crises of Eliot's life and career. To make sense of *Four Quartets* as a stage in Eliot's overall development is, of course, neither to explain fully the poems nor quite probably to satisfy either of the warring critical extremes. Let me suggest, accordingly, that those who wish to extend and deepen their understanding of these four poems are obliged to begin their study with a book by Helen Gardner, *The Composition of Four Quartets,* which offers materials and insights nowhere else available.[11] If I have not made much use of that indispensable book in the pages that follow, it is not because I have not read nor because I do not value it, but only because my purposes are so different that it is not of primary relevance.

Burnt Norton, published in 1935, takes its title from an old manor house in Gloucestershire, which has a stunning garden, a garden visited by Eliot in 1935 at a time when both house and garden were unoccupied. The poem's opening lines seem to have been written originally for *Murder in the Cathedral,* and dropped from that play only to find a permanent home in this first of the *Quartets:*

> Time present and time past
> Are both perhaps present in time future,
> And time future contained in time past.
> If all time is eternally present
> All time is unredeemable.
> What might have been is an abstraction
> Remaining a perpetual possibility
> Only in a world of speculation.
> What might have been and what has been
> Point to one end, which is always present.

Apart from the theological conclusion to this passage, which asserts that God is always in control and is always immanent in the world, Eliot has in one way not advanced past the elaborately overwritten passages of a similar sort in *Ash-Wednesday*. The literal content here is, like those earlier passages, not in fact elaborate at all. There is a kind of poetic mummification going on, a process sometimes known as lifting yourself by your own bootstraps. But in another sense, equally important, *Burnt Norton* does signal a substantial advance, for the tone of these lines is almost serene and certainly does not labor and strain as *Ash-Wednesday* so often does. And it is in this second sense, too, that the theological conclusion of the passage has a more resonant ring and carries a good deal more conviction than almost anything in the earlier poem.

There is, significantly, no material from the physical, external world, in this passage. What Eliot is able to accomplish, however, is partially to detach himself from the necessity of dealing with that world. No one, I suspect, is completely able to so detach himself; Eliot in particular is not capable of that degree of detachment without, as it were, leaving parts of himself behind. But what he can and does do is to lighten the "mummification" I spoke of a moment ago, making it not only more affirmative in nature and tone, but also more palatable and more readily comprehensible. He is not so insistent as he was in *Ash-Wednesday,* nor does he stay so long in any one key. "Footfalls echo in the memory," has a three-dimensional solidity which connects the poem to the external world at the same time as it connects back to the abstractions already detailed for us in the opening lines. We follow him all the more readily, therefore, "down the passage which we did not take / Towards the door we never opened. . . ." There is a sudden shift into indeterminacy in the quick introductory reference to "the rose-garden," but he backs off, deftly, with a "Gerontion"-like phrase, "My words echo / Thus, in your mind." When he immediately swings back to the "bowl of rose-leaves," and to the "other echoes / [which] inhabit the garden," we feel ourselves on very much more solid ground than at any point in *Ash-Wednesday.* There is a narrative progression in the process of creation, a movement back and forth between external and internal worlds. It does not parallel the polarities of a similar sort, which fueled and gave drama and power to his earlier poetry, but it promises at least the possibility of renewed drama and renewed power, perhaps not as tension-filled and memorable as what came before, but distinctly worthwhile.

The promise is both fulfilled and negated. Whether one sees the speaking bird ("Quick, said the bird, find them, find them, / Round the corner") as an evocation of childhood urgencies or as a mythological creature out of, say, Richard Wagner's operas, it is neither an invention we are prepared for nor a trail the poet himself intends to follow. As we go "through the first gate, / Into our first world," we are asked to consider "the deception of the thrush." I do not think it will do to observe, as Spender and virtually all other commentators do at this point in the poem, that "There is much that is mysterious in the passage, just as there is much that is mysterious in such a moment."[12] Nor do I find myself convinced that Eliot is "encouraging us to look back and discover in childhood memory a brightness and meaningfulness which many adults find more easily in their past than in the present."[13] If this is, as Spender claims it is, "a good part of the 'deception' of the thrush," I would like to know where he acquired that information. Surely he did not find it in the poem: can we even be sure from the poem itself that the "bird" and the "thrush" are the same? Are we being invited to follow a deceitful speaker, or does Eliot intend us to believe the bird and be wary of the thrush? These are not captious queries. The poem simply does not locate us, does not give us the data we need in order to understand its terms with reasonable clarity. How then are we to proceed into that "first world," ready to follow whatever we may find there?[14]

And what we find there is a scene that might be described, perhaps, as written by someone who combined the concerns of Lewis Carroll with the concerns of St. Augustine, and tinted his poetry with a deft and consistently surrealistic point of view. *Who* moves "without pressure, over the dead leaves"? It seems to me a fairly basic question; no critic has to my knowledge addressed it head-on, and though I have tried, I cannot discover any verifiable answer. *Why* is there "unheard music hidden in the shrubbery," and from what source does it emanate? The bird responds to it, but what does that response signal to us? Persona, and bird, and invited guests (we the readers?), and even the flowers growing in the garden, proceed to stare into "the drained pool." But why? Is this a *Waste Land* pool, with water symbolic of salvation? There is a vision of water, abruptly, "out of sunlight," in which a "lotus rose, quietly, quietly," which suggests that the water has indeed some larger significance in Eliot's scheme of things. The lotus is not a Christian symbol, but an Oriental one, centered principally in Buddhism. Why is it in this suddenly liquified pool? "Then a cloud passed, and the pool was empty." The leaves are "full of children," the bird warns us to leave the garden, since "human-kind / Cannot bear very much reality." But one must dig in one's heels: for all that this bird-wisdom may be accurate, in some contexts, what makes it relevant here? That is, if "reality" is what Eliot has been presenting to us, then indeed, as Eliot puts it in the last part of *Burnt Norton,* "Words strain, / Crack and sometimes break, under the burden. . . ." There is a sense of charm and of delight in the passage; there is, as there almost always is with Eliot's poetry, a sense of very great verbal mastery at work. But there is also, at least on the page in front of us, less than meets the eye. Eliot is offering us a great deal less than either he or some of his critics would have us believe. And whether he is deceiving himself or us is less important than the realization, which close reading seems to me to force upon us, that this is simply not fully realized poetry.

And the opening lines of the second part of the poem seem to me to strongly reinforce that judgment. "Garlic and sapphires in the mud / Clot the bedded axle-tree. / The trilling wire in the blood / Sings below inveterate scars / And reconciles forgotten wars." Kenner assures us that "there is no need" for these lines "to occasion puzzlement. The axle-tree appears to be that of the turning heavens, its lower end, like the bole of Yggdrasill, embedded in our soil."[15] Never mind how this astronomical image came to be in the poem, or how Norse-saga-like imagery came to be in the poem, for Elizabeth W. Schneider also assures us of the demonstrable clarity of the lines, except in a direction roughly 180° different from Kenner's. Her comments require extended quotation, for reasons which I will explain in a moment:

The lines have been incompletely and sometimes misleadingly glossed. . . . Everybody knows sapphire skies and emerald grass, which of course a self-respecting poet does not now mention. But spring in the country or on the fringes and in the unpaved byways of town used to mean—in Cambridge (Mass.) or elsewhere—deep mud from the spring thaw, miring a wagon or car up to its axletree; puddles reflecting blue sky; and garlic—just common wild garlic or onion, the earliest spring green along roadside or in pasture, and the earliest spring weed to rise up in the brown lawn. In damp woods or swamps skunk cabbage comes first, but Eliot knew where to draw the line.[16]

It is a lovely bucolic scene, but what does it have to do with Yggdrasill, and for that matter what does it have to do with *Burnt Norton?* Everyone may know of emerald grass, but Eliot speaks of "garlic and *sapphires* in the mud" (emphasis added), and a quick sleight-of-hand inclusion of "sapphire skies" simply will not help, not when the poet has so securely placed his jewels "in the mud." Whether self-respecting or not, no poet of any stature confuses the sky and the mud, and Eliot does not do so here. "But Eliot knew where to draw the line," Schneider assures us, with an apparent confidence that, in fact, she withdraws immediately, adding "Or did he?"

"Garlic and sapphires in the mud," whatever symbol-hunters may think or say, is plainly a forced and unsuccessful attempt to link (a) that which is common and ordinary, "garlic," with (b) that which is precious and relatively rare, "sapphires." The linkage has, however, no context, it comes to us without preparation, and there is no way at all that we can understand what Eliot may have meant, much less any way that we can be moved by the attempted linkage. Even the movement of the verse seems to me heavy and forced. Critics have spoken of the dominant four-stressed line in *Burnt Norton,*[17] but they have not called attention to what seems to me obvious, namely, that at points the four-stress line turns jarringly unpleasant. Read aloud, the first two lines of this second part of *Burnt Norton* are not just obscure and forced, they are quite simply bad verse.

What has gone wrong, here and it seems to me in much of the rest of the four-poem cycle, is not so much Eliot's poetic craft as his grip on his material. *Four Quartets,* as finally published, is meant to celebrate Eliot's new-found faith. The poems were "inevitably religious, since his religion had become his central experience."[18] But as I have indicated, there is a significant difference between wishing to believe and believing; there is a gap, that is, between desire and ability, a hiatus between what the conscious mind tells the rest of the organism and what that organism will accept—for as I have also indicated, and as everyone knows, different aspects of being and artistic expression stem from different sources and involve different levels of acceptance. Eliot had been practicing his new faith in its assorted external manifestations for long enough to feel visibly more comfortable in and with it. He could and he did appear in public and in private as a sincere and committed churchman. On such levels, let me say emphatically, there can be no question whatever that he *was* a sincere and committed churchman. But poetry involves other levels than the outer and the rational; it stems from places that even the poet cannot fully control, whether he wants to or thinks he can. There is, to put it differently, a variety of "truth" in poetic expression, as to be sure there is in all artistic expression, which is beyond the power of the conscious mind alone to regulate. And this level of "truth" manifests itself, finally, in exactly such passages as these, revealing to the properly observant eye its own messages, which may not always be those the poet hoped to convey.

Lines 3–5, which I have also quoted but not yet discussed ("The trilling wire in the blood . . ."), says Schneider, are "all part of the ascending motion—this is recovery from illness in blood, artery, lymph; and it is the now unreluctant revival of life in spring."[19] I can only ask, bluntly: what "ascending motion"? What "illness"? And if in part one of the poem we have been told that we are "in the autumn heat," how do we get to spring here? Kenner—to confine ourselves to the same two critics— tells us that these "lines move into a lyric extrapolation from the Women of Canterbury's discovery [in *Murder in the Cathedral*] that what is woven on the loom of fate is woven also in their veins and brains."[20] Kenner and Schneider cannot both be right, plainly, and I am inclined to think both are wrong—though neither they nor I can be sure. The poem has failed us: *that* is the nub of it, the true "still point of the turning world." Eliot was not a mystic. All commentators are agreed upon that. But it is a rather more complicated problem. Eliot struggled hard and long, and in part successfully, to withdraw himself from the external world, to shelter himself behind the safe and protective walls of the Church. Once more or less securely lodged in that protective shelter, he could readmit aspects of the external world into his inner universe. He could not ever again control, or even permit himself fully to react to, the world in its totality, and he could not fully control, in himself, the deeper aspects of belief. He tried, manfully and patiently and, I want to make very clear, sincerely. He was not in any way a fraudulent Christian, as he was not in any way a fraudulent Englishman. But just as, again by common consent, he never quite became an Englishman, remaining in many aspects an American to the day of his death, so too he never quite became a Christian, never fully accepted at the deepest levels of his being those truths to which he paid such devout worship. Poetry, in a way, is a mirror which the

poet holds up, willy-nilly, to those deeper levels, and it
does not lie.

Despite critical enthusiasts who write of "the interre-
lationship . . . between the various sections of each of the
Quartets [, which] is strengthened by a structural pattern
of reiterated, if loosely developed themes by which they
are further united,"[21] and critics who claim that "there is
not a passage in *Four Quartets* that can be attributed to
chance,"[22] and those critics who see "in *Four Quartets*
. . . a perfect articulation of sound and movement and
meaning,"[23] and the critics who proclaim "it is impossible
not to recognize that they constitute a unity,"[24] it is a
simple fact that when writing *Burnt Norton* Eliot had
neither a plan for a cycle of poems nor even the intention
of following this poem with another one. "In 1939 if there
hadn't been a war I would probably have tried to write
another play."[25] In 1940 John Hayward, who was so close
to Eliot that he had "constituted himself in some measure
'Keeper of the Eliot Archive'," wrote to Frank Morley
that Eliot "is making a little progress with a new poem in
succession to 'Burnt Norton'—the second of three qua-
tours [quartets]—provisionally entitled 'East Coker'.
. . ."[26] Some months later, Eliot is reported to have said,
"during the writing of *East Coker* . . . the whole sequence
began to emerge . . ."[27]

Burnt Norton, then, both in its inception and in its
publication, was for half a decade understood both by its
readers and by its author as a separate poem, not as the
doorway to a cycle of poems. It has, I think, two main
themes, one being the possibility of Christian redemption,
the other being the difficulty of dealing with redemption,
or indeed with anything else, using the slippery inexact-
ness of mere words. Inevitably, in handling these two
themes, Eliot is drawn, as he has been drawn before, into

a consideration of the effects of time on a poet trying to cope with immensely serious matters. Inevitably too, *Burnt Norton* is linked both to *Murder in the Cathedral* and to *Ash-Wednesday* by more than the mere presence of lines cancelled from both the latter. *Burnt Norton,* as I have already noted, makes and at the same time does not make an advance, in particular, over the strained artificialties of *Ash-Wednesday.*

"The still point of the turning world," the key phrase I have already quoted, is described in part two of the poem, in an eight-line strophe of singular abstraction: "And do not call it fixity, / Where past and future are gathered. Neither movement from nor towards, / Neither ascent nor decline." But Eliot only succeeds in poetically embodying this "inner freedom from the practical desire," as he calls it, in a thirteen-line strophe which does not advance the cause very much (*"Erhebung* [exaltation] without motion, concentration / Without elimination"), when he links it, movingly and very beautifully, to the things of the external world:

> To be conscious is not to be in time
> But only in time can the moment in the rose-garden
> The moment in the arbour where the rain beat,
> The moment in the draughty church at smokefall
> Be remembered . . .

There is a dignity (some critics have quite properly referred to the "transparency" of much of the poetry in the *Quartets*) to this verse which is deeply, if somewhat wistfully, convincing. So too, in the third part of the poem, Eliot is turgidly unconvincing, writing of "a place of disaffection," so long as he fumbles about in quasi-philosophical, intensely abstract terms. "Time before and time after / In a dim light: neither daylight / Investing form with lucid stillness / Turning shadow into transient beauty /

With slow rotation suggesting permanence. . . ." But two
lines, in a passage twenty-four lines in length, come to
light in a blaze clearly drawn, in good part, from the same
source as "Preludes." "Men and bits of paper, whirled by
the cold wind / That blows before and after time.
. . ." And just as abruptly, Eliot extinguishes that light, in
a miasma of vague generalization: "Wind in and out of
unwholesome lungs . . . Eructation [belching] of unhealthy
souls. . . ." Even the flattened-out specificities of "The
Hollow Men" fairly glow in comparison with *Burnt Norton*'s presentation of "World not world, but that which is
not world," offered to us as "Internal darkness, depriva-
tion / And destitution of all property, / Dessication of the
world of sense, / Evacuation of the world of fancy, /
Inoperancy of the world of spirit. . . ." Nothing catches
fire, when the poet's forge has to draw its heat from such
tepidities. *Burnt Norton* proceeds to its end in a cold and
distinctly repetitive wash of much this sort. The final lines
—"Ridiculous the waste sad time / Stretching before and
after"—are sad indeed, coming from a poet of Eliot's
stature.

   East Coker (1940) takes its title from yet another old
English manor house, this time one with which Eliot has
a very real connection, for it was the place of origin of the
Eliot family. The opening words of the poem, "In my
beginning is my end," thus have a weight and a context
for the poet, and promise well. And this time the promise
is much more fully vindicated. "In succession / Houses
rise and fall, crumble, are extended, / Are removed, destroyed, restored, or in their place / Is an open field, or
a factory, or a by-pass," is not verse of the first intensity;
it labors and tries to make too much of the more or less
abstract fact that Eliot's ancestors, and not the poet himself, came from the house being described. The echoes of
Ecclesiastes, too, seem distinctly oversolemn, even con-

trived. But in the second strophe Eliot moves to a "still point" he himself occupies, as "the light falls / Across the open field, leaving the deep lane / Shuttered with branches, . . . [and] you lean against a bank while a van passes. . . ." He first establishes this solid, worldly scene, then draws on his ancestor, Sir Thomas Elyot, and his *The Governor* (I:21), to construct a vivid and oddly charming scene of the rustic folk of Sir Thomas' era, "Keeping time, / Keeping the rhythm in their dancing / As in their living. . . ." He slows this scene to its conclusion with rhythms that echo *Sweeney Agonistes,* but to a very different purpose and with a totally dissimilar rhetoric: "The time of the coupling of man and woman / And that of beasts. Feet rising and falling. / Eating and drinking. Dung and death." And having brought himself to this new-old, and historically heightened "still point," Eliot proceeds to four of the greatest lines he or, in my view, anyone else has ever written:

> Dawn points, and another day
> Prepares for heat and silence. Out at sea the dawn wind
> Wrinkles and slides. I am here
> Or there, or elsewhere. In my beginning.

I would say of passages like this what Kenner says, I think erroneously, of *Burnt Norton,* namely that they bring "the generalizing style of the author of *Prufrock* and the austere intuitions of the disciple of Bradley for the first time into intimate harmony. Suggestion does not outrun thought, nor design impose itself on what word and cadence are capable of suggesting."[28]

But it does not last. The *Quartets* regularly oscillate between passages given vivid embodiment and passages which lie inertly on the page. "What is the late November doing . . . Thunder rolled by the rolling stars / Simulates triumphal cars / Deployed in constellated wars / Scorpion

fights against the Sun / Until the Sun and Moon go down.
. . ." Written though they are by a great poet, these lines
are little more than clumsy doggerel. "That was a way of
putting it—not very satisfactory," as Eliot himself notes
some few lines farther along, "Leaving one still with the
intolerable wrestle / With words and meanings." And, he
then asserts, with a truer sense of his own limitations than
many of his critics have credited him with, "The poetry
does not matter." Indeed: in his own wrestling with himself, and with the doubts and urgencies and problems of
faith, Eliot *had* moved to some extent beyond poetry. It
is in no way accidental that his career as a poet was to end
with these *Quartets,* which were in some significant degree
made possible only by the coming of World War II and
the fact that it made further theater work for the moment
impossible. Nor is it accidental that, after *Little Gidding*
in 1942, Eliot's final twenty-three years were occupied
with a few plays, some social and political criticism, and
many, many ripe and lapidary talks on literary and religious matters.

   Part three of *East Coker,* after some prosaic eulogiz-
ing of the virtues of humility ("humility is endless"),
breaks into a surprisingly Whitmanesque paean to "the
captains, merchant bankers, eminent men of letters" and
their like, who "all go into the dark." It is only eleven lines
in length, and when it ends Eliot moves, without indication of any formal change, into yet another interminable
and prosey discussion of the goodness of faith (". . . as,
when an underground train, in the tube, stops too long
between stations / And the conversation rises and slowly
fades into silence. . . ."). But while the Whitman-in-
fluenced lines last, they work with a fine, brisk pace toward the nasty conclusion that "we all go with them, into
the silent funeral, / Nobody's funeral, for there is no one
to bury." We will meet with Whitman again, in the *Quar-*

tets, most notably perhaps in *The Dry Salvages* (1941—
and pronounced, says Eliot's note, "to rhyme with *as-
suages*"), but the influence of Whitman anywhere in this
late poetry seems to me distinctly notable. There are to be
sure other influences at work, especially the effects of
Eliot's now fairly considerable theatrical experience, but
the Whitman component is clear—and important.

Eliot's struggle with his origins, with (in a sense) his
nonelective affinities, grafted onto him by the accidents of
birth and rearing and early education, led him virtually all
of his life to work at concealing, not revealing, his un-
breakable ties with those American stances and heritages.
This is especially important, as I shall explain later in this
book, for a true understanding of much of Eliot's literary
criticism. But it is important, too, in understanding the
inner struggles which underlay his poetry at its best. For
the "classicist, royalist, and catholic" Eliot to thus acknowledge the untraditional, democratic, and Quaker-
Protestant Whitman is no small matter.[29] Roy Harvey
Pearce argues, forcefully and I believe correctly, that "Eliot's relation to Whitman, like Pound's, marks an impasse,
or crossroads, in the continuity of American poetry.
. . . Eliot could not avoid being 'influenced' by Whitman
. . . either directly or indirectly . . . Moreover . . . when
Eliot thought of Pound's achievement, he perforce
thought of Whitman's. He would seem to have been aware
of Pound's concern to do right what Whitman, for all his
noble intentions, had done wrong."[30] Or as Hyatt H. Waggoner puts it, after first quoting Eliot's 1959 observation
that "my poetry has obviously more in common with my
distinguished contemporaries in America, than with anything written in my generation in England," "It had required a long journey to reach a point not far from where
we might suppose he could have started, had conditions
in 1910 been different from what they were."[31] It is worth

noting, too, that Eliot not only wrote an essay introducing
an edition of Mark Twain's *Huckleberry Finn,* but said of
that most quintessentially American of writers that
"Twain, at least in *Huckleberry Finn,* reveals himself to be
one of those writers, of whom there are not a great many
in any literature, who have discovered a new way of writing, valid not only for themselves but for others. . . . There
is in Twain, I think, a great unconscious depth . . . a
symbolism all the more powerful for being uncalculated
and unconscious."[32]

The middle portions of *East Coker,* most of part three
and all of part four, thrash about, asserting that "the
darkness shall be the light, and the stillness the dancing,"
and that a variety of things are all "pointing to the agony
/ Of death and birth." Eliot's own interjection is virtually
all the commentary these lines need: "You say I am repeating / Something I have said before. I shall say it again.
/ Shall I say it again?" But the extended meditation of part
five, though it lapses at times into prosaic dullness, collects
and expatiates on some of the themes and some of the
image materials of the better parts of the poem. "So here
I am, in the middle way, having had twenty years—/
Twenty years largely wasted, the years of *l'entre deux
guerres* [the time between two wars] . . . ," the section
begins, and it arrives, at its midpoint, at the conclusion
that "perhaps [there is] neither gain nor loss. / For us,
there is only the trying. The rest is not our business." And
moving past that conclusion, with the observation, hark-
ing back to the very opening of the poem, that "Home is
where one starts from," Eliot proceeds to consider some
of the moments which compose "a lifetime burning in
every moment." One of those moments, fascinatingly, is
virtually adapted from "Prufrock." "There is a time for
the evening under starlight, / A time for the evening under
lamplight / (The evening with the photograph album)."

Here too we see the "buried" Eliot rising, fragmentarily, to the surface. And the poem ends, reasonably satisfyingly, with a straightforward repetition of its start, except in reverse order: "In my end is my beginning."

The Dry Salvages (1941) has been savagely attacked by Donald Davie: "it is quite simply *rather a bad poem.*"[33] The attack is mistaken, I think, only because the poem is on the whole neither better nor worse than the other *Quartets*, though Davie is convinced that it "sticks out among the rest like a sore thumb." The first strophe, for example, is embarrassingly bad. "I do not know much about gods; but I think that the river / Is a strong brown god. . . ." This most emphatically does not "do right what Whitman, for all his noble intentions, had done wrong." Eliot maunders on about "the brown god . . . Keeping his seasons and rages, destroyer, reminder / Of what men choose to forget," assuring us portentously that "The river is within us, the sea is all about us," and that "the sea has many voices, / Many gods and many voices." This is all deeply unmemorable. But three lines farther along, as so often in the *Quartets*—composed, we need to remind ourselves, very much in bits and pieces and as and when Eliot found time for them—there is a section as magnificent as any critic could require, twenty-three lines about "The sea howl / And the sea yelp," cadenced so extraordinarily that the ending of the passage breaks on us much as the sea itself might do. "And the ground swell, that is and was from the beginning, / Clangs / The bell." Time, in this beautifully developed strophe, is measured by "time not our time . . . time / Older than the time of chronometers." We are located, firmly and precisely, "Between midnight and dawn, when the past is all deception, / The future futureless, before the morning watch / When time stops and time is never ending." Eliot's poetic focus is equally firmly on the sea: issues of faith and philosophy are sec-

ondary, or simply put to the side while the meditation
lasts. The second part of the poem is on the whole long-
winded and uninteresting, with rather too much faith and
philosophy and rather too little poetry, with "I have said
before" and "we come to discover." But here too there is
a superb though somewhat smaller passage which catches
fire:

> Time the destroyer is time the preserver,
> Like the river with its cargo of dead Negroes, cows and
>   chicken coops,
> The bitter apple and the bite in the apple.
> And the ragged rock in the restless waters,
> Waves wash over it, fogs conceal it;
> On a halcyon day it is merely a monument,
> In navigable weather it is always a seamark
> To lay a course by: but in the sombre season
> Or the sudden fury, is what it always was.

And the phenomenon of such brilliant successes, set in a
context of much lesser work, and much of that lesser work
essentially dross, is what C. K. Stead addresses himself to
in the following fine summary judgment:

> *Four Quartets* alternates between, on the one hand the 'first
> voice' of poetry, the voice of 'The Waste Land,' less perfect now
> because directed into a conscious mould; and on the other the
> 'second voice,' the voice of the man 'addressing an audience' in
> verse barely distinguishable from prose. The poem is the expres-
> sion of a personality so fine, so mature, and so supremely intelli-
> gent, that to question the achievement may seem only to quibble.
> But however wise and admirable the man it displays, the poem
> remains, in this view, imperfectly achieved, with large portions
> of abstraction untransmuted into the living matter of poetry.[34]

Or as Stead says of one of the prosier passages in *East
Coker,* "There is truth in this, but not imaginative truth:
it remains *pure* discourse. If the feeling . . . is truly there,

it is there unused; it has not been transmuted by imagination into something larger than itself."[35] Again, that is the problem throughout all of the *Quartets*, and *The Dry Salvages* seems to me to suffer from it neither more nor less than the other poems in the cycle.

I have said that the two main themes of the *Quartets* are the possibility of Christian redemption, and (in a sense) the impossibility of approaching that possibility using only words. Meditations on the effects of time are an important subtheme; as Kristian Smidt nicely says, "More and more in Eliot's later work the idea of timelessness is connected with the Christian revelation."[36] But over and over, it seems to me, the meditations on time are, by virtue of their strength and their intensely moving nature, de facto the center of the entire cycle. Though one cannot put too much weight on it, Helen Gardner reports that Eliot himself seems to have recognized, and at one time intended to acknowledge, this centrality of his meditations on time. "Mrs. Valerie Eliot tells me that Eliot had thought of prefixing as epigraph to the volume as a whole [i.e., to all four *Quartets*] an observation by a modern philosopher, Mr. Roker of the Fleet prison: 'What a rum thing time is, ain't it, Neddy?' "[37] This observation, like the projected early title for the poem which became *The Waste Land*, is from Dickens, in this case *The Pickwick Papers* (chapter 42). And the final passage of fully realized poetry in *The Dry Salvages* is once again a meditation on time, a nine-line passage in the poem's fifth part—fully realized, let me emphasize once more, because Eliot has not limited himself to "discourse" or to abstractions, but has fertilized his conceptualizations with matter from the sometimes unlovely but, for all that, ineluctable external world:

> For most of us, there is only the unattended

> Moment, the moment in and out of time,
> The distraction fit, lost in a shaft of sunlight,
> The wild thyme unseen, or the winter lightning
> Or the waterfall, or music heard so deeply
> That it is not heard at all, but you are the music
> While the music lasts. These are only hints and guesses,
> Hints followed by guesses; and the rest
> Is prayer, observance, discipline, thought and action.

Eliot has come to this passage after a long disquisition on communicating "with Mars," and dissecting "the recurrent image into pre-conscious terrors," and the "distress of nations and perplexity / Whether on the shores of Asia, or in the Edgware Road." He leaves this passage, similarly, by launching into a treatise of sorts on what "the hint half guessed" and "the gift half understood" are, namely the "Incarnation," which Eliot proceeds to explain to us in terms of "the impossible union / Of spheres of existence" and "daemonic, chthonic [underworld] / Powers." The goal is "right action"; we, however, must be content "If our temporal reversion nourish / (Not too far from the yew-tree) / The life of significant soil." It is not, I'm afraid, either moving or inspiring. About such passages Mr. Davie is plainly right—but there is an abundance of them throughout the cycle, and *The Dry Salvages* need be neither singled out nor exempted.

Little Gidding (1942), Eliot's effective farewell to the serious composition of poetry, is in some ways the oddest of the four poems in the cycle. Spender calls it "the darkest, most wintry, most death-saturated" of the poems; "it is also," he adds, in my view more accurately, "the culminating point. . . ."[38] I find it the most consistent of the poems. Its verse, though sometimes a bit too highly worked (the long sequence in a sort of *terza rima* is competent but not much more), remains generally on a fairly even keel. But that makes it, in the terms I have been employing so far, also the dullest of the poems. "You are not here to verify, / Instruct yourself, or inform curiosity / Or carry report. You are here to kneel / Where prayer has been valid." That seems to me not so much dark and wintry as sedate, and resigned, earnest and calm rather than moving or truly strong. "A people without history," says the fifth part of *Little Gidding* (which was an Anglican religious community founded by Nicholas Ferrar and visited by George Herbert and Richard Crashaw—as well as, much later, by T. S. Eliot), "Is not redeemed from time, for history is a pattern / Of timeless moments." This is sober and possibly true; it is certainly not passionate. Even the lines which I take to be the central thrust of the poem, in this fifth part, are at best soberly reflective. "We shall not cease from exploration / And the end of all our exploring / Will be to arrive where we started / And know the place for the first time." Thoughtful, intelligent, this sort of thing can make useful reading, even at times good reading. It simply does not excite, as great poetry should. But then, Eliot might reply, "The poetry does not matter." Bergonzi (and others agree) tells us that the setting of the long terza rima passage, in part two, is a London street "just after an air raid," and the "familiar compound ghost" "is partly Brunetto Latini, Dante's old teacher, from *Inferno* XV, and partly Swift, but primarily Yeats. . . . In this passage, suggests Richard Ellmann, Eliot felt himself finally reconciled with Yeats, after lifelong differences. . . ."[39] But how much of the true Yeats—who was, I need not add, quite as great a poet as Eliot, and probably finer on the whole—is there, in fact, in the actual writing of the scene?

> . . . last year's words belong to last year's language
> And next year's words await another voice.
> But, as the passage now presents no hindrance

>To the spirit unappeased and peregrine
>Between two worlds become much like each
>   other. . . .

This is stiff, and borders on the pompous; it is neither good
Yeats nor good poetry, though *(pace* Mr. Davie) it could
have been worse. "This section of a poem," wrote Eliot
himself, "not the length of one canto of the *Divine Comedy*
—cost me far more time and trouble and vexation than
any passage of the same length that I have ever written."[40]
But "time and trouble and vexation" are not touchstones
by which to judge poetry, and comparisons with Dante's
great *Divine Comedy* are unfortunately out of place. It is
not I think disrespectful to observe that Eliot, at age sixty-
two, found it difficult to preserve an objective distance
from this last of his serious poems. "All shall be well and
/ All manner of thing shall be well," he intoned in the
third part of *Little Gidding,* "By the purification of the
motive / In the ground of our beseeching." The "purification of the motive," alas, may be dispositive in the Church;
it is essentially irrelevant in poetry, where it is the deed
and not the doer at which we must look.

Postscriptum on Possum

"Possum" was one of Eliot's nicknames; "the man in
White Spats," whose assistance is acknowledged in the
dedication to *Old Possum's Book of Practical Cats* (1939)
is apparently John Hayward.[41] The fourteen nonsense
poems collected in the little volume are pleasant, inoffen-
sive, and unremarkable. I want to comment, however, not
so much on the poems, which need no commentary, but
on the fact of a major poet having all his life written
nonsense verse of one kind or another, not all of it by any

means collected in *Possum*. Conrad Aiken, who was at Harvard with Eliot, records a mock epic entitled (or at least about) a "singular and sterling character known as King Bolo, not to mention King Bolo's Queen, 'that airy fairy hairy-'un, who led the dance on Golder's Green with Cardinal Bessarion'."[42] In London Eliot was for many years a member of a group, which met at John Hayward's home (for this purpose Hayward's nickname was "Tarantula" and Eliot, "though he retained his old nickname of Possum," was transformed into "the Elephant, presumably because he 'never forgot' "[43]) and seems to have discussed, principally, Conan Doyle's Sherlock Holmes stories. A collection of their verses, apparently comic, was privately printed in 1939 in an edition of twenty-five copies; it is called *Noctes Binanianae*—Hayward's home was at 22 Bina Gardens—and I see on the evidence available to me no reason to think that any of the poems approached even the level of *Possum*. The point is, rather, that Eliot had dropped the habit which had earlier produced King Bolo and (according to Wyndham Lewis) two poems called "Bullshit and the Ballad for Big Louise," and which Lewis characterized as "excellent bits of scholarly ribaldry" and intended, if he could, to see into print in his magazine, *Blast*.[44] Grover Smith mentions "an unpublished draft of a comic poem about a pig named, like a character in *Nicholas Nickleby*—Dickens again!—Mr. Pugstyles," and indicates that a typewritten copy is in the Harvard library along "with the holograph of 'Usk' (1934) on its reverse." "Usk" seems to have been "a parody of Wordsworth's 'The Reveries of Poor Susan'."[45]

The significance of these miscellaneous, undistinguished, but genial comic verses lies not in the verses themselves, but in the light they may shed on a side of Eliot sometimes made too little of. Raymond Preston, for example, says "That the *Love Song of J. Alfred Prufrock* is a fine comic poem is, I believe, its essential quality, and the quality that most of us who began to read T. S. Eliot as adolescents almost completely missed."[46] "Various reviewers [of Eliot's play, *The Confidential Clerk*] immediately noted analogies with [Gilbert and Sullivan's] *H.M.S. Pinafore* and [Oscar Wilde's] *The Importance of Being Ernest.* "[47] In a letter thanking a young clergyman for sending him the *Pogo Papers,* which he seems to have enjoyed, Eliot went on to discuss with obvious enthusiasm the cartoons of Rube Goldberg and George Herriman, dwelling at some length on Herriman's cartoon character, Krazy Kat, and also invoking "the peculiar nonsense verses of the German poet, Christian Morgenstern."[48] And Jay Martin nicely sums up what, in this brief postscriptum, I should like to emphasize. "Curiously, although writers who deal with Eliot as a person speak uniformly of his wit and good humor, literary critics have treated him with dead seriousness—perhaps in compensation for earlier attacks upon *[The Waste Land]* as a hoax. In some ways it *is* a hoax, in that Eliot treats the most serious issues in comic ways: he is flippant in the face of the ghastly, offhand concerning 'The Horror!' while yet (most apparently in his 'Notes') seriously deadpan about trivia. . . . This is high comedy, in the extravagant traditions of Chaucer, the American tall tale, *Candide,* [and] *Don Quixote.* "[49]

6

*From the
Middle Ages to
Broadway:
Eliot as
a playwright*

In his *Memoir* of Eliot, Robert Sencourt notes that "He could assume disguises and throw himself into fictitious characters as though from the beginning a playwright."[1] Jay Martin, on the other hand, commenting on Eliot's "Possum" nickname, says that it "alludes to the opposum's ability to fade into the background."[2] And E. Martin Browne, who produced all of Eliot's dramatic work, from *The Rock* to *The Elder Statesman,* and who worked more closely with Eliot the playwright than anyone else, has said that "This shy, slow-spoken man would not move easily among the ebullient, ephemeral people of the theatre."[3] Robert Speaight, who has acted the lead role, Becket, in *Murder in the Cathedral* "more than a thousand times" (and in more than one language), and has acted in other Eliot plays as well, confesses that "I cannot pretend to admire the plays of Eliot as much as I admire his poetry, and the interpretation of his poetry has given me more pleasure than the interpretation of any of his parts—Becket himself not excepted."[4] Stevie Smith, herself a fine poet, wrote of *Murder in the Cathedral* (all in all Eliot's best play) that "Mr. Eliot's play does not seem to me to be quite plausible, but to be very interesting. . . ."[5]

Eliot is, indeed, an "interesting" playwright—and the description has, inevitably, much of the force and the irony of Sonya's observation, in act III of Chekhov's *Uncle Vanya,* that "When a woman is not beautiful, they always say: 'You have beautiful hair, you have beautiful eyes'."[6] Had Eliot continued with the sort of experimentation begun in *Sweeney Agonistes,* he might have made a deeply original contribution to the theatre, "a new poetic drama which should be at once timeless and contemporary. . . . T. S. Eliot has arrived in Shaftesbury Avenue [home of the commercial theatre, in England] and the English

actor owes him much. But if he had chosen to go elsewhere, I think that gratitude might have been even greater."[7] But just as Eliot's desire to use background
drumming was a derivative notion, so too was virtually
everything about his plays. (Even the use of verse in modern stage works was not his invention.) "Our new dramatic poetry in the English theatre did not begin (as is often
supposed) with the production of *Murder in the Cathedral*
at Canterbury and the Mercury [Theatre]."[8] Eugene
O'Neill, who was arguably the greatest playwright in
English of this century, was writing bad poems and magnificent poetic drama long before Eliot.[9] Indeed, even "the
conception [of *The Rock*]," which began Eliot's formal
career as a playwright, "was not Mr Eliot's own. . . ."[10]
The Anglican churches of London were launching a fund-
raising drive for the construction of buildings; a pageant
had been conceived of to assist in that effort; and after
some hesitation—Eliot was "too modern: too difficult" in
the view of the Reverend R. Webb-Odell, who was direct-
ing the fund raising[11]—and the realization that the pageant was stiff and dull, Eliot was offered in the fall of 1933
a commission to write parts of *The Rock,* which he accepted. His own note to the pageant as published, dated April
1934, says forthrightly that "I cannot consider myself the
author of the 'play' . . . I wrote the choruses and dialogues
. . . [but] of only one scene am I literally the author."[12]

The Rock is not an inconsiderable achievement; there
are moments of some dramatic power, and moments even
of well-fashioned wit and humor. "The 'play' makes no
pretence of being 'a contribution to English dramatic literature'," Eliot wrote in reply to a review published in *The
Spectator.* "It is a *revue.* My only serious dramatic aim was
to show that there is a possible *rôle* for the Chorus."[13] And
it is only the choruses which are printed in the volumes
of Eliot's collected poems. But it *is* in fact a "review," with

Cockney dialogue and jokes and so on, and though Eliot shows no overwhelming theatrical gift, he is surely competent. "Use me brains, indeed! If I 'ad as little brains as 'im I might be a contractor myself by now; but bein' a intellectual, I'm only a foreman." And the choruses, too, though for the most part they are written in a suitably elevated tone, are not above sharply pointed speech. "Will you build me a house of plaster, with corrugated roofing, / To be filled with a litter of Sunday newspapers?" The "time-kept city" is memorialized by the wind in similar terms. "Here were decent godless people: / Their only monument the asphalt road / And a thousand lost golf balls." The chorus asks, pungently, at one point, "What does the world say, does the whole world stray in high-powered cars on a by-pass way?" And there is, of course, considerable evidence of the preoccupations that were evident in Eliot's verse: "Then came, at a predetermined moment, a moment in time and of time, / A moment not out of time, but in time, in what we call history. . . ." Just as meditations on time are in *The Rock,* so too are passages on the difficulties of verbal expression. "Out of the sea of sound the life of music, / Out of the slimy mud of words, out of the sleet and hail of verbal imprecisions, / Approximate thoughts and feelings, words that have taken the place of thoughts and feelings, / There spring the perfect order of speech, and the beauty of incarnation."

But competency, and familiar themes, do not make for high drama, verbal brilliance, or memorable formulations. *The Rock* is of interest to us chiefly because it truly began Eliot's career in the theatre, and because it led, quite directly to the invitation which produced in 1935 *Murder in the Cathedral,* which was written for the Canterbury Festival of that year. As Eliot later wrote, "my play was to be produced for a rather special kind of audience—an audience of those serious people who go to 'festivals' and expect to have to put up with poetry—though perhaps on this occasion some of them were not quite prepared for what they got. And finally it was a religious play, and people who go deliberately to a religious play at a religious festival expect to be patiently bored and to satisfy themselves with the feeling that they have done something meritorious."[14] What they got was an odd but sometimes arresting assemblage of disparate elements, drawn from classical Greek tragedies, medieval mystery plays, the Bible, and the pulpit traditions of men like Lancelot Andrewes, and more. The most innovative part of the play, the final speeches by the murderous knights, Eliot acknowledges to "have been slightly under the influence of *St. Joan,*" by George Bernard Shaw.[15] Even the title was borrowed: according to E. Martin Browne it was "offered" to Eliot by his (Browne's) wife, and "gratefully accepted."[16]

I want to briefly consider *Murder in the Cathedral* from two viewpoints: first as a drama, and second as a drama in verse. As a drama it is distinctly competent, if not inspired. Characters are moved about and situations presented, with considerable technical facility. "Here let us stand," says the chorus as the play opens, "close by the cathedral. Here let us wait. / Are we drawn by danger?" The subject matter of the entire play is in a sense contained in those few words. When the assassins first come upon Becket, they are prepared to kill him on the spot, but priests come on the scene and the suspense is maintained. It is further maintained, later, when the assassins' purpose has heated up, and been liquified as well, once again by the intervention of priests, this time forcibly removing Becket from the scene. These simple but effective devices keep the drama from sagging; Eliot is more than competent enough to see and to make use of such opportunities. The dialogue does not, in the nature of things, have much snap and crackle in it, but Eliot has managed a few moments of useful flippancy. When the assassins first arrive, and are pressed to stay for dinner, the priest who speaks to them asks, "Do you like roast pork?", having just pronounced, probably a bit sententiously, "Dinner before business." The First Knight replies, vigorously, "Business before dinner. We will roast your pork / First, and dine upon it after." There is often a degree of dramatic tension in the exchanges, especially as between Becket and his four Tempters, and as between Becket and the Knight assassins, but it is by no means an invariable tension. For the merits of *Murder in the Cathedral* ultimately are in good part pageant-like: it is in a sense *The Rock* intensified and made more like a play and less like a review.

The verse is of much greater significance, not only in a book like this one, which is concerned with a great poet, and not only because in Eliot's plays as a whole "everything depends upon language,"[17] but because so much has been made of Eliot as a pioneer in the use of verse in the theatre. If it is true that, in some of the choruses, he uses "the technique of organizing his verse rhythms by units corresponding to breath impulses,"[18] it is also true that at many crucial moments he flattens both the verse and its dramatic impact in what I can only describe as unfortunate ways. When one of Becket's priests, before the Archbishop's return from exile, welcomes that return, the best that Eliot is able to come up with is the affirmation that "Our Lord [Becket] is at one with the Pope, and also the King of France. / We can lean on a rock, we can feel a firm foothold / Against the perpetual wash of tides of balance of forces of barons and landholders. / The rock of God is beneath our feet." This is slack, predictable. Eliot perceived that, in the great verse plays of Shakespeare, the "verse is not merely a formalization, or an added decoration, but . . . intensifies the drama." And he felt, too, "the importance of the unconscious effect of the verse upon us," or as he also put it, "that the verse rhythm should have its effect upon the hearers, without their being conscious of it."[19] But as he also said, specifically about *Murder in the Cathedral,* "The style . . . had to be *neutral*" and, as for the versification of dialogue, it had "in my opinion, only a *negative* merit: it succeeded in avoiding what had to be avoided, but it arrived at no positive novelty. . . ."[20] When Thomas makes his first entrance, a moment which should impress itself strongly on the audience, the verse is indeed neutral and negative. The priests have been scolding the women of the chorus; Thomas appears:

> Peace. And let them be, in their exaltation.
> They speak better than they know, and beyond your
>   understanding.
> They know and do not know, what it is to act or suffer.
> They know and do not know, that acting is suffering
> And suffering is action. Neither does the actor suffer
> Nor the patient act. But both are fixed
> In an eternal action, an eternal patience
> To which all must consent that it may be willed
> And which all must suffer that they may will it,
> That the pattern may subsist, for the pattern is the
>   action
> And the suffering, that the wheel may turn and still
> Be forever still.

It is not surprising that, first shown the play, the actor who was to play Becket found him "a very passive protagonist. . . . This Becket, I thought, was more of a figure than a part. . . ."[21]

There is much in the choral writing, too, of the same flattened-out sort. Fearing danger, the chorus says: "We do not wish anything to happen. / Seven years we have lived quietly, / Succeeded in avoiding notice, / Living and partly living. / There have been oppression and luxury, /

There have been poverty and licence, / There has been minor injustice." The rhythmic gains, here, are exceedingly slight; it could easily be argued that the losses involved in casting these lines in verse form actually outweigh the gains. If, as Eliot has said, "poetic drama has anything potentially to offer the playgoer, that prose drama cannot, . . . it must justify itself dramatically . . . No play should be written in verse for which prose is *dramatically* adequate."[22] I do not mean that *Murder in the Cathedral* would have been better had it been written in prose nor do I mean to suggest that most of the verse is dramatically inadequate. Most of it is adequate; some of it is exceedingly fine; some of it is slack. The mixture, in short, is neither bad nor good, but sometimes one and sometimes the other. And the final effect is, to quote Stevie Smith once more, "interesting." That overall effect can be seen, for example, in a long choral speech toward the end of the play, just before Becket's murder:

> I have smelt them, the death-bringers, senses are quickened
> By subtile forebodings; I have heard
> Fluting in the nighttime, fluting and owls, have seen at noon
> Scaly wings slanting over, huge and ridiculous. I have tasted
> The savour of putrid flesh in the spoon. I have felt
> The heaving of earth at nightfall, restless, absurd. I have heard
> Laughter in the noises of beasts that make strange noises: jackal, jackass, jackdaw; the scurrying noise of mouse and jerboa; the laugh of the loon, the lunatic bird. I have seen
> Grey necks twisting, rat tails twining, in the thick light of dawn. I have eaten
> Smooth creatures still living, with the strong salt taste of living things under sea; I have tasted
> The living lobster, the crab, the oyster, the whelk and the

prawn; and they live and spawn in my bowels, and my
bowels dissolve in the light of dawn. I have smelt
Death in the rose, death in the hollyhock, sweet pea, hyacinth, primrose and cowslip. I have seen
Trunk and horn, tusk and hoof, in odd places;
I have lain on the floor of the sea and breathed with the
breathing of the sea-anemone, swallowed with ingurgi-
tation of the sponge. I have lain in the soil and criti-
cised the worm. In the air
Flirted with the passage of the kite, I have plunged with the
kite and cowered with the wren. I have felt
The horn of the beetle, the scale of the viper, the mobile
hard insensitive skin of the elephant, the evasive flank
of the fish. I have smelt
Corruption in the dish, incense in the latrine, the sewer in
the incense, the smell of sweet soap in the woodpath,
a hellish sweet scent in the woodpath, while the
ground heaved. I have seen. . . .

There are twenty-four more lines to the speech; it im-
proves in those final lines. But it seems to me terribly clear
that, in these seventeen lines, we do not have a poet writing at the top of his form. We have, rather, a poet half out
of control, struggling to find what it is he wants to say,
repeating himself too often, saying too much, and never
simply cutting through—as Shakespeare for example
regularly did—to the heart of the matter, the dramatic
essence, the straightforward core of action and tension.
Nor is that dramatic core either obscure or even subtle, in
this historical confrontation between church and state.
That is, the materials available to Eliot should have presented him with a much clearer insight into the dramatic
core of the affair. The fact that he could not find such a
core, or could find it at best intermittently, in so ready-
made a body of material, is, I think, not encouraging for
his future as a playwright.

Nor, despite all the interest aroused, and the produc-

tions mounted, was that future any improvement on what
we have already seen. *The Family Reunion* was brought
to E. Martin Browne's house in November of 1937, where,
after supper, Eliot proceeded to read aloud his draft.

> When he finished, there was a long pause. He looked up,
> disappointed at our slow reaction: and we caught a sudden
> glimpse of the young poet [Eliot was then forty-nine], sensitive
> and unsure of himself. Our minds were divided between fascina-
> tion and doubt. We were at once fascinated by the authenticity
> of the family and of the verse-form created for it; we were doubt-
> ful whether the central scenes of the play, which seemed cloudy
> compared to those in the family atmosphere, could emerge into
> full drama with their characters clearly defined and their pur-
> pose comprehensible.[23]

These doubts did not disappear: shown a "finished" version early in 1938, Browne still felt "the play to be weak
in plot," which Eliot admitted, though his Faber and
Faber partner, Frank Morley, shown both play and criticisms, said that "It is *not* weak in plot: it is if anything
surcharged with too much plot: but too much remains
hidden. . . ."[24] Revisions and yet more revisions followed,
until, early in 1939, *The Family Reunion* was staged with
a first-rate cast that included Michael Redgrave in the
lead, playing Harry Monchensey. It "was not a theatrical
success,"[25] and the explanation is not hard to come by.
"The total effect was intended to be the presentation of a
modern counterpart to the universal experience of religious purgation. The audience was to leave the theater
having seen an action in modern existence which duplicat-
ed the age-old religious pattern and returned to the theater
its original function of expressing God's presence."[26] In
Kenner's pithy phrase, however, "the work contains a
situation rather than a plot,"[27] and since Eliot plainly
"lacks that intense interest in human behavior in everyday

living which makes realism interesting in a playwright like Ibsen,"[28] it is up to the verse to carry the burden. And as C. L. Barber wrote in 1940, "the poetry often has a sighing, tired quality, the lines ending in a gratuitous dying fall. And the iteration of key words which characterizes much of this type of verse occurs frequently when what is re-echoed is of no significance. Although the diction is never pretentious, the presence of such excess of form over content, unobtrusive but pervasive, leaves one with a feeling of being clogged with unevacuated language. . . ."[29]

Not all the reliance on Greek mythology in the world —the play retells the Orestes story, and makes use of the Furies—could prop up a drama with these and other weaknesses. Contrast, for example, the "Vivienne" scenes in *The Waste Land* with their pale progeny in *The Family Reunion*. The speaker is Harry's mother, the Dowager Lady Monchensey:

> Not yet! I will ring for you. It is still quite light.
> I have nothing to do but watch the days draw out,
> Now that I sit in the house from October to June,
> And the swallow comes too soon and the spring will be over
> And the cuckoo will be gone before I am out again.
> O Sun, that was once so warm, O Light that was taken for granted
> When I was young and strong, and sun and light unsought for
> And the night unfeared and the day expected
> And clocks could be trusted, tomorrow assured
> And time would not stop in the dark!

The verse is not all quite so slack as these opening lines, the first spoken in the play. But the verse is poor enough, and the play is confused and dull enough, so that I want to spend no more time on it, here, but pass rapidly on to Eliot's more commercially oriented comedies, *The Cock-*

tail Party (1949) and *The Confidential Clerk* (1953), and his last play, *The Elder Statesman* (1958). These are, perhaps, not better plays; they are however in some ways different, and as I have indicated the first of them was very successful on both sides of the Atlantic. Just as importantly, the verse may not be any better, but it too is different, and the nature of that difference seems to me well worth comment.

> I like that story.
>   I love that story.
>   *I'm* never tired of hearing that story.
> Well, you all seem to know it.
>   Do we all know it?

This is by no means the jazz-influenced verse of *Sweeney Agonistes:* it is generally agreed that that experiment had no direct progeny. And yet one aspect of *Sweeney* is echoed here, namely its attempt to capture real speech, its attempt to use the diction and rhythm of speech for its own purposes. Both early and late, what Eliot seems most to have heard in colloquial language was its bare, mechanical quality, its emptiness, its sterility. But in *The Cocktail Party* and its two successors, he does turn that brittle chatter into frequently quite entertaining theatrical moments—and in the commercial theater, entertainment is, of course, the name of the game.

Eliot means to do much more than entertain; he is not after all Noel Coward nor was meant to be. He wants us to hear under the brittle pattering the more ominous spiritual facts, which are in all these late works at the heart of his purpose.[30] Edward Chamberlayne, for example, "breaks down" toward the end of the play, and asks the mysterious Sir Henry Harcourt-Reilly, surely one of the oddest "psychiatrists" ever seen on or off stage, if he can be locked away in Sir Henry's sanitorium. There is much relatively satisfying mumbo-jumbo performed; Sir Henry confronts Edward with Lavinia, his wife, and some interesting sparks fly. But Eliot has dimmed the entire proceeding from the start, putting into Edward's mouth such speeches as this:

> I once experienced the extreme of physical pain,
> And now I know there is suffering worse than that.
> It is surprising, if one had time to be surprised:
> I am not afraid of the death of the body,
> But this death is terrifying. The death of the spirit—
> Can you understand what I suffer?

The brittle verse cannot carry ideas of such intensity. By stylizing his poetry, thinning it to the point where, indeed, it almost ceases to be poetry at all, Eliot has surrendered even the opportunity to make such speeches convincing, even in a context where Edward is not meant to be fully believed, neither by Sir Henry nor by the audience. "By adopting this pattern of ironic social comedy, Eliot placed upon his genius a regrettable limitation," as E. Martin Browne, Eliot's longtime collaborator, writes at the end of his thoughtful study of Eliot's theatrical work. "He put his poetry, as he says, 'on a thin diet.' We have seen the progressive diminution of poetry in these plays, quite deliberately achieved. The poet's skill is still supremely evident in the choice of language, and his inspiration often peeps through it; but too much of his energy is devoted to the expression of unimportant social niceties. The comedy is often delightful, but one pays too great a price for it in prolixity. . . ."[31] Browne adds that, "in one form or another" what Eliot needed was "ritual . . . which he had used so satisfyingly in *Murder in the Cathedral*. . . ."

I do not think that *Murder in the Cathedral* is quite so satisfying as does Mr. Browne. I do, however, think it on the whole the best of Eliot's plays. And to my mind the reason why it succeeds relatively well, and the other plays (after *The Rock*) do not, is that Eliot was trying in all those plays to do what earlier and more basic decisions had made it impossible for him to do. That is, having turned his back to the external world in those momentous years of the 1920s, he was now trying to face toward it again—but without the same equipment he had once been possessed of, the equipment which had carried him from "Preludes" to *The Waste Land* and beyond it, as far as "The Hollow Men." The poetic failure of *Ash-Wednesday,* and the comparative poetic failure of *Four Quartets,* is thus paralleled, if not precisely mirrored, in Eliot's plays. Eliot's religious convictions, had they taken hold deeply enough, could have brought him back into the world as, in a way, a new man. As I have said, those religious convictions never took hold to anything like that extent. He went out into the world as a playwright with—figuratively speaking—one hand tied behind his back. He groped and struggled, and he worked surpassingly hard, but without any possibility of true success. Whether Eliot could ever have been a successful playwright I do not know, and it is, of course, impossible for anyone to say with conviction what might have happened had he not taken the turn he did take. But surely, once he had gone the way of *The Waste Land* and of "The Hollow Men," and even more the way of *Ash-Wednesday,* his theatrical attempts were bound to end, as they did end, in barrenness and frustration.

The farce of *The Confidential Clerk,* based on the *Ion* of Euripides, owes a good deal, also, to such earlier playwrights as Oscar Wilde. But it distinctly lacks the drive and the power of either of its progenitors:

That is the way it must have happened.
Oh, Claude, you know I'm rather weak in the head

> Though I try to be clever. Do try to help me.
>
> . . . .
>
> I told Colby, never learn to mix cocktails,
> If you don't want women always dropping in on you.
> And between a couple of man-eating tigers
> Like you and Lizzie, he's got to have protection.
>
> . . . .
>
> I suppose that's true of you and me, Claude.
> Between not knowing what other people want of one,
> And not knowing what one should ask of other people,
> One does make mistakes! But I mean to do better.

These examples, chosen entirely at random, illustrate the problem. It almost does not matter who is speaking; all the characters are so exceedingly flat that the viewer (and the reader) does not know them, and does not care to make distinctions which the author himself has not bothered to make. David E. Jones, well inclined to Eliot as a playwright, refers to the "mechanical smoothness" of this play.[32] C. L. Barber refers to the "paucity of invention in *The Confidential Clerk,*" and though he concludes "that it is not undramatic, except for a few barren places, . . . it is, until the last act, exceedingly difficult to act."[33] Browne, writing as a theater professional, feels that "The verse is perhaps the most consistent of that in any of the modern plays [of Eliot]. There are very few peaks; there is little variation in tone; there is no artificiality." He speaks also of "a narrower range of diction," and adds that "the play contains less interesting characters."[34] I agree.

The Elder Statesman, finally, is for two acts a reasonably pleasant melodrama, more or less Victorian (as more than one critic has noted). Even in these largely successful two acts, however, there is almost no poetry—and what attempts at poetry are made do not come off:

> How did this come, Charles? It crept so softly
> On silent feet, and stood behind my back

> Quietly, a long time, a long long time
> Before I felt its presence.

As love poetry, which it is meant to be, this little speech
falls as flat as anything one might imagine from the pen
of, say, Rupert Brooke or any other Edwardian poet. On
the other hand, when the lines deal with social rather than
emotional matters, they are often effective, if not powerful:

> My obituary, if I had died in harness,
> Would have occupied a column and a half
> With an inset, a portrait taken twenty years ago.
> In five years' time, it will be the half of that;
> In ten years' time, a paragraph.

It is, as I say, pleasantly done—not inspired, not moving,
but very competent. Eliot's apprenticeship in the theatre
has to this extent paid off quite well: he knows how the
thing is done. All the same, it is on the whole a subdued
competence, neither reaching high nor falling low. When
it reaches, it fairly regularly fails. "Perhaps I've never
really enjoyed living / As much as most people. At least,
as they seem to do." Lord Claverton, here, is pretty plainly
a marionette, manipulated for the expression of things his
creator wants said. At the end of the second act the same
character speaks in the same elevated but disconnected
fashion:

> I said I knew from experience. Do I understand the
>   meaning
> Of the lesson I would teach? Come, I'll start to learn
>   again.
> Michael [his son] and I shall go to school together.
> We'll sit side by side, at little desks
> And suffer the same humiliations
> At the hands of the same master. But have I still time?
> There is time for Michael. Is it too late for me . . .?

Nothing in the play prepares us for this burst of humility; similar bursts, in the third act, are still less prepared for.

But the third act, in which the playwright is obliged to bring the various strands of his plot to some conclusion, jointly and severally, exposes the play as the tired invention it unfortunately is. Lord Claverton's speeches grow longer, and less interesting; the other characters dash about, this way and that; and the impression is distinctly one of loss of control, almost at times of desperation.

> *Monica:* It is time to break the silence! Let us share your ghosts!
> *Charles:* But these are only human beings, who can be dealt with.
> *Monica:* Or only ghosts, who can be exorcised!

It is the playwright, we feel, who is anxious for some exorcism; the characters, to the extent they actually exist, seem unmoved. Monica's father, Lord Claverton, replies to her outburst with a blandness of unsurpassable quality. "And yet they've both done better for themselves / In consequence of it all." When therefore he tells us, toward the end of the act (and of the play) that "I feel at peace now. / It is the peace that ensues upon contrition / When contrition ensues upon knowledge of the truth," it is neither moving nor meaningful. It comes out of nowhere, and goes to the same destination, as does the play itself.

But Eliot's career as a playwright cannot be left without a word as to its extrinsic importance. By the time he ventured into the theatre, Eliot was a literary and a cultural figure of international significance. The mere fact of his attempting to write plays, accordingly, had an importance and an influence beyond anything the plays themselves might have merited. That he attempted serious subjects, and attempted them in a sort of verse, was also influential. That is, no matter how unoriginal Eliot may have been as a playwright, the presence in the theater, and especially in the commercial theater, of a man of his standing could not help but be a potent fact both for those already involved in theater, and also for those who might in the future be involved. In that sense, then, Eliot's playwrighting career could be nothing but beneficent, and useful, and on the whole important. Those extrinsic dimensions are not of direct relevance, in a discussion such as this. But they exist, and they ought to be noted.

7

The Harvard
Sam Johnson:
Eliot as
a literary critic

Unlike Matthew Arnold, whose career is fairly neatly divided between a poetic first phase and a critical second, Eliot wrote critical prose all his life. And like those other great poet-critics, John Dryden before him, and W. H. Auden after him, Eliot dealt with an immense variety of subjects, sometimes in connection with a particular literary assignment, whether a book review or an invitation for a speech, sometimes himself initiating matters. There are subjects Eliot dealt with both early and late, other subjects are dealt with only once, and some subjects which might have seemed inevitable for a man of his interests are not dealt with at all, except in passing or in an essay devoted to other matters. As I have said, much of Eliot's critical prose stems from his work as a literary journalist and editor: he was neither a scholar, in the usual sense of the term, nor an academic, able to pick and choose. He wrote a late essay on "Johnson as Critic and Poet" (1944), and yet never wrote either on Swift or on Alexander Pope, both of whom were important to him. He also produced an essay on Goethe (1955) though, according to Ronald Duncan, Eliot declared "I can't stand his stuff," even as he was writing it.[1] There is, as I have noted, an essay on Mark Twain's *Huckleberry Finn,* not a book most critics would automatically associate with Eliot, but there is no essay on Mallarmé, no essay on Charles-Louis Philippe, no essay on Flaubert or Proust. He wrote of Dickens, of immense importance to him, only once in an essay entitled "Wilkie Collins and Dickens," which is in fact more about Collins than Dickens. Loyal as he was to Ezra Pound, he wrote in 1917 an important small book, *Ezra Pound: His Metric and Poetry,* but his judgment (conveyed to Conrad Aiken in an undated letter) was that though "Pound is rather intelligent as a talker: his verse is touchingly incompetent."[2]

Not a systematic critic, Eliot is nevertheless a very great critic, capable of performing, and performing supremely well, the two most important tasks of all criticism, namely (1) elucidating the work in front of him, and (2) igniting the reader. Pedantic petulants will continue to maintain that "errors can be found in most of Eliot's earlier critical essays," and that, although "the lapses from scholarly precision become noticeably fewer in the later essays . . . , the critical interest of the literary essays decreases in an almost exact proportion to the absence of factual error."[3] This makes as much sense as arguing that circumstances "launched Eliot into premature pre-eminence,"[4] rather than talent or hard work or any other native quality, or that comments made by Irving Babbitt in 1928 or 1929, in informal conversation, to the effect that Eliot as an undergraduate was " 'a vurra poor stoodent',"[5] need to be taken seriously, or indeed ought to be retailed in print at all. W. F. Jackson Knight, a very professional classicist, has said with authority that Eliot's "classical knowledge is no outsider's knowledge";[6] John Crowe Ransom declares that "the learning behind [Eliot's criticism] is perfectly regular, and based generally on the academic sources of learning."[7] And Austin Warren observes, with immense propriety, that although "Eliot tactfully desists from naming himself as . . . [Matthew] Arnold's successor . . . the Harvard auditors of 1933 who listened to the first series of Norton Lectures *[The Use of Poetry & The Use of Criticism]* . . . were ready to supply the name."[8]

This is not the place for an elaborate or fully systematic survey of Eliot's large critical output.[9] And since my primary concern is the poetry, I want to use this brief discussion of Eliot's literary criticism to shed some light both on the poetry and some of the underlying forces which gave rise to it. Eliot himself wrote, with that edge of ironic self-deprecation that often seems to underlie his prose, that "the critical writings of poets . . . owe a great deal of their interest to the fact that the poet, at the back of his mind, if not as his ostensible purpose, is always trying to defend the kind of poetry he is writing, or to formulate the kind that he wants to write."[10] (The other side of this, also formulated by Eliot—and in the same essay—is that "the meaning of a poem may be something larger than its author's conscious purpose, and something remote from its origins."[11]) I should like to conduct my examination under two chief heads, first Eliot's approach to and use of history, and second his more theoretical formulations about who and what the poet is and how he ought, more or less ideally, to operate.[12]

The essay most usually referred to in any discussion of Eliot's approach to history (and also the essay most widely anthologized) is, of course, "Tradition and the Individual Talent," published in 1919 but written two years earlier, when Eliot was not quite thirty. Eliot himself gave the essay pride of place in his most important single volume of criticism, his *Selected Essays,* a book of a solid 460 pages. The principal assertion, here, is that "the historical sense compels a man to write not merely with his own generation in his bones, but with a feeling that the whole of the literature of Europe from Homer and within it the whole of the literature of his own country has a simultaneous existence and composes a simultaneous order."[13] In his 1964 reprinting of *The Use of Poetry & The Use of Criticism,* he rather wearily referred to this essay as "perhaps the most juvenile and certainly the first to appear in print," and added that "I reprint [this book] in the faint hope that one of these lectures may be [anthologized] instead. . . ."[14] But on the score of the "historical sense," as here defined, there is abundant evidence that Eliot never changed his judgment. In "Euripides and

Professor Murray" (1920) he says, for example, that "We need a digestion which can assimilate both Homer and Flaubert . . . an eye which can see the past in its place with its definite differences from the present, and yet so lively that it shall be as present to us as the present."[15] In "What is Minor Poetry" (1944), Eliot gives the idea a fine reverse twist: "I should not trust the taste of anyone who never read any contemporary poetry, and I should certainly not trust the taste of anyone who read nothing else."[16] In "The Classics and the Man of Letters" (1942), he affirmed that "The continuity of a literature is essential to its greatness . . . [and] this continuity is largely unconscious, and only visible in historical retrospect."[17] And yet another corollary of the general notion appeared in one of his last essays, "To Criticize the Critic" (1961). "We cannot discount the influence upon our formation of the creative writing and the critical writing of the intervening generations [in trying, that is, to understand earlier criticism], or the inevitable modifications of taste, or our greater knowledge and understanding of the literature preceding that of the age which we are trying to understand."[18]

Much of Eliot's literary criticism, of a more or less historical nature, can be viewed in some part as a product of this fundamental and unchanging concern for the pattern and the continuity of history. "The best of my *literary* criticism . . . consists of essays on poets and poetic dramatists who had influenced me. It is a by-product of my private poetry-workshop; or a prolongation of the thinking that went into the formation of my verse."[19] Indeed, Eliot goes even further than this: "What has no relation to the poet's own work, or what is antipathetic to him, is outside of his competence [as a critic]."[20] Or, finally, "The critic must be the whole man. . . ."[21] And I should like to reverse the polarities employed by a fine critic of matters intellectual, John D. Margolis, who writes that Eliot's "early poetry . . . is of limited value in illuminating the intellectual concerns that were exercising Eliot during the first years of his career. . . ."[22] My concern, that is, is with the poet who writes superb criticism, and not with the critic who is also a poet. I prefer to examine the criticism, once again, in order to shed some light on the poetry.

What then do we find that may be illuminating to that poetry, in Eliot's consistently historical approach as a critic? Eliot's situation as a poet, and Eliot's situation more generally, as a man, as an American, and as a student of ideas and letters, ought to provide us with the background against which this deep drive toward historicism can be evaluated. He gives us one part of the answer in an essay written in 1953, "American Literature and the American Language": "In the first decade of the century the [poetic] situation was unusual. I cannot think of a single living poet, in either England or America, then at the height of his powers, whose work was capable of pointing the way to a young poet conscious of the desire for a new idiom."[23] Eliot's resolution to this difficulty was to look elsewhere, notably to the literature of France. "His serious exploration of French poetry had ebbed by the early 1920s," as Francis Scarfe points out; what mattered to him in French poetry "was mainly . . . what he had read at an early, impressionable age . . ."[24] But it was, of course, Europe as a whole to which he turned, as he turned away from America. "If [the Classics] are to survive, to justify themselves as literature, as an element in the European mind, as the foundation for the literature we hope to create, they are badly in need of persons capable of expounding them," he wrote in 1920.[25] And in his essay on Dante nine years later, he explained with some particularity that "Dante can do less *harm* to anyone trying to learn to write verse than can Shakespeare. . . . The language of each great English poet is his own language; the language of Dante is the perfection of a common language."[26]

Insofar as he still thought of himself as an American in 1933 (he had as I have noted become a British subject in 1927), Eliot declared that "I speak as a New Englander." And so speaking, to a Virginia audience, he went on to explain that "The Civil War was certainly the greatest disaster in the whole of American history; it is just as certainly a disaster from which the country has never recovered, and perhaps never will . . . Yet I think that the chances for the re-establishment of a native culture are perhaps better here than in New England." And his reasons for this judgment are of considerable interest. "You are farther away from New York; you have been less industrialized and less invaded by foreign races; and you have a more opulent soil."[27] It is no secret, surely, "that Eliot's departure from America may reflect his response to a cultural deadlock with extensive implications. And . . . it is [even] possible to see in the shadowy Jew whose rootlessness and vulgarity offends Eliot's inherited culture, a scapegoat for his own expatriation."[28] Gabriel Pearson links Eliot's movement *away from* America and his movement *toward* England and Europe generally. "For Eliot, Symbolism is a poetic inheritance but also the manifestation of a predicament. The inheritance is complicated by the way that Symbolism is itself a formulated resistance against the debasements of bourgeois democratic mass society."[29] Pearson's analysis continues:

The career of poetry seems, then, to have necessitated the remove to England and the abandonment of America. William Carlos Williams recognised as much when he recalled in his *Autobiography* the first impact of *The Waste Land:* "Eliot had turned his back on the possibility of reviving my world. And being an accomplished craftsman, better skilled in some ways than I could ever hope to be, I had to watch him carry my world off with him,

the fool, to the enemy."(p.174) This comment is brilliantly precise. Eliot did carry off not only Williams's but his own world
with him, perhaps more of it than he realised. The defeat of his
social values moved him out of America and led him to construct
the counter-universe of symbolist aesthetic. Yet within the poetry that societal defeat remains fiercely alive. Apparently impersonal procedures are fuelled by some very raw emotions, the
more violent for their being locked up inside a verbal prison."[30]

Two of Eliot's formulations from his Norton lectures
at Harvard in 1932–1933 seem to bear directly on Pearson's acute analysis. First, Eliot's evaluation of poetry's
importance to a culture: "The people which ceases to care
for its literary inheritance becomes barbaric; the people
which ceases to produce literature ceases to move in
thought and sensibility. The poetry of a people takes its
life from the people's speech and in turn gives life to it; and
represents its highest point of consciousness, its greatest
power and its most delicate sensibility."[31] It would be
difficult to state a more sweeping case, or to express it
more dramatically. Eliot then goes on to discuss the importance of culture to the poet, observing with his frequent flippant seriousness that "the poet aspires to the
condition of the music-hall comedian. Being incapable of
altering his wares to suit a prevailing taste, *if there be any,*
he naturally desires a state of society in which they may
become popular, and in which his own talents will be put
to the best use."[32] (Emphasis added).

Viewing Eliot's historically oriented literary criticism
as the "private poetry-workshop" that he himself called it
("or a prolongation of the thinking that went into the
formation of my verse"), there are clear patterns which
relate those essays to his own poetic output. There are
thirty-seven essays in his most-used and largest collection,
Selected Essays, and no less than fifteen of these deal with
seventeenth-century poets, one additional essay being on

the seventeenth-century divine, Lancelot Andrewes. As Hugh Kenner says, "If Prufrock is the sort of *persona* entailed by the viewpoints and methods of Laforgue, it is from the resources of Jacobean rhetoric that [Eliot] is invested with such momentous and paradoxical magnitude. . . ."[33] Eliot's use of, and indeed his borrowings from, Elizabethan and Jacobean authors have been a commonplace in the criticism written about his poetry from the very start of his career.

When he leaves the seventeenth century, Eliot tends to move back in time to Dante and the Classics, by which he usually means Virgil or Seneca, or forward in time to nineteenth-century poets like William Blake, Algernon Swinburne, and Tennyson, as well as Baudelaire and Poe, and to twentieth-century poets like Kipling, Yeats, and, of course, Ezra Pound. His only eighteenth-century essay is as I have noted on Samuel Johnson—and as he moves into the 1930s, it is remarkable how few historical essays of the earlier sort Eliot writes at all. That is, he is now occupied in his criticism, as he tends to be in his poetry, with generalizations, rather than with investigations of specific figures. His need for the poetic education, and the sense of poetic support he did not think he could obtain in America, waned at this stage in his career. It is not difficult to correlate this decreased need for historicity with Eliot's conversion and the poetic consequences attendant thereon.

Eliot's more theoretical formulations also correlate extremely well with his drive toward historicity and his aversion to America and his own immediate past. Virtually all those formulations revolve around the *need* for (he puts it as the *requirement* of, but the difference is only one of emphasis) impersonality in poetry, that is, upon the poet's need for impersonality. "The emotion of art is impersonal," he asserted in "Tradition and the Individual

Talent," explaining that "the more perfect the artist, the
more completely separate in him will be the man who
suffers and the mind which creates. . . ."[34] Thirty-five
years later, though he kept insisting that he did not dis-
avow "Tradition and the Individual Talent," Eliot's need
for the screen and the protection of impersonality had
diminished almost to the vanishing point—as, to be sure,
had his poetic output:

[The poet] has something germinating in him for which he must
find words; but he cannot know what words he wants until he
has found the words . . . He does not know what he has to say
until he has said it, and in the effort to say it he is not concerned
with making other people understand anything. . . . He is op-
pressed by a burden which he must bring to birth in order to
obtain relief. . . . In other words again, he is going to all that
trouble, not in order to communicate with anyone, but to gain
relief from acute discomfort. . . .

And he adds, in words sharply applicable to his own later
output from *Ash-Wednesday* on: "The most bungling form
of obscurity is that of the poet who has not been able to
express himself *to* himself; the shoddiest form is found
when the poet is trying to persuade himself that he has
something to say when he hasn't."[35] Or, as he says in a still
later essay written in 1961, "as for Classicism and Romanticism, I find that the terms have no longer the importance
to me that they once had."[36]

But the earlier importance is unmistakeable. Eliot's
famous notion of the "objective correlative," in his 1919
essay on "Hamlet," is simply an extension, a practical,
craftsmanlike application, of his overall need for impersonality and the shelter of history. "The only way of expressing emotion in the form of art is by finding an
'objective correlative'; in other words, a set of objects, a
situation, a chain of events which shall be the formula of

that *particular* emotion; such that when the external facts, which must terminate in sensory experience, are given, the emotion is immediately evoked."[37] Eliot grew rather tired of having this repeated back by the "student of contemporary literature, [who] putting pen to paper about my criticism, is certain to pass an examination on it if he alludes to the 'dissociation of sensibility' and the 'objective correlative'. . . ."[38] It remains, however, both a powerful (if surely a limited) analytical tool, and more importantly, a trace of Eliot's deeper needs as poet and man. One might argue that Eliot's conversion, no less than the directions of his poetry and of his criticism, pretty clearly well up from the same sources. And that has, of course, been in fact the argument of this book from start to finish. Eliot's poetry is to my mind primary, but it is impossible not to make use, in examining that poetry, of his plays and his literary and social criticism. A play and an essay are indirect tools for the analysis of a poem, but they remain, for all that, useful tools.

It should be added, finally, that as an intellectual— that is, when operating as a critic—Eliot remained all his life a product of Harvard University. His kinsman, President Charles W. Eliot, had prophetically written, the year before his selection as the new leader of Harvard, that "the priceless gift of our fathers [ought to] be transmitted to our children, not only unimpaired, but constantly renewed. . . ." The future President of Harvard concluded his essay with the resounding declaration that the University ought, accordingly, to "be devoted to Christ, the great teacher of truth, and to his Church, the great means of human education."[39] The poet did not share this burgeoning optimism, but as we have seen his own intellectual program was not terribly different. As Harvard's greatest historian, Samuel Eliot Morison, described President Eliot, it is hard not to think of the poet as well. ["President]

Eliot's mind was Roman rather than Greek or Hebraic. . . ."[40]

But Harvard has not for at least a century represented solely an intellectual or even a spiritual center. Eliot never thought of himself as someone from Missouri: he declared himself to be "a New Englander." The center of New England has always been the city of Boston, and it has always been true that "The atmospheres of the city of Boston and the University across the river have always influenced one another profoundly. . . ."[41] The biographer of Eliot's Harvard classmate, Walter Lippmann, traces in some detail the sense of possibility, of excitement, of almost unbounded opportunity which came almost automatically to the Harvard student.[42] In even blunter terms, "Harvard meant prestige, status, connections. . . ."[43] What Richard Hofstadter neatly calls the "classic Groton-Harvard career"[44] was internalized as well as readily verifiable. When, for example, A. Lawrence Lowell exchanged letters with a Harvard alumnus, Franklin Delano Roosevelt, who was at the time President of the United States, he felt that as a former President of Harvard he could without hesitation feel, and act, as Roosevelt's superior. The occasion was the three-hundredth anniversary of the University's founding, and Roosevelt had agreed to speak. Wrote Lowell:

. . . President Conant tells me that you have kindly consented to speak on this occasion. Now, it being a meeting for the mutual congratulation of the graduates at the three hundredth anniversary of their alma mater, we hope you will choose for your theme for a brief address something connected with Harvard and the tercentary of higher education in this country, and feel that you would welcome this opportunity to divorce yourself from the arduous demands of politics and political speech-making. Do you not think it would be well to limit all the speeches that afternoon to about ten minutes?[45]

Roosevelt was, predictably, outraged. "I shall lose my temper completely," he wrote, "and find it necessary to stay in Washington . . . instead of going to Cambridge! . . . Damn."[46] But how like Eliot, once again, is the tone taken by Harvard's emeritus President!

In short, though this is not the place to elaborate the point, it is virtually impossible to imagine Eliot the critic as, say, a Princetonian, or a graduate of Columbia, or Yale, or indeed of any intellectual and social environment but that of Harvard. I would myself argue that Eliot is far more the Harvard Sam Johnson than the London sort: for better and for worse, "the university supplied a reservoir of ideas on which he [drew] for fifty years."[47]

8

God's Word in
man's world:
Eliot's social
criticism

Although there are elements of what I have here called "social criticism" in many of Eliot's essays after about 1930, there are only two books which seem to me worthy of separate discussion under that heading, namely *The Idea of a Christian Society* (1939) and *Notes towards the Definition of Culture* (1949).[1] Part seven of Eliot's *Selected Essays* includes a number of essays which would need to be considered in a full examination of his views; several of the essays in *Poetry and Poets* and in *To Criticize the Critic* would similarly be relevant, and several of the unreprinted essays from *For Lancelot Andrewes* (subtitled "essays on style and order") would also need to be looked at. There is much in *After Strange Gods,* too (subtitled "a primer of modern heresy"), which would need examination, though all in all it seems more a literary than a social discussion. Much the same might be said of *The Use of Poetry & the Use of Criticism.* Indeed, in a fascinating little book, *Theory and Personality: The Significance of T.S. Eliot's Criticism,*[2] all of Eliot's literary essays are approached from an essentially social perspective. And any proper examination of Eliot's socially oriented writings would surely need to take account of his now-published Harvard doctoral dissertation, *Knowledge and Experience in the Philosophy of F. H. Bradley.* All manner of fugitive essays, some of them collected (and some only excerpted) in John Hayward's edition of Eliot's *Selected Prose,*[3] would need examination. And there are Eliot's many, many letters to editors, some of them dry and uninteresting, some full of surprising turns and twists.[4]

It is worth emphasizing from the start that some fine social critics, especially British social critics, take Eliot's major work in this area very seriously. Raymond Williams, for example, devotes a long chapter to Eliot in his *Culture and Society, 1780–1950.*[5] "If Eliot is read with attention," he observes, "he is seen to have raised questions which those who differ from him politically must answer, or else retire from the field. In particular, in his discussion of culture, he has carried the argument to an important new stage, and one on which the rehearsal of old pieces will be merely tedious."[6] Williams states his central objection as follows: "The 'free economy' which is the central tenet of contemporary conservatism not only contradicts the social principles which Eliot advances [and in particular the notion of culture as 'a whole way of life'], . . . but also, and this is the real confusion, is the only available method of ordering society to the maintenance of those interests and institutions on which Eliot believes his values to depend."[7] These arguments will become clearer, in a moment: I want to state them, before discussing what Eliot himself has said, largely to indicate that on these subjects Eliot is frequently "read with attention."[8] And I want to emphasize, as well, that Eliot's standing as "perhaps the most important literary critic in the English-speaking world"—words used of him by Edmund Wilson as long ago as 1929[9]—affects but does not determine the respect with which his social criticism has been at times received. It is not universally so received, but that is not now relevant. Eliot is a serious social critic, and must be taken seriously, no matter whether one agrees with him or not.

The Idea of a Christian Society is generally considered his major statement in this area; *Notes towards the Definition of Culture,* though significant, is commonly taken as more discursive, less sharply focused, and even something of a footnote to the earlier book. Eliot's concern in *The Idea of a Christian Society* is clearly formulated in his preface, namely, "that the current terms in which we discuss international affairs and political theory may only tend to conceal from us the real issues of contempo-

rary civilisation."[10] It is not his concern either to bring
about a religious revival, he says quite explicitly, or to
indicate or evaluate "the means for bringing a Christian
Society into existence."[11] Rather,

my primary interest is a change in our social attitude, such a
change only as could bring about anything worthy to be called
a Christian Society. That such a change would compel changes
in our organisation of industry and commerce and financial
credit . . . I feel certain.[12]

He does not want to advocate "any particular political
form," in fact, "but whatever State is suitable to a Christian Society, whatever State a particular Christian Society
develops for itself."[13]

In order to define that ideal society, Eliot begins by
dismissing "Democracy" as a notion "so universally sanct-
ified . . . [that] I begin to wonder if it means anything,"
and Liberalism as something which works "to relax, rather than to fortify," something which tends toward "the
artificial, mechanised or brutal control which is a desperate remedy for its chaos."[14] He sees the Liberal attitude,
indeed, as something so dangerously corrosive that it can
"infect opponents as well as defenders."[15] And without
defining that attitude, he asserts that "the attitudes and
beliefs of Liberalism are destined to disappear, are already
disappearing."[16] And what does it leave behind, he asks,
except a sense of being against something rather than truly
for something? (His fundamental objection to fascism, incidentally, "is that it is pagan."[17]) But in that context,
"We have less excuse than our ancestors for un-Christian
conduct, because the growth of an un-Christian society
about us . . . has been breaking down the comfortable
distinction between public and private morality." Accordingly, "the problem of leading a Christian life in a non-
Christian society is now very present to us. . . ." Chris-

tians, he says flatly, are now faced with "institutions the operation of which appears no longer neutral, but non-Christian."[18] Eliot thus concludes that "the only possibility of control and balance is a religious control and balance," which seems to him to mean "that the only hopeful course for a society which would thrive and continue its creative activity in the arts of civilisation, is to become Christian."[19]

The balance of his small book is devoted to an exposition of the fundamentals of a truly Christian state. Eliot indicates forthrightly that he is not too much concerned with "the great mass of humanity," who, since "their capacity for *thinking* about the objects of faith is small," need for the most part to be set in a reliable context of "customary and periodic religious observances, and in a traditional code of behaviour towards their neighbors."[20] It is clear, I think, that though he disclaims "advocating any *complete* reversion to any earlier state of things"[21] (emphasis added), he is looking backward a good deal harder than he is looking forward. "A great deal of the machinery of modern life," he admits a few pages farther along, "is merely a sanction for un-Christian aims," and he asserts "that it is not only hostile to the conscious pursuit of the Christian life in the world by the few, but to the maintenance of any Christian society *of* the world."[22] Masses and "rulers" alike, he says, must be bound by "a unified religious-social code of behaviour"; one can to a degree "include persons of exceptional ability who may be indifferent or disbelieving" and also "a proportion of other persons professing other faiths than Christianity," but there will have to be "limitations imposed upon such persons. . . ."[23] An established or "National" Church, inevitably, must in Eliot's view underlie this ideal Christian society. He acknowledges the possibility of danger to the arts, but cannot worry about activities which "are probably by-products for which we cannot deliberately arrange the conditions." In any case, "a strong and even tyrannous government may do no harm, . . . so long as it limits itself to restricting the liberties, without attempting to influence the minds, of its subjects." He does a bit grudgingly recognize, however, that "a régime of unlimited demagogy *appears* to be stultifying."[24] (Emphasis added). He acknowledges, too, that "a wholly Christian society might be a society for the most part on a low level."[25]

Eliot insists that he is not simply contributing "one more amateur sketch of an abstract and impracticable future. . . ."[26] And no one can be surprised that, in a "Postscript," he reveals that "a distinguished theologian" feels that "The main theses of this book seem . . . so important, and their application so urgently necessary, that [he] want[s] to call attention to two points which . . . need further emphasis. . . ."[27] But it is not, in my view, social criticism at all, though plainly it has social implications. *The Idea of a Christian Society* seems to me, rather, a variety of social theology. Roger Kojecky, author of a book-length study of *T. S. Eliot's Social Criticism,* uses the term "social philosophy."[28] And though he recognizes Eliot's "deeply felt desire for orthodoxy," he finds this book in good part "forced . . . In fact, it could be said that it was written with less than half an eye to the whole contemporary situation, and was in the nature of a homily."[29]

Though I find myself totally unable to agree with Raymond Williams, who goes so far as to claim that "The next step, in thinking of these matters, must be in a different direction, for Eliot has closed almost all the existing roads,"[30] I think this book "in the nature of a homily" is in many ways deeply revealing. For one thing, its intense nostalgia for a better and a now-vanished world fits perfectly with Eliot's stances as poet, playwright, and literary critic. The book positively yearns for the peace and composure of "order," and in this, too, it complements Eliot's other work. The abstract, even remote, style comports extremely well with the sharp swing toward abstraction which I have described from about 1930 on in most of Eliot's work. And there is another aspect to this rather dry, stuffily English style: it indicates just how hard Eliot was working to *become* English, how extremely important it was to him—though he never quite reached his goal. "From the first he fitted naturally into English clothes and English clubs, into English habits generally. In fact, *if anything gave him away it was an Englishness that was a shade too correct to be natural.*"[31] (Emphasis added). Summarizing Eliot's activities after World War II broke out, Kojecky writes, with a significance I do not think he intended:

During the war Eliot was elected to a group called simply The Club. Founded in the eighteenth century, its members had included Dr. Johnson, Charles James Fox and Edmund Burke. Dinners were held about ten times a year, and the members, in all about three dozen, were almost exclusively peers. . . . There were no formal proceedings, simply an opportunity for conversational exchange. Associations such as these were regarded by Eliot as of some importance.[32]

And what Allen Austin calls Eliot's frequent obliviousness to "the necessity of evidence or even argument," a "dogmatism" which Austin correctly finds "increases in his later religious and sociological works,"[33] seems to me of significance too. I do not mean to raise the issue of Eliot's sincerity, or in any way to argue issues of belief. I mean, instead, that for all that this book can be seen as "in the nature of a homily," it must also be seen as not a discussion of matters of belief. Eliot assumes so neatly

closed a stance, indeed, and makes it so superabundantly
clear that he is addressing only those who already believe,
and believe essentially as he does, that Kristian Smidt,
writing specifically on *Poetry and Belief in the Work of T.
S. Eliot,* makes only a single, passing, and unimportant
reference to *The Idea of a Christian Society.*[34] Eliot is
dogmatic, in my view, because he no longer seriously
concerns himself with finding answers: the answer has
been found, and his only imperative is to promulgate it.
But he is dry and uninspiring in his promulgations precisely because his belief is not at issue—or, to put it less
pleasantly, because, in fact, it is still very much at issue in
his own mind and heart, but he simply cannot face or deal
with that fact. He could not face or deal with it in his
poetry; there ought to be no surprise that he cannot face
or deal with it in his social criticism (or religious philosophy).

   Notes towards the Definition of Culture is less dogmatic, on the whole, in part because it assumes what has
already been said in the earlier book and in part because
Eliot's purpose is considerably less focused. In trying to
define "culture," he sets out three conditions for its surviv-
al and growth: (1) an "organic" structure, "such as will
foster the hereditary transmission of culture within a
culture: and this requires the persistence of social classes"[35]; (2) levels within society, both hierarchical and geo-
graphical (i.e., regional); and (3) what in one place he calls
"the balance of unity and diversity in religion—that is,
universality of doctrine with particularity of cult and de-
votion"[36]—and later on explains as a process in which "as
a religion divides into sects, and as these sects develop
from generation to generation, a variety of cultures will be
propagated."[37] This third condition seems vastly less dogmatic than almost anything in the earlier book, and also
considerably vaguer. Eliot is capable, a decade after *The*

Idea of a Christian Society, of formulations like the following:

One need not be a cynic to be amused, or a devotee to be saddened, by the spectacle of the self-deception, as well as the frequent hypocrisy, of the attackers and defenders of one or another form of the Christian Faith. But from the point of view of my essay, both mirth and sorrow are irrelevant, because this confusion is just what one must expect, being inherent in the human condition.[38]

And not only has tolerance and good humor spread thus far, and brought with it a substantially less stuffy prose style, but Eliot now argues—with more aplomb than he argued the opposite point of view a decade before—that religious "reunion facilitated by the disappearance of the cultural characteristics of the several bodies reunited might accelerate and confirm the general lowering of culture."[39] What had not unduly troubled him earlier, now bothers him a good deal; the increased realism of this second book is both marked and salutary. Could one imagine, in *The Idea of a Christian Society,* Eliot going out of his way to praise Leon Trotsky's *Literature and Revolution* as "a book which merits republication"?[40] Is there—I would argue that there is not—a single sentence in *The Idea of a Christian Society* so supple and so sensitive as this one: "Culture can never be wholly conscious—there is always more to it than we are conscious of; *and it cannot be planned because it is also the unconscious background of all our planning.*"[41] (Emphasis added).

Had Eliot gone on from *Notes towards the Definition of Culture,* he might have become something rather like the academic philosopher he started out to be in the early years of this century. He was over sixty when the book appeared: new beginnings of so massive a nature are not frequent at that age. And the parallel with his poetry must again be drawn. Had Eliot been able to continue on with the partially healing direction he took in *Four Quartets,* who can say what poetry he might have been able to write? But just as there are reasons why *Four Quartets* marks an end rather than a beginning—reasons which are not simply matters of Eliot's age: he was after all only in his middle fifties when the last of *Four Quartets* appeared—so too there are non-chronological reasons why the comparative ease and much increased sophistication of *Notes towards the Definition of Culture* could not be pursued. "We all agree about the 'cultural breakdown',"[42] Eliot notes in the final chapter, but he also affirms "that we cannot directly set about to create or improve culture—we can only will the means which are favorable to culture. . . ."[43] And Eliot had, in this as in his poetry, gone as far as "will" could carry him.

9

Eliot's reputation and influence, briefly considered

The *fact* of Eliot's vast reputation and influence is spread wide across the record. If it is a relatively simple matter in the case of many literary figures to separate the writer from the man, and the critical standing ("reputation") from the potency ("influence"), in dealing with Eliot no such compartmentalization makes much sense. He is surely more potent to some poets and critics than to others; his reputation surely varied from one period to another. But for more than half a century, roughly from the publication of *The Waste Land,* Eliot has loomed on the literary horizon like a staple, classic, enduring, and multifold landmark. Whether he is seen as beneficent or malign, whether he is viewed as inspiration or obstacle, he cannot be avoided. Other poets, other critics, must deal with him—and they know perfectly well that if they do not, others will do the job for them, comparing this and that to what Eliot has written, and often evaluating later writers' success or failure by the touchstone of Eliot's performance.

Rather than the fact, or even the extent, of Eliot's pervasiveness, I want to concentrate on the *quality* of that pervasiveness. Consider, for example, John Berryman's essay, "Prufrock's Dilemma," originally published in 1960. After setting out and commenting upon the first two lines of "Prufrock," he quotes the third line, "Like a patient etherised upon a table." And he then ends the first paragraph of his essay with the brief, flat assertion, "With this line, modern poetry begins."[1] It is a dramatic assertion, and a totally deliberate one. But the dramatic force depends on two principal assumptions: (1) that Eliot is of an importance—something like, say, that of Moses delivering the Ten Commandments, or Martin Luther nailing his theses to the Wittenberg church door—which readily justifies high drama, and (2) that his readers agree with him and do not require any convincing. There is no argument: the balance of Berryman's essay is textual exegesis of the poem at issue. In a sense, so large and potent does Eliot seem to him, and by extension to his readers, that Berryman can and does employ Eliot as a sort of symbol, a cultural force of universal validity.

Nor does one need to like or even approve of Eliot to make such stances possible. Martin Seymour-Smith, who is quite clear that "Eliot is a minor poet, . . . the enormous edifice of [whose] authority stands on a pin-point of actual poetic achievement," makes at the same time no bones about the fact that Eliot "is a vitally important influence, . . . [of] enormous extrinsic importance."[2] Even Allen Ginsberg, whose poetry and whose poetic and cultural theories stand in about as direct an opposition to Eliot as it is possible to be, has confessed that, when he is noodling rather than truly writing, he is apt to "look at [what] I wrote and say, 'Ah, my attention was wandering,' or, 'I was thinking about writing like T. S. Eliot'."[3] Or as Edith Sitwell, openly an admirer of Eliot, said in a letter to him, written June 26, 1935: "I have just read the unpublished poems of a young man called Thomas Driberg. They seem to me to show really remarkable promise, and, at moments, achievement. He is very greatly under your influence (though not in form; he needs more shaping). But then, who is not?"[4]

Nor does that pervasiveness stop at national or linguistic boundaries. There are poets, in particular, who seem forever locked into their own languages. The German Georg Trakl, for instance, or (despite many attempts at translation, including, I must admit, a recent volume of my own[5]) the Russian Alexander Pushkin, seem destined never to have elsewhere the great and fructifying effects they have in their own homelands. Eliot's power has reached, like some glowingly compelling beacon, into al-

most all corners of the globe. The greatest poet of modern
Indonesia, Chairil Anwar, not only read but worked hard
to translate Eliot's poetry. The translations are fragmentary, but one can hear, even in a tongue so utterly unlike
English as is Indonesian, that the rhythms and phrasing
of Eliot have been deeply felt and to a considerable extent
recreated.[6] The Nigerian poet, Christopher Okigbo, was
so overwhelmed by Eliot that one needs to talk, in his
early work, of a "thick Eliot flavour," and to say of a poem
that it "smacks of a page from *The Hollow Men.*"[7] The
Nigerian critic, Sunday O. Anozie, says forthrightly that
"for a young poet-aspirant, graduating from the University of Ibadan in the late 1950s, to be modern, elegant and
intellectually difficult, meant not only courting Eliot's poetry but also wooing his prose writing."[8] The quality of
pervasiveness, once again, is every bit as significant as the
fact of it.

Even in the closed system of contemporary Russia,
young poets worship at the shrine. Joseph Brodsky,
refused admission to the Writer's Union, denied the possibility of publishing a book of his own work so long as he
remained in Russia, was so moved by Eliot's death that he
wrote "In Memory of T. S. Eliot," and Russian official-
dom was so keenly aware of Eliot that the journal *Den
Poezii* actually published this poem in the late 1960s.[9] It
was a brave step, for Brodsky was regarded as a criminal,
a socially aberrant vagrant, and was some years later ex-
pelled from Russia as an undesirable. Modern Greek poetry is a different sort of battleground, but a fiercely
contested one, with the possibility of political reprisals,
including jail sentences, never far from poets' minds. And
when George Seferis, lecturing at the British Institute in
Athens in 1946, wanted to convey some notion of the
greatness of Constantine Cavafy, he found no more appropriate method than to link Cavafy with Eliot. There is in

truth not much of a link, as Seferis is himself at pains to point out. Neither man was of any importance, and certainly was of no influence, for the other. But "one can," Seferis maintains, "legitimately speak about a parallel between the works of these poets, . . . as we speak in navigation of places which are on the same parallel and have the same climate, although they are on separate points of the globe."[10] This is pretty far-fetched stuff; the significance of it is the evocative power contained in Eliot's standing, in Athens as elsewhere around the world. As early as 1922, disinterested friends are warning young poets to be wary of that long and potent reach. "Be strong," Edmund Wilson advised John Peale Bishop on December 13 of 1922, "and for heaven's sake do read somebody besides Eliot for a little while—he is enslaving your style and your imagination."[11] Or as the poet and critic Allen Tate bluntly put it:

What I owe to T. S. Eliot is pervasive. . . . The two first lines of 'The Love Song of J. Alfred Prufrock' were the first gun of the twentieth-century revolution: the young Tom Eliot pulled the lanyard and quietly went back to his desk in a London bank. But it was a shot heard round the world. I also owe to Eliot . . . gratitude for furnishing me a model of what the non-academic man of letters ought to be.[12]

No matter that perhaps the fiercest of Eliot's antagonists, Yvor Winters, went straight for the jugular. "T.S. Eliot is probably the most widely respected literary figure of our time; he is known primarily as the leader of the intellectual reaction against the romanticism of which he began his career as a disciple. It is my purpose to show that his intellectualism and his reactionary position are alike an illusion."[13] Many listened to Winters, and surely many agreed. But once a man has attained the heights on which

Eliot stood, dislodging him is the very farthest thing from a rational procedure.

Is Eliot's standing in truth deserved? When we find him being employed as a prophetic symbol, as a political symbol, as a model in his life as well as in his work, the question must I think be asked. Vladimir Nabokov was quite sure that the answer had to be No. "Have been looking through Eliot's various works," he wrote on April 17, 1950, "and reading that collection of critical articles about him and am now more certain than ever that he is a fraud and a fake. . . ."14 Eight years later, when Edmund Wilson had reprinted an essay, "T. S. Eliot and the Church of England," originally published in 1929 as a review of *For Lancelot Andrewes,* Nabokov fairly chortled with delight. The essay, he wrote to Wilson, March 24, 1958, "is one of your very best essays, lucid, acid and wise. I realize you still think a lot of [Eliot] as a poet, and I disagree with you when you say that his verses lodge in one's head (they never did in mine—I always disliked him)—but you have pricked a ripe amber pimple and from now on, Eliot's image will never be the same."15 But for all his shock at Eliot's then-recent conversion, Wilson's essay was the farthest thing from a demolition job. Speaking of Eliot's potency as a literary critic, Wilson says:

T. S. Eliot has now become perhaps the most important literary critic in the English-speaking world. His writings have been brief and few [this was of course written in 1929, and left unchanged], and it is almost incredible that they should have been enough to establish him as an intellectual leader; but when one tries to trace the causes of the change from the point of view of the English criticism of the period before the war to the point of view of our own day, one can find no figure of comparable authority. And we must recognize that Eliot's opinions, so cool and even casual in appearance, yet sped with the force of so intense a seriousness and weighted with so wide a learning, have stuck oftener and sunk deeper in the minds of the post-war generation of both England and the United States than those of any other critic.[16]

Wilson's contemporary, E. E. Cummings, supplies the answer to both Wilson's query and to mine. "Before an Eliot we become alive or intense as we become intense or alive before a Cézanne. . . ."[17] And yet another American poet takes the argument still further. Writing to Gorham Munson, January 5, 1923, Hart Crane expands things in his own terms:

There is no one writing in English who can command so much respect, to my mind, as Eliot. However, I take Eliot as a point of departure toward an almost complete reverse of direction. His pessimism is amply justified, in his own case. But I would apply as much of his erudition and technique as I can absorb and assemble toward a more positive . . . goal. . . . I feel that Eliot ignores certain spiritual events and possibilities as real and powerful now as, say, in the time of Blake. Certainly the man has dug the ground and buried hope as deep and direfully as it can ever be done. He has outclassed Baudelaire with a devastating humor that the earlier poet lacked.[18]

Plainly, no one has ever needed to agree with Eliot in order to recognize his power and his potency. James Atlas, biographer of the poet Delmore Schwartz, offers us yet another instance:

. . . it devolved upon Eliot to become Delmore's model; he was, after all, the quintessential Modernist, and, what was perhaps more significant, he provided an example of the recognition conferred upon those who managed to establish a new poetic idiom. And yet Eliot was, in another sense, the very antithesis of what Delmore thought the poet should be. Authoritarian, dignified, remote, Eliot had achieved a stature that infuriated Delmore even as it filled him with envy . . . Eliot may have explored [his] experience in his poetry, . . . but in Delmore's era he represented the very type of high culture and society; and as

such, he had become the enemy, a 'cultural dictator,' as Delmore
later described him.[19]

It is one of the basic assumptions of this book that no
one needs to see, or to react to, the work of Eliot in any
single perspective. I have been generous, throughout, with
the views of other critics, precisely because they too are an
important part of Eliot's place in our world. I do not think
Eliot a chameleon; most assuredly, I do not think him a
fraud. It should be apparent to anyone who has read this
far that I do not consider Eliot any sort of demi-god,
immune to negative commentary. What I have tried to
recognize, however, is the unusual and profound multiplicity of both the man and his works. If there is nothing
duplicitous about multiplicity, neither is there anything
necessarily useful about it. In Eliot's case, it has been my
argument, multiplicity is part and parcel of what he is
about, as man and as writer. His restlessness, his incom-
pletions, his failures even, all seem to me in this sense
integral. And he seems to me, in Martin Seymour-Smith's
words, "vitally important," precisely because in his multiplicity and his restlessness he embodies so much of what
our century revolves around. He posits the questions that
demand to be asked. One does not need to like his responses to those questions in order to recognize the
searching power of the questions and of the questioner.
Yet another American poet, Louise Bogan, reviewing the
1936 edition of Eliot's *Collected Poems,* puts it so very well
that I want to close with her comments:

Eliot . . . brought back into English poetry the salt and the range
of which it had long been deprived. From Dante through the
Symbolists, he took what he needed from the varied stream of
poetic resources; he swung the balance over from whimpering
Georgian bucolics to forms wherein contemporary complexity

could find expression. The *Collected Poems* are more than a work of poetic creation; they are a work of poetic regeneration.[20]

Notes

Preface

1. I would argue, though it is not directly relevant to this book, that Stevens was far more an intellectual than Eliot ever was. In a way, the two poets stand in relationship to one another much as do Coleridge and Wordsworth. Coleridge, too, was, like Stevens, a true intellectual. Though critics have tended to talk about Wordsworth's "philosophy," he, like Eliot, seems to me much more basically a poet of passion than of ideas.

2. Elisabeth W. Schneider, a first-rate reader and analyst of contemporary poetry (and perhaps the finest critic ever to tackle yet another "difficult" poet, Gerard Manley Hopkins), has only two casual references to "Preludes" in her 1975 study, *T. S. Eliot: The Pattern in the Carpet* (Berkeley: University of California Press). She wonders, in fact, if the sequence actually is "one poem or many?" (p.73). And an even more recent study, Derek Traversi's very detailed discussion of what he terms Eliot's "major works," totally ignores "Preludes," dealing only with *The Waste Land, Ash-Wednesday,* and the *Four Quartets. T. S.*

Eliot: *The Longer Poems* (N.Y.: Harcourt, Brace, Jovanovich, 1976).
3. See note 2, above.

Chapter One: "Preludes"

1. The standard dating has been 1915: see e.g. George Williamson, *A Reader's Guide to T. S. Eliot* (N.Y.: Noonday
paperback, 1953), p.79. The sequence was first printed in
Blast No.2, edited by Wyndham Lewis in 1915, which
probably accounts for the 1915 dating. Hugh Kenner,
however, dates the first two poems in the sequence from
"Harvard in 1909–1910, just after *Conversation Galante*
and a little before *Portrait of a Lady*," the third poem from
"a year later in Paris," and the fourth poem from "Harvard, 1911." Hugh Kenner, *The Invisible Poet: T. S. Eliot*
(N.Y.: Harbinger paperback [Harcourt, Brace], 1959),
pp.33-34. Grover Smith, who also notes that "neither Eliot
himself . . . nor anyone else seems to know precisely in
what sequence the poems of 1915–19 were written, or, for
that matter, those of 1909–11," agrees with Kenner's dating. Grover Smith, *T. S. Eliot's Poetry and Plays: A Study
in Sources and Meaning* (Chicago: Phoenix paperback
[Univ. of Chicago Press], 1956), pp.vii, 20, Georges Cattaui dates the poems from "about 1910, in Harvard or
Paris. . . ." Georges Cattaui, *T. S. Eliot* (N.Y.: Funk &
Wagnalls, 1968), p.28. Dating of "Preludes" is on the
whole fudged in Herbert Howarth *Notes on Some Figures
Behind T. S. Eliot* (Boston: Houghton, Mifflin, 1964), and
the evidence offered by both poems and footnotes in *T.S.
Eliot, Poems Written in Early Youth* (London: Faber and
Faber, 1967), seems to me to indicate that some fudging,
at least, may be in order. Some of the poems unquestionably dating from 1909 and 1910, that is, may be suggestive
of an inability in those years for Eliot to write anything so
complex as "Preludes." Let me, however, close this brief
discussion by quoting the distinguished and generally in-

fallible bibliographer, Donald Gallup, to the effect that "Preludes" were "written 1910–1911." Donald Gallup, "T. S. Eliot and Ezra Pound: Collaborators in Letters," *The Atlantic,* January 1970, p.50.

2. Schneider, p.73. Smith points out, perhaps a bit grudgingly, that they "are better unified than Eliot's method of composing them might seem to have permitted." Smith, p.21. This observation seems to me to ignore both the fact that Eliot habitually composed his poems in segments, often publishing those segments under titles which, in the event, were dropped in favor of the title by which we now know the larger structure, and also to ignore what I take to be the indisputable fact that methods of composition frequently have little or nothing to do with the final product of composition.

3. Smith, pp.20–23. The two novels cited from, and quoted by, Smith are *Barbu de Montparnasse,* for which Eliot wrote a preface when it was published in English translation in 1932, and *Marie Donadieu.*

4. It is of course legendary that contemporary readers who mistook poems like "The Hippopotamus" (1917) for anticlerical manifestoes were, in short order, proven totally in error. But is it after all surprising to find that Eliot takes the trouble to criticize that which deeply concerns him, · that for which he wishes to feel more affection and loyalty than the current situation permits him to feel? The same, I submit, is true of "Preludes."

5. It must be said that the separation / heightening—here and also with the poem's final three-line segment—is delicately assisted by the paragraphlike indentation of the first line in the segment. The rhetorical effect, further, is assisted both by the comma after "images," which comma enforces a kind of caesura, and also by the absence of a comma after "gentle," which lack of punctuation seems to me to emphasize the continuity and necessary identity of "infinitely gentle" and "infinitely suffering." I do not want to make too much of effects like these, but as a poet and

teacher of poets I find it impossible to pass over them in silence.

6. "But unlike Cassirer, the philosopher, Mr. Eliot retains a hint of the Tree on the top of Mount Purgatory, half-remembered, half-forgotten, a hint of the mystery of love which is at the heart of creation: *The notion of some infinitely gentle / Infinitely suffering thing.*" Genesius Jones, O.F.M., *Approach to the Purpose: A Study of the Poetry of T. S. Eliot* (New York: Barnes & Noble, 1965), pp.80–81.

7. Readers of "Preludes" have often been unattentive to the text in front of them, let alone to its significance in any larger context. Lyndall Gordon, *Eliot's Early Years* (Oxford: Oxford University Press, 1977), e.g., not only speaks of the third poem in the sequence as offering us "rather improbable thoughts," but ascribes those thoughts to "a grimy *woman* . . . [who] lies on her back in a poor suburb of Boston, staring at the ceiling, where she projects 'a thousand sordid images' from her miserable mind . . ." Gordon, p.45; italics added. So rigorous and perceptive a critic as Hugh Kenner can dismiss the poem as presenting "sensate fact just stirring toward a unity chiefly pictorial . . . the meaning of *Preludes* is expressly that the natural object is nothing of the kind." Kenner, pp.33, 35. We hear from other critics that "Preludes" is "written in a tone of jaded cynicism and mild regret" (Donald Barlow Stauffer, *A Short History of American Poetry* [N.Y.: Dutton paperback,1974], p.267), or that "In *Preludes,* written about 1910, Eliot constantly evokes the tedium of Puritan provincial life, the gloom of the winter evening . . ." Cattaui, p.5. Grover Smith, who like Lyndall Gordon misses entirely the deliberately unfixed gender of the human creature in the third poem of the sequence, goes off into an odd fantasy about "both woman and street [as] individual substances, so that each peculiarly registers the images they share. . . . Woman and street alike are earthbound: she supine in bed, 'he' trampled under foot . . ."—and so on. Smith, p.22. So fine a critic as Elizabeth Drew, indeed, can assert flatly —and as we have seen, erroneously—that in Eliot's first

volume "*Prufrock* is the only poem in which a conflict
between contemporary isolation, disintegration and sterility is even hinted at . . ." Elizabeth Drew, *T. S. Eliot: The
Design of His Poetry* (New York: Scribner's, 1949), p.37.
Not many critics have seen, as Bernard Bergonzi nicely
puts it, that " 'Preludes' contain some of the most memorable epiphanies of urban experience in English. . . ." Bernard Bergonzi, *T. S. Eliot* (New York: Macmillan, 1972),
p.20.

The point of this overlong footnote is that Eliot's work
has frequently seduced critics into varieties of inebriate
delirium. This book will not deal much with those deliri-
ums, but I think their existence needs to be at least pointed
out, if only in so subterranean a style as footnote debate of
this sort. Hopefully, almost a hundred years after Eliot's
birth, we can finally begin to practice what Matthew Arnold, dead in the year in which Eliot was born, so zealously
advocated, namely "To press to the sense of the thing itself
with which one is dealing, [and] not to go off on some
collateral issue about the thing. . . ." Matthew Arnold, *On
Translating Homer* (London: John Murray, 1896), p.116.

*Chapter Two: From St. Louis to London: Prufrock to
"Geronition"*

1. T. S. Eliot, *Notes towards the definition of culture,* in T.S.
   Eliot, *Christianity and Culture* (N.Y.: Harcourt, Brace
   paperback, 1968), p.115.
2. Memorandum dated September 30, 1963 and attached to,
   but not proved with, Eliot's will. Donald Adamson, "Fore-
   word," in Robert Sencourt, *T. S. Eliot: A Memoir* (London: Garnstone Press, 1971), p.13 n.4.
3. In her Introduction to the facsimile edition of *The Waste
   Land* manuscript, Valerie Eliot, the poet's widow, quotes
   from a good many letters, and surely there are many many
   more. (John D. Margolis spoke in 1972 of "the forthcom-
   ing edition of his letters [edited] by Mrs. T. S. Eliot." John

D. Margolis, *T. S. Eliot's Intellectual Development, 1922–1939* [Chicago: University of Chicago Press, 1972], p.xv.) See T. S. Eliot, *The Waste Land: A Facsimile and Transcript of the Original Drafts* . . . (London: Faber and Faber, 1971).

4. Howarth, p.10. The fullest source of information on Eliot's family and background remains Howarth's sometimes rambling but always fascinating book.
5. Howarth, p.19.
6. Gordon, pp.8, 9.
7. Howarth, pp.33, 30.
8. Gordon, p.4.
9. Gordon, p.3.
10. Howarth, p.33.
11. Gordon, p.2; Howarth, p.33.
12. Stephen Spender, *T. S. Eliot* (N.Y.: Penguin paperback, 1975), pp.46–47.
13. Gordon, pp.6, 7.
14. T. S. Eliot, *Knowledge and Experience in the Philosophy of F. H. Bradley* (N.Y.: Farrar, Straus, 1964).
15. Gordon, p.74.
16. Spender, p.49. "Eliot believed she was sane, but that she talked herself into an unbalanced state." Gordon, p.80.
17. Spender, p.49. In an essay, "Beyle and Balzac," published in May 1919, Eliot mightily praised these two French novelists for the way they "suggest unmistakeably the awful separation between potential passion and any actualization possible in life . . . They indicate also the indestructible barriers between one human being and another." Quoted in David Ward, *T. S. Eliot Between Two Worlds* (London: Routledge & Kegan Paul, 1973), p.16.
18. Spender, pp.46–47.
19. Spender, p.48. Kenner, p.76, notes that after 1916 and "for the next ten years this at first involuntary expatriate was condemned to labor at no profession in particular under constant strain."
20. "One of Eliot's friends, Mary Hutchinson, who read *The Waste Land* soon after its completion, said it was 'Tom's

autobiography.' Eliot himself said it was only 'the relief of a personal . . . grouse against life'." Gordon, p.86.

21. F. V. Morley, "T. S. Eliot as a Publisher," in *T. S. Eliot,* ed. Richard March and Tambimuttu, (London: Editions Poetry, 1948), p.61.

22. Kathleen Raine, "The Poet of Our Time," in March and Tambimuttu, p.78. Miss Raine's generation was precisely twenty years later than Eliot's: she was born in 1908.

23. E. R. Curtius, *Essays on European Literature* (Princeton: Princeton University Press, 1973), p.371. Curtius translated *The Waste Land* into German. Note too, as an Australian critic has written, that "It is certain that Eliot's prose made people sooner aware that he was a man to be taken seriously than would have been the case had he written only poetry." C. K. Stead, *The New Poetic: Yeats to Eliot* (Harmondsworth: Penguin paperback, 1967), pp.115–116.

24. Gordon, p.18.

25. Gordon, pp.38, 40.

26. Gordon, p.71.

27. Gordon, pp.122, 132.

28. Gordon, pp.134, 138, 139.

29. F. O. Matthiessen, *The Achievement of T. S. Eliot* (N.Y.: Oxford University Press paperback, 1959), p.104. Matthiessen's pioneering study was first published in 1935.

30. Kenner, p.3.

31. Eliot's image is both the ultimate source and, to my mind, the superior of Hart Crane's almost equally famous, "Love [is] / a burnt match skating in a urinal . . ." Part VII, "The Tunnel," of Crane's long poem, *The Bridge* (1930).

32. The best discussions of the influences on Eliot are by Kenner (especially pp.13–69) and Howarth. See also the superbly balanced general discussion in Margolis. And there is an interesting chapter, "Landscape as Symbol in Eliot, Tennyson, and Baudelaire," in Nancy Duvall Hargrove, *Landscape as Symbol in the Poetry of T. S. Eliot* (Jackson: University of Mississippi Press, 1978).

33. *The Letters of Ezra Pound, 1907–1941,* ed. **D. D.** Paige (N.Y.: Harcourt, Brace paperback, 1950), p.40.

34. *Letters,* p.50.

35. *Letters,* pp.44-45.

36. Schneider, p.28. She adds, in a footnote: "A trivial detail, but one that has led to some comically ingenious interpretations. Robert Llewellyn solved the difficulty some years ago in the *Explicator.*"

37. Hargrove, p.48.

38. Conrad Aiken, "King Bolo and Others," in March and Tambimuttu, pp.21–22.

39. Although Eliot is a vastly greater poet than is Ezra Pound, Pound's poem, "Portrait d'une Femme" [i.e., Portrait of a Lady], written at about the same time as Eliot's identically titled poem, is to my mind very much superior.

40. Genesius Jones, p.230.

41. Smith, p.33.

42. Helen Gardner, who makes much of Eliot's metrics, states flatly, and totally erroneously, that "Gerontion" is in "blank verse." Helen Gardner, *The Art of T. S. Eliot* (London: Cresset, 1949), p.18.

43. It may be worth noting, as some measure of Eliot's continuing influence and quotability, that the title of my own 1982 novel, *After Such Ignorance,* is a blatantly parodistic reference to this line.

44. T. S. Eliot, *After Strange Gods* (N.Y.: Harcourt, Brace, 1934), pp.19–20. The book's subtitle is "A Primer of Modern Heresy." As Spender, p. 149, notes revealingly, "after [its] first publication, he never allowed [*After Strange Gods*] to be reissued."

45. All the same, it *was* taken literally. "And I am made a little tired at hearing Eliot, only in his early forties, present himself as an 'agèd eagle' who asks why he should make the effort to stretch his wings." Edmund Wilson, *Axel's Castle* (N.Y.: Scribner's, 1931), p.13.

46. Drew, p.47.

47. Spender, pp.48–49.

48. Margolis, p.12.

49.   Bergonzi, p.37.
50.   F. V. Morley, in March and Tambimuttu, p.60.
51.   Donald Davie, "Anglican Eliot," in *Eliot in His Time*, ed. A. Walton Litz (Princeton: Princeton University Press, 1973), p.182.
52.   Clive Bell, "How Pleasant to Know Mr. Eliot," in March and Tambimuttu, p.18. See also Conrad Aiken, "King Bolo and Others," in the same volume, pp.20–23, and Elizabeth Sewell, "Lewis Carroll and T. S. Eliot as Nonsense Poets," in *T.S. Eliot*, ed. Neville Braybrooke (N.Y.: Farrar, Straus & Cudahy, 1958), pp.49–56.
53.   Margolis, p.3.
54.   Genesius Jones, p.98 n.1. Sir Edmund Gosse, who introduced Eliot and others at a wartime poetry reading in 1917, "was rather shocked by . . . the blasphemous 'Hippopotamus' . . ." Gordon, p.85.
55.   Facsimile *Waste Land*, pp.x, xi. He had earlier in the letter to his brother indicated that, though his wife wanted him to continue in the manner of "Prufrock," "I often feel that [it] is a swan-song."
56.   Smith, p.45.
57.   Burton Raffel, *"The Waste Land:* A Common Sense Exegesis," *Yes,* December 1964 [unpaginated], n.12.
58.   Williamson, p.98.
59.   Facsimile *Waste Land*, p.1.
60.   Letter to Henry Eliot, February 15, 1920, quoted in facsimile *Waste Land*, p.xviii.
61.   Kenner, p.87.
62.   Smith, p.45.
63.   Bergonzi, p.50.
64.   F. W. Bateson, "The Poetry of Learning," in *Eliot in Perspective*, ed. Graham Martin (N.Y.: Humanities Press, 1970), p.36.
65.   Ward, p.31.
66.   Spender, pp.54, 53.
67.   Spender, p.55.
68.   Cattaui, p.41.

69. David Perkins, *A History of Modern Poetry* (Cambridge: Harvard University Press paperback, 1979), p.497.
70. Curtius, p.359.
71. For a close exegesis see, *inter alia,* Kenner, pp.87–88, or Smith, pp.43–45.
72. See facsimile *Waste Land,* p.xviii.
73. Williamson, p.106. I must confess that my own copy of Eliot's *Collected Poems* bears, in the margin next to "A Cooking Egg," the following comment: "Who is Pipit? nurse? little girl? bride and spiritual guide? who cares?"
74. Quoted from Margolis, p.xi.
75. Margolis, p.13.

Chapter Three: The Waste Land

1. Facsimile *Waste Land,* p.xxii. Donald Gallup indicates, in the *Atlantic* essay referred to earlier, that in fact Pound had "finally put the manuscript for a book of Eliot's poems into shape, and sent it off to [the publisher] Alfred Knopf in early September, 1918." Gallup, p.53. Indeed, though details are lacking, it is apparent that Pound also had a hand in Eliot's first marriage. Writes Valerie Eliot: "Pound encouraged [Eliot] to settle [in England], and to marry an Englishwoman, Vivien[ne] Haigh-Wood, which he did . . ." Facsimile *Waste Land,* p.ix.
2. Pound, *Letters,* p.171.
3. Pound, *Letters,* p.169.
4. Pound, *Letters,* p.170.
5. Gallup, p.54.
6. *Letters,* p.180. He had written earlier, that Eliot's "*Waste Land* [was] a series of poems, possibly the finest that the modern movement in English has produced, at any rate as good as anything that has been done since 1900 . . ." *Letters,* p.175, n.1. Pound was remarkable both for his ᴜnthusiasm and generosity and also for his ready ability to talk himself into (and out of) virtually any position.
7. Gallup, p.54.

210   *T. S. Eliot*

8. Gallup, p.59.

9. Gallup, p.60.

10. See T. S. Eliot, "William Blake," in *Selected Essays of T. S. Eliot* (N.Y.: Harcourt, Brace, 1960), pp.275–280. The essay was written in 1920.

11. See *Blake's Complete Writings,* ed. Geoffrey Keynes (London: Oxford University Press, 1972), pp.172–173, 214, and 214 n.1.

12. Unpaginated note on "Editorial Policy," facsimile *Waste Land.*

13. Helen Vendler, *Part of Nature, Part of Us* (Cambridge: Harvard University Press, 1980), p.85. "*The Waste Land* is about sexual failure as a sign of spiritual failure." Robert Langbaum, in Litz, p.113.

14. This is Eliot's 1928 recollection of Pound's comments, which I quote from facsimile *Waste Land,* p.127 col. 1, n.1, which is headed "This . . . passage was written in imitation of *The Rape of the Lock.*"

15. Quoted by Vendler, p.85. Jarrell's comments were written in 1963 and are cited with approval, also, by James E. Miller, Jr., *T. S. Eliot's Personal Waste Land* (University Park: University of Pennsylvania Press, 1977), pp.45–46.

16. Facsimile *Waste Land,* p.127, col.1 n.3.

17. Facsimile *Waste Land,* p.127, col.2 n.2, and p.128, col.1.

18. Facsimile *Waste Land,* p.127, col.2 n.1.

19. Facsimile *Waste Land,* p.37, prints a singularly heavily worked-over version, again in pencil, of this same passage, and there is yet another version printed on p.43, this time in typed form. Plainly, it meant a good deal to Eliot and he struggled mightily both to perfect and to find a place in the poem for it. I for one rather regret that he did not in the end succeed. These fifteen lines are perhaps the finest, all in all, of the many canceled from the poem as printed.

20. It is worth noting that, in his translation of the Old English "Seafarer," Pound not only suppresses the prayer at the end of the poem, but quite ruthlessly transforms any and every religious reference to a secular one, throughout the portion of the poem which he does translate. These are not

casual matters. Nor, on the evidence, did Pound take them
casually.

21. Facsimile *Waste Land,* p.55 n.
22. Kenner, pp.147–48.
23. Gallup, p.53; Margolis, p.13 n.13.
24. Kenner, p.149.
25. Spender, p.94.
26. Sencourt, pp.88–89.
27. Spender, p.94.
28. See facsimile *Waste Land,* p.63 n.
29. Facsimile *Waste Land,* p.129, col.1 n.2 (to text page 71).
30. Facsimile *Waste Land,* p.129, col.2 n.1 (to text page 95).
31. *Letters,* p.169.
32. *Letters,* p.169.
33. *Letters,* p.169.
34. Helen Vendler calls it "repellent" and I do not think it possible to disagree. Vendler, p.82.
35. *The Waste Land: A Collection of Critical Essays,* ed. Jay Martin (Englewood Cliffs: Prentice-Hall paperback, 1968), p.5.
36. John Press, *A Map of Modern English Verse* (London: Oxford University Press, 1969), p.73.
37. Robert Langbaum, in Litz, p.95.
38. Richard Ellmann, in Litz, p.51.
39. Stephen Spender, "The Dilemma of the Modern Poet in a Modern World," *New York Times Book Review,* January 4, 1948.
40. See e.g. Kenner, pp.150–152.
41. Perkins, pp.499, 501.
42. Vendler, p.77.
43. Edmund Wilson, pp.113–114.
44. Quoted in Miller, p. 9. Mr. Miller argues, along with a very small group of other critics, that Jean Verdenal, killed in World War I, and to whom Eliot dedicated *Prufrock and Other Observations,* was at the center of a distinct homosexual strand in Eliot's makeup. Mr. Miller goes a good deal farther than this: I do not myself find the argument persuasive, and therefore will not take it up here.

45. Ezra Pound, *Personae* (New York: New Directions, 1926), p.191.

46. See Gordon, pp.107–108. It seems not to have been much noted, but Eliot was apparently enough of a pianist, early on, to "tackle Beethoven sonatas." Sencourt, p.52.

47. Gordon, p.109. Miss Gordon goes on to assert, I think very fairly, that "Pound effectively blocked, at several points, Eliot's impulse to exhibit the whole truth—the strength as well as the sickness of a suffering soul." Gordon, p.117.

48. In Pound's work between 1915 and 1920, notes Perkins, "he adopted for the first time the extraordinarily compressed, oblique, learned, elliptical, allusive style that still baffles most readers." Perkins, p.473.

49. Raffel, *Yes,* unpaginated.

50. I cannot accept Robert Langbaum's suggestion that "the poem's awareness makes us remember consciously what the protagonist, in recalling the Hyacinth garden, remembers unconsciously—that Hyacinth was a fertility god." In Litz, p.101. It seems to me that at this point we have left the realm of poetry and entered the kingdom of scholarship, and I think it is seriously erroneous to thus confuse two such different approaches.

51. "For an instant he held the principles of lost or potential order and actual disorder in balanced, violent antipathy . . . He was imbued with a sense of discordant gestural rhythm, partly intuitive, partly derived from recent music, ballet, and cinema (Stravinsky and Massine); and he had newly looked into the great primitive phantasmagoria revealed by the Cambridge anthropologists . . ." Robert M. Adams, in Litz, p.145.

52. In Litz, p.125.

53. In Litz, p.124.

54. Hargrove, p.61.

55. Cleanth Brooks, "*The Waste Land:* An Analysis," in *T. S. Eliot: A Study of His Writings By Several Hands,* ed. B. Rajan (New York: Haskell House, 1964), p.14.

56. Kenner, p.161.

57. Such lines as "My nerves are bad to-night. . . . Speak to

me," have been frequently and probably correctly associated with Vivienne Eliot.

58. There is in fact a jazz-age song entitled "Shakespearian
Rag." Elisabeth Schneider acknowledges the man in "the
Library of Congress's Music Division, who with the sheet
music in front of him sang part of that rag to me over the
long distance telephone." Schneider, p.ix.

59. In Litz, p.136 and n.8.

60. Spender, p.111.

61. Vendler, p.81.

62. See, e.g., Eliot's essay on "Marie Lloyd," written at just
about this same time (1923). It is reprinted in his *Selected
Essays*, pp.405–408, and displays an intense if unsentimen-
tal appreciation of this and of other music-hall performers.
See also Bergonzi, pp.100–101.

63. Ian Hamilton, in Martin, p.104.

64. Introductory paragraph to Eliot's own *Waste Land*
"Notes."

65. Smith, pp.86–87.

66. Hugh Kenner's *The Invisible Poet* is one of the very best
books yet written on Eliot, but he too succumbs at times
to this sort of esotericism. "Part three, *The Fire Sermon*,
the most explicit of the five sections, surveys with grave
denunciatory candor a world of automatic lust, in which
those barriers between person and person which so troubled Prufrock are dissolved by the suppression of the person and the transposition of all human needs and desires
to a plane of genital gratification." And about the opening
lines in particular, which I have here called portentous,
Kenner writes that "The 'tent', now broken would have
been composed of the overarching trees that transformed
a reach of the river into a tunnel of love; the phrase beck-
ons to mind the broken maidenhead; and a line later the
gone harmonious order, by a half-realizable metamorpho-
sis, struggles an instant against drowning." Kenner,
pp.164, 165.

67. Smith, pp.69–70, 71.

68. Drew, p.82.

69.   Kenner, p.172.
70.   Facsimile *Waste Land,* p.130, col.2 n. to text page 113.
71.   Williamson, p.149. Smith reports, more compellingly, that
      Eliot attributed these lines in part to "a painting from the
      school of Hieronymous Bosch." Smith, p.95. The informa-
      tion is, I admit, interesting, but I do not think it either does
      help, or can help, the *poem.*
72.   At Harvard Eliot studied both Sanskrit and Eastern
      philosophy. Gordon, p.57. Howarth, who discusses Eliot's
      Oriental studies, pp.199–209, indicates that it was a two-
      year course of study. "He became rather mystical," says
      Spender, during his Oriental studies, "though distrusting
      this tendency in himself. But Buddhism remained a life-
      long influence in his work and at the time when he was
      writing *The Waste Land* he almost became a Buddhist
      . . ." Spender, p.20. But Spender immediately adds, "or so
      I once heard him tell the Chilean poet Gabriele [sic] Mis-
      tral, who was herself a Buddhist." Eliot was capable of
      extravagant politeness: I think the context of his remark
      about becoming a Buddhist, as thus explained, makes it
      considerably less literal and serious.
73.   See Isaiah 38:1: "Set thine house in order: for thou shalt
      die, and not live."
74.   Ward, p.91.

Chapter Four: The road to religion

1.   Quoted in Gordon, p.117.
2.   *The Waste Land: A Collection of Critical Essays,* p.13.
3.   Gordon, p.124. See, generally, B. L. Reid, *The Man From
     New York: John Quinn and His Friends* (N.Y.: Oxford
     University Press, 1968).
4.   Spender records not only Eliot's belief at the time, "that
     Western civilization was confronted by impending ruin,"
     but also a remark in 1929, that Eliot expected "internecine
     warfare," by which he explicitly meant "People killing one
     another in the streets." Spender, pp.119–120.

5. *"The Hollow Men* is a kind of coda to *The Waste Land."* Spender, p.123.
6. Facsimile *Waste Land,* p.xxv.
7. Gordon, pp.63, 122.
8. Gordon, p.130.
9. Gordon, p.120.
10. Smith, p.114.
11. Carol H. Smith, *T. S. Eliot's Dramatic Theory and Practice* (Princeton: Princeton University Press, 1963), p.13. Mrs. Smith also believes that "Eliot is first and last a religious poet." p.viii. See E. Martin Browne's explanation for not including *Sweeney Agonistes* in his *The Making of T. S. Eliot's Plays* (Cambridge: Cambridge University Press, 1969): ". . . though I believe that some of the experiments made in the *Sweeney* fragments would have enriched his playwrighting had they been followed up, . . . only traces of them can be discerned in the later plays." p.x.
12. Arnold Bennett, *The Journals* (Harmondsworth: Penguin paperback, 1971), pp.482–483. Eliot later told Hallie Flanagan that "I had intended the whole play to be accompanied by light drum taps to accentuate the beats . . ." Quoted by Carol Smith, p.52. This sort of experiment was, of course, in no way original to Eliot, Eugene O'Neill having used the drum accompaniment more thoroughly, and more effectively, in *The Emperor Jones,* first produced in 1920 and published in 1921.
13. Bennett, p.505.
14. David E. Jones, *The Plays of T. S. Eliot* (Toronto: University of Toronto Press, 1960), p.36.
15. Gardner, p.132.
16. Carol Smith, p.51.
17. Quoted by Carol Smith, p.53 n.28.
18. ". . . the author of *Ash-Wednesday* is a Christian while the author of *The Waste Land* was not." Gardner, p.103.
19. T. S. Eliot, *For Lancelot Andrewes* (London: Faber and Gwyer, 1928), p.ix.
20. Kenner, pp.242 ff.
21. Bergonzi, p.136.

22. Smith, p.128.
23. Harvey Gross, *Sound and Form in Modern Poetry* (Ann Arbor: University of Michigan Press, 1965), p.169.
24. *The Diary of Virginia Woolf,* vol. 2 (N.Y.: Harcourt, Brace, Jovanovich, 1978), p.178.
25. Cited from Eliot's essay on Andrewes, *Selected Essays,* p.307. The passage is also quoted by Matthiessen, p.197 n.9, who introduces it with the remark that "How prose may be transformed into poetry is illustrated by the comparison . . ."
26. *Selected Essays,* pp.299, 303, 305.
27. *Selected Essays,* pp.308–309.
28. Matthiessen, p.92. Matthiessen notes, accurately, that "to an even greater extent than most poets, Eliot has been sensitively responsive to the rhythms of other writers." See pp.93 ff.
29. Luke 2:25–26.
30. Mario Praz, *The Flaming Heart* (Garden City: Doubleday Anchor paperback, 1958), p.364.
31. Smith, p.127.
32. Genesius Jones, p.268 n.1.
33. Genesius Jones, p.241.
34. *Selected Essays,* pp.218–219.
35. *The Letters of Virginia Woolf,* vol. 3 (N.Y.: Harcourt, Brace, Jovanovich, 1977), pp.457–458.
36. Letter dated February 7, 1928, to Clive Bell, p.455.
37. E. M. Forster, *Abinger Harvest* (London: Edwin Arnold, 1965), p.112.
38. Martin Jarrett-Kerr, in Martin, p.233.
39. *Axel's Castle,* p.126.
40. Thomas McGreevy, *Thomas Stearns Eliot* (N.Y.: Haskell House, 1971 [first published 1931]), p.68.
41. R. P. Blackmur, *Form and Value in Modern Poetry* (Garden City: Doubleday Anchor paperback, 1957), pp.135, 136.
42. Traversi, p.58.
43. Drew, pp.100-101.
44. Genesius Jones, p.111. See also the admirably objective

discussion in Ward, pp.148–163. Matthiessen's discussion, *passim,* is also finely unprejudiced one way or the other.

45. Spender, p.130.
46. Smith, p.144.
47. Gardner, p.122.
48. Howarth, p.294. See also T. S. Eliot, *On Poetry and Poets* (N.Y.: Noonday paperback, 1961), p.98: "I seemed to myself to have exhausted my meagre poetic gifts, and to have nothing more to say."
49. McGreevy, p.1.
50. Smith, p.130.
51. Ward, p.171.

Chapter Five: Last poems and partial recovery

1. Vendler, p.82.
2. Vendler, pp.81–82.
3. Bateson, in Martin, p.43. Bateson finds only one worthwhile passage in any of the four poems, "the half-translation from Mallarmé in the beautiful Dantesque episode in 'Little Gidding'."
4. In Litz, pp.192, 195, 194, and 195 (again). Davie's fierce attack on the third poem in the cycle, *The Dry Salvages,* should be noted here, though I will not discuss it until later in this chapter: *T. S. Eliot: A Collection of Critical Essays,* ed. Hugh Kenner (Englewood Cliffs: Prentice-Hall paperback, 1962), pp.192–205.
5. Hargrove, pp.131, 184, 206.
6. Gardner, p.2.
7. Drew, p.144.
8. In Rajan, p.95. Father Genesius Jones, similarly, claims that "The only long poem in Modern English which is comparable with *Four Quartets* in organic complexity is [Spenser's] *The Faerie Queen.* . . . Once removed from the light of Milton's biography, *[Paradise Lost]* does not have the organic meaning which is to be found in *The Faerie Queen;* and structurally it is so uncertain that argument

218 T. S. Eliot

still rages over its central theme. . . . *Four Quartets* tackles
the task that was mooted in *The Faerie Queen* and brings
it off triumphantly." Genesius Jones, pp.321–322.
9. Bergonzi, p.163.
10. Stead, p.178.
11. Helen Gardner, *The Composition of* Four Quartets (N.Y.:
Oxford University Press, 1978).
12. Spender, p.167.
13. Ward, p.233.
14. "The requirements for reading [Ezra Pound's] *Cantos* are
as modern as the poem itself: one would do well to read
the *Cantos* with a home computer terminal plugged in by
one's side, programmed with large chunks of civilization's
economic, political, philosophical, and literary history,
able to translate simultaneously from as many classical and
contemporary languages as possible." Richard Hamasaki,
"The *Cantos* of Ezra Pound: East vs. West," *Hawaii Review,* Spring / Fall 1980, p.173. This seems to me funda-
mentally to confuse poetry and crossword puzzles, and I
for one reject any such identification out of hand.
15. Kenner, p.297.
16. Schneider, pp.180–181.
17. See e.g. Gardner, pp.29 ff.
18. Spender, p.158.
19. Schneider, p.181.
20. Kenner, pp.296–297. On the seasonal identification, see
Eliot's letter to Hayward, August 5, 1941, quoted in *Composition of* Four Quartets, p.29: " 'Autumn weather' only
because it *was* autumn weather . . ."
21. Traversi, p.93.
22. Cattaui, pp.62–63.
23. Drew, p.205.
24. Rajan, in Rajan, p.78.
25. *Composition of* Four Quartets, p.15.
26. *Composition of* Four Quartets, pp.5, 16.
27. *Composition of* Four Quartets, p.18. Interestingly, Eliot
wrote to Hayward, September 3, 1942, that the overall
"title I have always had in mind . . . was KENSINGTON

QUARTETS. I have had a fancy to have Kensington [where he had lived in the 1930s] in it." *Composition of Four Quartets*, p.26.

28. Kenner, p.301.
29. Eliot of course acknowledged Whitman very openly in his 1953 address, "American Literature and the American Language," reprinted in T. S. Eliot, *To Criticize the Critic* (London: Faber and Faber, 1965), pp.43–60. But poetry is not criticism.
30. Roy Harvey Pearce, *The Continuity of American Poetry* (Princeton: Princeton University Press paperback, 1967), p.303. Pearce refers to a book I have never seen, S. Musgrove, *T. S. Eliot and Walt Whitman,* published in New Zealand in 1952.
31. Hyatt H. Waggoner, *American Poets From the Puritans to the Present* (N.Y.: Delta paperback, 1968), p.418.
32. *To Criticize the Critic,* p.54. For Eliot's essay on *Huckleberry Finn,* see Kenneth S. Lynn, ed., *Huckleberry Finn: Text, Sources, and Criticism* (N.Y.: Harcourt, Brace paperback, 1961), pp.198–202.
33. See note 4, above.
34. Stead, p.179.
35. Stead, p.179.
36. Kristian Smidt, *Poetry and Belief in the Work of T. S. Eliot* (N.Y.: Humanities Press, 1961), p.179.
37. *Composition of* Four Quartets, p.28.
38. Spender, p.179.
39. Bergonzi, pp.171–172.
40. *To Criticize the Critic,* p.129.
41. *Composition of* Four Quartets, p.8. It seems to have been Ezra Pound who gave Eliot the "Possum" nickname: William Turner Levy and Victor Scherle, *Affectionately, T. S. Eliot* (Philadelphia: Lippincott, 1968), p.29.
42. In March and Tambimuttu, p.22.
43. *Composition of* Four Quartets, p.7.
44. Bergonzi, p.31; see also Gordon, p.54.
45. Smith, pp.33–34.
46. In Braybrooke, p.163.

47. Kenner, p.339.
48. Letter dated December 14, 1953, in Levy and Scherle, pp.46–47.
49. In *The Waste Land: A Collection of Critical Essays,* pp.10–11.

Chapter Six: *From the Middle Ages to Broadway*

1.   Sencourt, p.67.
2.   *The Waste Land: A Collection of Essays,* p.7. Eliot once said, of *The Invisible Poet,* Hugh Kenner's book on his work, that "I especially like the title of Kenner's book . . . it's very appropriate." Levy and Scherle, p.105.
3.   In March and Tambimuttu, p.196.
4.   In Braybrooke, pp.73, 77.
5.   In Braybrooke, p.175. Hugh Kenner speaks of Eliot "contriving plays." Kenner, p.327.
6.   Anton Chekhov, *Uncle Vanya,* in *Chekhov: The Major Plays,* trans. Ann Dunnigan (N.Y.: Signet paperback, 1964), p.204. According to E. Martin Browne, Chekhov was one of the playwrights most carefully studied by Eliot: "Chekhov [was] a notable modern influence." Browne also lists as major influences the Greeks, Shakespeare, and the Bible. In March and Tambimuttu, pp.196–197.
7.   Speaight, in Braybrooke, p.78. The commercial theatre paid Eliot very well indeed: see, e.g., Browne, *The Making of T. S. Eliot's Plays,* p.247.
8.   Ashley Dukes, in March and Tambimuttu, p.111.
9.   See Arthur and Barbara Gelb, *O'Neill* (N.Y.: Dell paperback, 1965). Portions of *Marco Millions* (1927) are in verse, though O'Neill was strongly opposed to "heavy blank verse [and] soggy symbolism . . ." Letter to George Jean Nathan [1920?], quoted in Gelb and Gelb, p.220.
10. Browne, in Braybrooke, p.57.
11. Browne, *The Making of T. S. Eliot's Plays,* p.6.
12. T. S. Eliot, *The Rock* ["book of words by T. S. Eliot"]

(London: Faber and Faber, 1934), unpaginated "Prefatory Note."

13. Quoted in Jones, p.39.
14. *On Poetry and Poets,* p.84.
15. *On Poetry and Poets,* pp.86–87. And "it was also Ashley Dukes," not Eliot, "who had the idea of allowing the First Knight, as chairman of the 'meeting' after the murder, to characterize each of the speakers by an introductory phrase." Browne, *The Making of T. S. Eliot's Plays,* p.74.
16. Browne, *The Making of T. S. Eliot's Plays,* pp.55–56.
17. Kenner, p.331.
18. C. L. Barber, in *T. S. Eliot: A Selected Critique,* ed. Leonard Unger (N.Y.: Rinehart, 1948), p.423.
19. *On Poetry and Poets,* pp.81, 78.
20. *On Poetry and Poets,* p.85.
21. Robert Speaight, in Braybrooke, p.71.
22. *On Poetry and Poets,* pp.75–76.
23. Browne, *The Making of T. S. Eliot's Plays,* p.90.
24. Browne, *The Making of T. S. Eliot's Plays,* pp.102–111.
25. Carol Smith, p.112.
26. Carol Smith, p.117.
27. Kenner, p.333.
28. Spender, p.220.
29. In Unger, pp.423–424.
30. See e.g. Jones, pp.127–128.
31. Browne, *The Making of T. S. Eliot's Plays,* p.343.
32. Jones, p.178.
33. C. L. Barber, "The Power of Development . . . in a Different World," being a 1958 essay appended to Matthiessen, pp.218, 226.
34. Browne, *The Making of T. S. Eliot's Plays,* p.305.

Chapter Seven: The Harvard Sam Johnson

1. Quoted by Bergonzi, p.179, who calls the essay "a strangely rambling and even incoherent performance."
2. Quoted by Aiken, in March and Tambiumuttu, p.23. It is,

I think, revealing of Eliot's loyalty, and his generosity, that when in 1959–1960 Pound wrote him, expressing "grave doubts about the quality of his own work . . . Eliot . . . told Pound not to worry, that he was one of the immortals, and that part of his work was sure to survive. Pound was relieved . . ." C. David Heymann, *Ezra Pound: The Last Rower* (N.Y.:Viking, 1976), p.268. Eliot also edited Pound's *Literary Essays* (1954), writing a strong and very positive introductory essay, although in Eliot's earlier *After Strange Gods* (N.Y.: Harcourt, Brace, 1934) he said, among other things, that Pound "is attracted to the Middle Ages, apparently, by everything except that which gives them their significance." See pp.44–47.

3.   F. W. Bateson, in Martin, p.34. His "scholarship," concludes Professor Bateson, was only skin-deep . . ." p.44.

4.   Gabriel Pearson, in Martin, pp.100–101.

5.   F. W. Bateson, in Martin, p.32. Bateson's careful reproduction of how he heard Babbitt's American accent is revealingly hostile.

6.   In Braybrooke, p.120.

7.   In Unger, p.53.

8.   Austin Warren, in *T. S. Eliot: The Man and His Work,* ed. Allen Tate (N.Y.: Delacorte, 1966), p.287.

9.   For a rough counting of pages see F. W. Bateson, "Criticism's Lost Leader," in *The Literary Criticism of T. S. Eliot,* ed. David Newton-De Molina (London: Athlone Press, 1977), p.11.

10.   *On Poetry and Poets,* p.17.

11.   *On Poetry and Poets,* p.22.

12.   Eliot of course wrote about prose, including prose fiction, as well as about poetry. But most of his critical work dealt with poetry, and Spender recalls him saying, in private conversation, "that if one wanted to write poetry one should not write anything else creative." In Tate, p.48.

13.   *Selected Essays,* p.4.

14.   T. S. Eliot, *The Use of Poetry and the Use of Criticism* (London: Faber and Faber paperback, 1964), p.9. As the very first paragraph of first lecture in the book demon-

strates beyond any doubt, Eliot was in later years somewhat troubled by this particular essay (and by its populari-
ty): "But I do not repudiate what I wrote in that essay any
more fully than I should expect to do after such a lapse of
time." p.15.

15. *Selected Essays,* p.50.
16. *On Poetry and Poets,* p.50.
17. *To Criticize the Critic,* p.147.
18. *To Criticize the Critic,* p.16.
19. *On Poetry and Poets,* p.117.
20. *On Poetry and Poets,* p.118.
21. *On Poetry and Poets,* p.130.
22. Margolis, p.13.
23. *To Criticize the Critic,* p.58.
24. In Martin, pp.46, 60.
25. *Selected Essays,* p.47. See Ezra Pound's poem, "Cantico del Sole," which is built almost entirely out of the repeated phrase "The thought of what America would be like / If the Classics had a wide circulation / Troubles my sleep . . ." *Personae,* p.183.
26. *Selected Essays,* p.213.
27. *After Strange Gods,* pp.16–17.
28. Martin, in Martin, p.25.
29. In Martin, p.94.
30. In Martin, p.99.
31. *The Use of Poetry and the Use of Criticism,* p.15.
32. *The Use of Poetry and the Use of Criticism,* p.32.
33. Kenner, p.22.
34. *Selected Essays,* pp.11, 7–8.
35. *On Poetry and Poets,* pp.106–108.
36. To Criticize the Critic, p.15. "So much for tradition and the community of European letters," says Graham Hough both tartly and accurately. In Newton-De Molina, p.60.
37. *Selected Essays,* pp.124–125.
38. Preface to 1964 edition, *The Use of Poetry & the Use of Criticism,* p.9.
39. Samuel Eliot Morison, *Three Centuries of Harvard* (Cambridge: Harvard University Press, 1946), p.327.

40. Morison, p.336.
41. Elliott Roosevelt, ed., *F.D.R, His Personal Letters: Early Years* (New York: Duell, Sloan and Pearce, 1947), p.419.
42. Ronald Steel, *Walter Lippmann and the American Century* (Boston: Little, Brown, 1980), pp.12 ff.
43. James MacGregor Burns, *Edward Kennedy and the Camelot Legacy* (New York: Norton, 1976), p.23.
44. Richard Hofstadter, *The American Political Tradition* (New York: Vintage paperback, 1958), p.323.
45. *Roosevelt & Frankfurter: Their Correspondence, 1928–1945,* ed. Max Freedman (Boston: Little, Brown, 1967), p.322.
46. *Roosevelt & Frankfurter,* p.326.
47. Howarth, p.65.

Chapter Eight: God's Word and Man's World

1. These were reprinted, under one cover, as T. S. Eliot, *Christianity and Culture* (N.Y.: Harcourt, Brace, Jovanovich paperback, 1968). All citations to both books will be to this edition.
2. Brian Lee, *Theory and Personality: The Significance of T. S. Eliot's Criticism* (London: Athlone Press, 1979). "The problem for which Eliot was trying to find an answer in his criticism," says Mr. Lee, is "how to be a poet in a world where all depth has shrunk." p.3. I do not agree with Mr. Lee that Eliot misled "himself into thinking . . . that *impersonality* is the opposite of *personality,* when it need not be." p.123. But his is a deeply suggestive book, sensitive and well-informed.
3. T. S. Eliot, *Selected Prose,* ed. John Hayward (Harmondsworth: Penguin paperback, 1953). See pp.209–251.
4. The invaluable guide to this material is Donald Gallup, *T. S. Eliot: A Bibliography* (N.Y.: Harcourt, Brace, 1969).
5. Raymond Williams, *Culture and Society, 1780–1950* (Harmondsworth: Penguin paperback, 1963), pp.224–238.
6. Williams, p.224.

7. Williams, p.237.
8. See also, e.g., Alexander Karanikas, *Tillers of a Myth: Southern Agrarians as Social and Literary Critics* (Madison: University of Wisconsin paperback, 1969), p.91: ". . . the subject of race was also relevant to the cultural unity of their ideal community, in which respect they received valuable guidance from T. S. Eliot. His proper Christian community rejected the presence of Negroes and Jews because they divided the otherwise monolithic social unity." In a 1931 letter to Allen Tate, Edmund Wilson scolds Tate because "You are still, I think, too much impressed with the dicta . . . of the Aquinas of *The Criterion* [i.e., T. S. Eliot], who has an obvious interest nowadays in disparaging scientific revelation in order to fortify religious revelation . . ." *Letters on Literature and Politics,* p.212. Richard Hoggart says that "Eliot's *Notes towards the Definition of Culture* . . . is one of the most formidable modern statements of the conservative case about culture . . ." Richard Hoggart, *Speaking to Each Other: About Society* (N.Y.: Oxford University Press, 1970), p.119.
9. Edmund Wilson, "T. S. Eliot and the Church of England," in *The Shores of Light* (N.Y.: Vintage paperback, 1961), p.436.
10. *Christianity and Culture,* p.3.
11. *Christianity and Culture,* p.6.
12. *Christianity and Culture,* p.8.
13. *Christianity and Culture,* p.9.
14. *Christianity and Culture,* pp. 11, 12. Indeed, Eliot later adds, speaking of General J. F. C. Fuller, "one of the two British visitors invited to Herr Hitler's birthday celebrations," that "From my point of view, General Fuller has as good a title to call himself a 'believer in democracy' as anyone has." pp.53–54, note to p.15.
15. *Christianity and Culture,* p.13.
16. *Christianity and Culture,* p.14.
17. *Christianity and Culture,* p.15.
18. *Christianity and Culture,* p.17.
19. *Christianity and Culture,* p.19.

20. *Christianity and Culture,* p.23.
21. *Christianity and Culture,* p.25.
22. *Christianity and Culture,* p.27.
23. *Christianity and Culture,* pp.27, 29.
24. *Christianity and Culture,* p.31.
25. *Christianity and Culture,* p.47.
26. *Christianity and Culture,* p.50.
27. *Christianity and Culture,* p.69.
28. Roger Kojecky, *T. S. Eliot's Social Criticism* (N.Y.: Farrar, Straus, 1972), p.126.
29. Kojecky, pp.127, 138, 141.
30. Williams, p.238.
31. Sir Herbert Read, in Tate, p.15.
32. Kojecky, p.152.
33. Allen Austin, *T. S. Eliot: The Literary and Social Criticism* (Bloomington: Indiana University Press paperback, 1971), p.54.
34. He connects *The Idea of a Christian Society* only to Eliot's "conclusion that the writer must take a direct interest in politics." Smidt, p.29.
35. *Christianity and Culture,* p.87.
36. *Christianity and Culture,* pp.87–88.
37. *Christianity and Culture,* p.147.
38. *Christianity and Culture,* p.151.
39. *Christianity and Culture,* p.154.
40. *Christianity and Culture,* p.165 n.1.
41. *Christianity and Culture,* p.170.
42. *Christianity and Culture,* p.182.
43. *Christianity and Culture,* p.186.

Chapter Nine: Eliot's reputation and influence

1. John Berryman, *The Freedom of the Poet* (New York: Farrar, Straus and Giroux, 1976), p.270.
2. Martin Seymour-Smith, *Funk & Wagnalls Guide to Modern World Literature* (New York: Funk and Wagnalls, 1973), pp.252, 253, 254.

3. *Allen Verbatim: Lectures on Poetry, Politics, Consciousness by Allen Ginsberg,* ed. Gordon Ball (New York: McGraw-Hill paperback, 1975), p.112.

4. Edith Sitwell, *Selected Letters, 1919–1964,* ed. John Lehmann and Derek Parker (New York: Vanguard Press, 1970), p.53.

5. Alexander Pushkin, *Selected Poems,* trans. Burton Raffel and Alla Burago (Calcutta: Writers Workshop, 1979).

6. Burton Raffel, *The Development of Modern Indonesian Poetry* (Albany: State University of New York Press, 1967), p.91.

7. Sunday A. Anozie, *Christopher Okigbo* (London: Evans Brothers paperback, 1972), pp.15, 33–34.

8. Anozie, p.102.

9. Suzanne Massie, *The Living Mirror: Five Young Poets from Leningrad* (Garden City: Doubleday, 1972), p.38.

10. Seferis, pp.123–124.

11. Edmund Wilson, *Letters on Literature and Politics, 1912–1972,* ed. Elena Wilson (New York: Farrar, Straus and Giroux, 1977), p.100.

12. Allen Tate, *Essays of Four Decades* (Chicago: Swallow Press, 1968), p.xi.

13. Yvor Winters, *In Defense of Reason* (Chicago: Swallow Press, n.d.), p.460.

14. *The Nabokov-Wilson Letters, 1940–1971,* ed. Simon Karlinsky (New York: Harper and Row, 1979), p.237.

15. *Nabokov-Wilson,* p.323.

16. Edmund Wilson, *The Shores of Light: A Literary Chronicle of the Twenties and Thirties* (New York: Vintage paperback, 1961), p.436.

17. E. E. Cummings, *A Miscellany Revised* (New York: October House, 1965), p.26.

18. *The Letters of Hart Crane, 1916–1932,* ed. Brom Weber (Berkeley: University of California Press, 1965), pp.114–115.

19. James Atlas, *Delmore Schwartz* (New York: Avon paperback, 1978), pp.124–125.

20. Bogan, *Poet's Alphabet,* p.108.

Bibliography

1. *Works by Eliot*
(For a full chronological listing of all the works, see Gallup's
    Bibliography; listed here are only editions currently in print
    and readily available.)

POETRY

Collected Poems, 1909–1962 (N.Y.: Harcourt, Brace, Jovano-
    vich, 1963) includes *Prufrock, Poems, 1920, The Waste
    Land, The Hollow Men, Ash-Wednesday, Ariel Poems,*
    "Unfinished Poems" (Sweeney Agonistes; Coriolan), "Mi-
    nor Poems," Choruses from *The Rock, Four Quartets,* and
    "Occasional Verses"
*The Waste Land: A Facsimile and Transcript of the Original
    Drafts . . . ,* ed. Valerie Eliot (N.Y.: Harcourt, Brace,
    Jovanovich, 1971)
Poems Written in Early Youth (N.Y.: Farrar, Straus & Giroux,
    1967)
Old Possum's Book of Practical Cats (N.Y.: Harcourt, Brace,
    Jovanovich, 1939; new ed., 1968)

PLAYS

The Complete Plays (N.Y.: Harcourt, Brace, Jovanovich, 1967)

228

includes *Murder in the Cathedral, The Family Reunion, The Cocktail Party, The Confidential Clerk,* and *The Elder Statesman*

ESSAYS

Selected Essays (N.Y.: Harcourt, Brace, Jovanovich, 1960) includes most of *The Sacred Wood, For Lancelot Andrewes, Essays Ancient and Modern, Dante, Homage to John Dryden,* as well as some essays not otherwise collected in book form

Selected Prose of T. S. Eliot, ed. Frank Kermode (N.Y.: Harvest / Noonday paperback, 1975)

On Poetry and Poets (N.Y.: Farrar, Straus & Giroux, 1957; Noonday paperback, 1961)

To Criticize the Critic (N.Y.: Farrar, Straus & Giroux, 1965)

SOCIAL CRITICISM

Christianity and Culture (N.Y.: Harcourt, Brace, Jovanovich paperback, 1968) includes *The Idea of a Christian Society,* and *Notes towards the Definition of Culture*

PHILOSOPHICAL WRITING

Knowledge and Experience in the Philosophy of F. H. Bradley (N.Y.: Farrar, Straus & Giroux, 1964)

2. *Works about Eliot:* books only, and only books of current importance and/or utility

BIBLIOGRAPHY

T. S. Eliot: A Bibliography, ed. Donald Gallup, 2nd ed. (N.Y.: Harcourt, Brace, Jovanovich, 1969)

CRITICISM: BIOGRAPHICAL

Lyndall Gordon, *Eliot's Early Years* (N.Y.: Oxford University Press, 1977)

Herbert Howarth, *Notes on Some Figures Behind T. S. Eliot* (Boston: Houghton, Mifflin, 1964)

William Turner Levy and Victor Scherle, *Affectionately, T. S. Eliot* (Philadelphia: Lippincott, 1968)

Robert Sencourt, *T. S. Eliot: A Memoir* (N.Y.: Dodd, Mead, 1971)

CRITICISM: ANTHOLOGIES

T. S. Eliot: A Symposium for his Seventieth Birthday, ed. Neville Braybrooke (N.Y.: Farrar, Straus & Giroux, 1958)

T. S. Eliot: A Collection of Critical Essays, ed. Hugh Kenner (Englewood Cliffs: Prentice-Hall paperback, 1962)

Eliot in His Time, ed. A. Walton Litz (Princeton: Princeton University Press, 1973)

T. S. Eliot, ed. Richard March and Tambimuttu (London: Editions Poetry, 1948)

Eliot in Perspective, ed. Graham Martin (N.Y.: Humanities Press, 1970)

The Waste Land: A Collection of Critical Essays, ed. Jay Martin (Englewood Cliffs: Prentice-Hall paperback, 1968)

The Waste Land in Different Voices, ed. A. D. Moody (N.Y.: St. Martin's, 1974)

The Literary Criticism of T. S. Eliot, ed. David Newton-De Molina (London: Athlone Press, 1977)

T. S. Eliot: A Study of his Writings by Several Hands, ed. B. Rajan (N.Y.: Haskell House, 1964 [first published, 1947])

T. S. Eliot: The Man and His Work, ed. Allen Tate (N.Y.: Delacorte, 1966)

T. S. Eliot: A Selected Critique, ed. Leonard Unger (N.Y.: Rinehart, 1948)

CRITICISM: POETRY AND GENERAL

Bernard Bergonzi, *T. S. Eliot* (N.Y.: Macmillan, 1972)

Georges Cattaui, *T. S. Eliot* (N.Y.: Funk & Wagnalls, 1968)

Elizabeth Drew, *T. S. Eliot: The Design of His Poetry* (N.Y.: Scribner's, 1949)

Northrop Frye, *T. S. Eliot: An Introduction* (Chicago: University of Chicago Press, 1963; Phoenix paperback, 1981)

Helen Gardner, *The Art of T. S. Eliot* (London: Cresset, 1949)

———— *The Composition of* Four Quartets (N.Y.: Oxford University Press, 1978)

Nancy Duvall Hargrove, *Landscape and Symbol in the Poetry of T. S. Eliot* (Jackson: University of Mississippi Press, 1978)

Genesius Jones, *Approach to the Purpose: A Study of the Poetry of T. S. Eliot* (N.Y.: Barnes & Noble, 1965)

Hugh Kenner, *The Invisible Poet: T. S. Eliot* (N.Y.: Harcourt, Brace, 1959; Harbinger paperback, 1959)

Thomas McGreevy, *Thomas Stearns Eliot: A Study* (N.Y.: Haskell House, 1971 [first published, 1931])

F. O. Matthiessen, *The Achievement of T. S. Eliot* (N.Y.: Oxford University Press, 1935; Oxford University Press paperback, 1959)

James E. Miller, Jr., *T. S. Eliot's Personal Waste Land* (University Park: University of Pennsylvania Press, 1977)

Gertrude Patterson, *T. S. Eliot: Poems in the Making* (Manchester: University of Manchester Press, 1971)

Elisabeth W. Schneider, *T. S. Eliot: The Pattern in the Carpet* (Berkeley: University of California Press, 1975)

Kristian Smidt, *Poetry and Belief in the Work of T. S. Eliot*, rev. ed. (N.Y.: Humanities Press, 1961 [first published, 1949])

Grover Smith, *T. S. Eliot's Poetry and Plays: A Study in Sources and Meaning* (Chicago: University of Chicago Press, 1956; Phoenix paperback, 1956; 2nd ed., 1975)

Stephen Spender, *T. S. Eliot* (N.Y.: Penguin, 1975)

Derek Traversi, *T. S. Eliot: The Longer Poems* (N.Y.: Harcourt, Brace, Jovanovich, 1976)

David Ward, *T. S. Eliot Between Two Worlds* (London: Routledge & Kegan Paul, 1973)

George Williamson, *A Reader's Guide to T. S. Eliot* (N.Y.: Noonday paperback, 1953)

CRITICISM: ESSAYS AND IDEAS

Harry T. Antrim, *T. S. Eliot's Concept of Language* (Gainesville: University of Florida Press, 1971)

Allen Austin, *T. S. Eliot: The Literary and Social Criticism* (Bloomington: Indiana University Press paperback, 1971)

Roger Kojecky, *T. S. Eliot's Social Criticism* (N.Y.: Farrar, Straus & Giroux, 1972)

Brian Lee, *Theory and Personality: The Significance of T. S. Eliot's Criticism* (London: Athlone Press, 1979)

John D. Margolis, *T. S. Eliot's Intellectual Development, 1922–1939* (Chicago: University of Chicago Press, 1972)

Jyoti Prakesh Sen, *The Progress of T. S. Eliot as Poet and Critic* (New Delhi: Orient Longman, 1971)

Rajendra Verma, *Royalist in Politics: T. S. Eliot and Political Philosophy* (London: Asia Publishing House, 1968)

CRITICISM: PLAYS

E. Martin Browne, *The Making of T. S. Eliot's Plays* (Cambridge: Cambridge University Press, 1969)

David E. Jones, *The Plays of T. S. Eliot* (Toronto: Toronto University Press, 1960)

Carol H. Smith, *T. S. Eliot's Dramatic Theory and Practice* (Princeton: Princeton University Press, 1963)

Index